TO THE LAST ROUND

TO THE
LAST ROUND

The South Notts Hussars

1939-1942

Peter Hart

Pen & Sword Books Limited, Barnsley

LEO COOPER

**This book is dedicated to
Battery Sergeant Major Jim Hardy
'Nellie'
Died 6 June, 1942, Age 24**

First published in Great Britain in 1996 by Leo Cooper
an imprint of Pen & Sword Books Limited
47 Church Street, Barnsley, South Yorkshire S70 2AS

*For up-to date information on other titles
produced under the Pen & Sword imprint,
please telephone or write to:*
Pen & Sword Books Limited
FREEPOST
47 Church Street
Barnsley
South Yorkshire
S70 2BR

Telephone (24 hours): 01226 734555

ISBN 0-85052-514-4

British Library Cataloguing in Publication Data

**Printed by Redwood Books Ltd
Trowbridge, Wiltshire**

Contents

Preface

I am greatly indebted to the old comrades of the South Notts Hussars without whom this book would not exist. My own role has been merely to select and link together within a historical context the various extracts from the remarkable recordings they have made for the Imperial War Museum. I must particularly thank – in alphabetical order – Ray Ellis, Bob Foulds, Harold Harper, Frank Knowles and John Walker to whom I have frequently turned for help over the last five years and have never been disappointed. I would also like to thank my tireless colleagues in the Sound Archive at the Imperial War Museum: Margaret Brooks, Kate Johnson, Laura Kamel, Rosemary Tudge and Conrad Wood. Together they have amassed an archive which is a fantastic treasury of human experience and knowledge for those willing to use it. I am grateful to my friend and colleague Nigel Steel from the Department of Documents who has brought his finely honed mind to bear on the many grammatical errors which littered this text. Of course my own natural stubbornness is responsible for any slips that remain! Paul Kemp and Dave Parry of the IWM Photographic Archive were extremely helpful in selecting many of the photographs in the text. Many thanks to Ted Whittaker for the use of his cartoons. Ragnar Coop assisted by reading a preliminary draft and his comments were as pithy as ever. Suzanne Bardgett was a great help in preparing an early version of the Knightsbridge chapter which appeared as an article in the *Imperial War Museum Review* of which she was the esteemed editor. Roni Wilkinson of Wharncliffe Books was responsible for almost everything else and is a pleasure to work with.

CHAPTER ONE

Early Days

A regiment is a strange organisation. It has a life separate from the experience of its serving members which reaches back in time and forward into the future. Although the men of the South Notts Hussars (SNH) who fought in the Second World War were not often aware of it, they were the direct descendants of the gentlemen yeomanry who had initially formed the regiment in response to Prime Minister William Pitt's speech in Parliament on 5 March 1794. 'As an augmentation of the cavalry for internal defence was a very natural object, they might, under certain circumstances, have a species of cavalry consisting of Gentlemen and Yeomanry, who would not be called upon to act outside of their respective counties except on the pressure of emergency, or in cases of urgent necessity'.[1] The emergency that concerned him was the successes of the Armies of Revolutionary France and the rise of Napoleon Bonaparte. The men of Nottinghamshire responded and the nucleus of the regiment was formed at a meeting on 10 June 1794. Their first active service was not in fact against the French but in dispersing the local men engaged in the Luddite riots of 1811-1812. This was not as distasteful a duty as it might seem to men who were defending the perceived interests of their own class.

> A Yeomanry regiment may be said to be an expression of the best of the county on horseback, and, like other Territorial units, partakes of that particular individuality that marks so distinctly every English shire, though it is hard enough to say sometimes where a county begins or ends. Nowhere, however, is this personal and intimate touch with its county more marked than in a Yeomanry regiment, with its ranks manned from the homesteads and farms whose tenure has often been held for several generations, and officered, as such regiments are, from the great houses.[2]
>
> ***Benson Freeman,*** **SNH Historian**

Under these circumstances it is not unnatural that they were enthusiastic in defending their privileged position within society and internal security was to be the main function of the unit during the turbulent early Nineteenth Century: the Brandreth riots of 1817; political unrest in 1819; the Reform Bill riots of 1831; the Chartist Riots and Demonstrations of 1839 and 1848 – at all these the SNH defended the status quo with vigour. The introduction of an effective police service by the 1850s meant that in subsequent periods of popular unrest

Yeoman taking their refreshment at a local hostelry.

they were merely brought to readiness in case of a complete breakdown in law and order. The regiment remained a viable unit enduring the multitudinous problems caused by government military reforms and associated cutbacks but slowly the demographical factors generated by the industrial revolution and agricultural depression began to change the composition of the force commanded by the officers. As the true country yeoman ceased to exist recruits began to come in increasing numbers from Nottingham and its suburbs as the Twentieth Century loomed.

The early disasters of the Boer War which began on 11 October 1899, brought the first opportunity for real active service. On 24 December 1899 an appeal was issued to form a SNH contingent within the 3rd Imperial Yeomanry Regiment and such was the response that a whole squadron was recruited under the leadership of Colonel Lancelot Rolleston. They embarked for South Africa in January 1900 and during

Colonel Lancelot Rolleston, a man with his own caption, at Summer camp, Aldershot, 1903.

Magnificently mounted, Trooper Gervase Wright during the period of the Boer War, 1900. Note the Long Lee-Enfield rifle seated in the special butt holster and the rifle sling around the trooper's right arm.

the next two years took a considerable part in a series of actions with the Boers across the veldt; until finally the last contingent returned home following the declaration of peace in June 1902.

For hundreds of years cavalry had been the shock troops of the

Troopers busily working on their saddles under the supervision of NCOs.

Impressing, rather than repressing, the crowds, the South Notts resplendent in their full dress uniforms, complete with bearskins and sabres, at an open air Church Parade at the turn of the century.

battlefield but their role was becoming more controversial as the tacticians argued as to the relative merits of 'pure' cavalry and mounted infantrymen. The experiences of the SNH in the First World War of 1914-1918 rather typified the confusion that existed over a precise role for horseman in modern warfare. After mobilization, training and coastal defence duties in England the SNH were sent out as part of the 2nd Mounted Division to Egypt in April 1915. After a period sweltering in Abbassia Barracks in Cairo the division was used to reinforce the faltering Allied campaign against the Turks at Gallipoli in August 1915. They were thrown pell mell into dismounted action in the assault on Scimitar Hill at Suvla Bay on 21 August but little was achieved in the blazing scrub covered hills. An unhealthy period in the line followed as dysentery and para-typhoid ravaged the ranks before the regiment returned to Egypt in November 1915. Re-united with their precious horses they were sent to the Balkans in February 1916 where they acted

Nottingham City Centre at the outbreak of the First World War, the South Notts Hussars parade before dignitaries in their khaki uniforms. After coastal defence duties they shipped out for Egypt in April 1915.

After serving in Gallipoli in an unmounted role they were reunited with their horses in 1916 and served in the Balkans before returning to the Middle East, where they took part in the last great cavalry campaign in Palestine. They were dismounted yet again and became part of the Machine Gun Corps.

as divisional cavalry to the 10th (Irish) Division on patrol and outpost duties where malaria at least varied the complex cocktail of disease. They returned to the Middle East in June 1917 to join the Desert Mounted Corps and took part in the last great cavalry campaign under General Sir Edmund Allenby in Palestine which culminated in the surrender of Jerusalem on 9 December 1917. In April 1918 they were again dismounted and amalgamated with the Warwickshire Yeomanry to form 'B' Battalion, The Machine Gun Corps. They embarked for the Western Front but were torpedoed and sunk aboard the *Leasowe Castle* in the Mediterranean on 27 May 1918. The survivors reformed at Alexandria before the journey was resumed and as 100th Battalion, Machine Gun Corps spent the rest of the war as infantry in France.

★ ★ ★ ★

In the post-war period the confusion over their role was finally resolved when it was decided to convert the regiment into an artillery unit. The First World War had been dominated by the massed guns and howitzers of the opposing forces which were dug in well behind the front lines and rained down high explosive and shrapnel on every move made by the long suffering infantry. As gunnery ranges had increased artillery had become impervious to conventional infantry or cavalry operations and could only be threatened effectively by the longer range guns of the enemy. There was an obvious need to develop more artillery units for any future wars and a corresponding question over the continuing relevance of cavalry of whatever kind in this kind of warfare. Nevertheless, as might be expected in such a traditionally minded regiment, there was considerable opposition to this proposed change in status. The Honorary Colonel Sir Lancelot Rolleston, as a true believer in 'pure' cavalry, was apoplectic at a meeting held to discuss the merger at the Regimental Drill Hall on 13 July 1920.

> It was unfortunate that seniority had been chosen instead of efficiency as the method of selecting the ten regiments which were to continue as yeomanry. The seniority of the South Notts Hussars was quite a false one. If they had had their due, they would have been as senior as any in the service, but as it were they were fifteenth. The ideas of the War Office were constantly changing. In the present disturbed state of Europe, and the way the Bolsheviks were framing, it was quite possible that before two years were over we should want twenty Yeomanry Regiments instead of ten.[3]
>
> ### *Colonel Sir Lancelot Rolleston*

His protests were ignored and in March 1922 the SNH became the 107 (The South Notts Hussars Yeomanry) Field Brigade, Royal Artillery, divided into 425 and 426 Batteries each with four 18 pounders. The only sop to regimental pride was that they were allowed to retain their traditional acorn and oak leaf cap badges. The two batteries had

Yet another role for the South Notts. The Great War, just finished, demonstrated the importance of artillery and the South Notts were selected to convert. Below: *Early attempts by the hussars at the art of firing big guns, seen here using various artillery pieces at Redesdale Camp in the 1920s*

Getting to grips with the 18 pounders on Redesdale firing range. The South Notts meet the challenge and begin developing the basic gunnery skills.

separate and distinct identities with 425 Battery recruiting largely from Nottingham, so gaining a high proportion of young grammar school boys and clerical workers; whilst 426 Battery was largely composed of miners from the outlying Hucknall and Eastwood areas. Understandably resentment at the change in status lingered for a while and was still apparent when young Second Lieutenant William Barber joined the regiment in 1924. 'We were furious. Our sister regiment – 'the Shirk-All-Dangers' (Sherwood Rangers) – we used to call them – they remained as cavalry.' But, despite their initial reluctance, the officers and men responded well to the challenge and soon acquired the basic skills of gunnery. As Rolleston resignedly commented, 'It is a regimental tradition that no task assigned to it is too hard to be undertaken, and the new duties are being zealously and successfully performed'.[4]

The unit struggled through the parsimonious inter-war years when the Government seemed almost oblivious to the threat posed by the resurgence of Germany under the Nazi Party. It was glaringly obvious to others.

> My father and I used to go and canoe in Germany. You could see the war coming when people were pooh poohing it and saying that of course there won't be any war. I remember sitting on the top of a hill and we looked down to the valley on the sports field and we could see these Hitler Youth with burnished shovels marching and counter-marching down there. They were not allowed to have arms. It was very difficult to have any other opinion – you could see this great cloud growing.
>
> ***Second Lieutenant Charles Laborde, 426 Bty***

The Munich crisis of September 1938 saw the British Prime Minister

Group of officers including umpires wearing white hat bands in the hills during exercises at Redesdale Firing Camp.

Neville Chamberlain return from his meeting with Adolf Hitler, which marked the apotheosis of 'appeasement', as he meekly acquiesced to the German acquisition of Czechoslovakia.

But it was soon realized that war was inevitable and, as part of the last minute rush expansion of the peacetime army, the SNH were converted into a fully fledged Regiment of the Royal Horse Artillery.[5] This entailed an increase in their establishment personnel, first from 170 to 230 and then to 480, effectively doubling the size of the batteries. Each was divided into two troops of four 18 pounders which were to be towed into action hooked on to the back of ordinary lorries. The final stage was the formation of a complete 'second line' regiment which was known as 150 (South Notts Hussars) Field Regiment, Royal Artillery. On the outbreak of war this new unit was to continue training whilst the 'first line' regiment went off to active service almost immediately.

To achieve this massive expansion, long established territorials were joined by a large number of young men who, aware of what was coming, wanted some control over their own destinies.

> We would rather choose what we would be in, rather than in the
> event of an impending war, being told to do something. I thought
> I didn't particularly feel like the sort of person who could willingly

16

stick bayonets into people. I felt that if I was going to fight an enemy I would rather fight it from a range of 2 or 3 miles with an artillery gun than I would hand to hand.

Gunner John Walker, **425 Bty**

Amongst the prospective recruits folk memories still lingered of the horrors that many of their fathers had suffered as infantrymen in the trenches during the Great War.

I'd listened to my father and my uncles talking for hours and hours about the horrors of the First World War so naturally you weren't looking forward to a war. All we knew was trench warfare and 60, 70, 80% casualties.

Gunner Charles Ward, **426 Bty**

Many were seduced by the glamour of the 'Hussars' with their exotic name and trappings.

The only regiment I knew about apart from the Guards was the Sherwood Foresters. Soldiers to me were men who wore khaki and fought. I went down one evening to join the Territorial Army as an infantry soldier and I was going to join the Sherwood Foresters. I got to the Derby Road Drill Hall and there was a sign which was to change my whole life. A simple sign hanging there, a very colourful thing which said, "South Notts Hussars". "South Notts Hussars", I thought – it sounded good I didn't quite know what a Hussar was – I knew he rode a horse and I knew I couldn't ride and I wondered if that would be some sort of detriment to me. Strangely enough no-one asked if I could ride a horse – not surprisingly! I joined just on the strength of that sign!

Gunner Ray Ellis, **425 Bty**

Ellis was not the only man who was unaware of the regiment's change in status since the First World War. Bill Hutton confessed that, 'To tell you the truth I thought I was joining a cavalry unit. I had visions of having a long sword and riding a horse with spurs and things like that.'

Naive young men were easy prey for the experienced old soldiers who had been entrusted with recruitment for *their* unit.

We finished up at the Derby Road Drill Hall and said we wanted to join. Eventually we were confronted with this splendid figure — riding breeches, puttees, spurs, what they called a 'cheese cutter' cap and bright leather belt. He introduced himself as Sergeant Bennett. Spud Baker who was a bit of a lad, he was instantly taken with this uniform and he said to us, "How about this then?" He said to Bennett, "Do we wear a uniform like that?", and, lying through his teeth, Bennett said, "Of course!"

Gunner Ted Whittaker, **425 Bty**

As the whole of the Territorial Army was expanding there was considerable competition between the units for promising looking recruits which was not always conducted on a level playing field. The SNH office was next to the drill hall's entrance.

I didn't go to join the South Notts Hussars. A pal of mine said, "I'm in the Signal Corps at the Drill Hall. You want to pop up there – it's lovely!" I walked through the door and a bloke said, "Can I help you?" I said, "I want to be a signaller!" He said, "Just the man – you come with me!" Of course I was only a lad and he was an imposing chap. He said, "Sit down there and I'll send someone to see you". A bloke came in and said, "You want to be a signaller?" "Yes!" "Right!" "Just sign there. Have you got your parents' permission?" "Oh, yes!" "Sign – that's it!

Signaller Albert Parker, **425 Bty**

New recruits were signed on and given a medical inspection to ensure that they would be up to the physical stresses of army life. Unfortunately the examination was by no means rigourous – especially when the myopic Gunner Hutton was 'helping' the Doctor.

I was between jobs so I helped in the battery office. I signed

Group of officers from 426 Battery in the hills during exercises at Redesdale Firing Camp. From left to right: *Tony McCraith, Charles Laborde, Colin Barber and Bob Hingston.*

people up – I had this form and I filled it in, "Do you suffer from coughing, bed wetting, spitting of blood? What's your mother's name..." When they were busy I helped them with the medical. If they couldn't see the board properly I let them stand a yard nearer so I think there was a lot of short sighted people in our regiment – I wasn't the only one!

Gunner Bill Hutton, 425 Bty

Such laxity was typical of the whole procedure.

We had the most rudimentary medical, 'Strip off, cough, get on the scale...' They had a look in your mouth and a look at your feet. They used to say, "Touch him, if he's warm he's in!" It wasn't quite like that but they didn't seem to be turning anyone away.

Gunner Bob Foulds, 425 Bty

Many of the recruits were from the Nottingham High School and therefore had had some basic training of questionable relevance in the Officer Training Corps.

We used to do exercises – platoon in attack, platoon in defence, storming all sorts of objectives, getting into all sorts of messes. Looking back I don't think they were particularly realistic. We were instructed by a Sergeant Major from the Fourteen-Eighteen war, and at least one of the masters from the High School was Fourteen -Eighteen war. All their ideas and thinking in those days were based not on the next war but the last war. We didn't occupy a position with all round defence or anything like that, we tended to go blindly on. Everyone was keen and enthusiastic but the principles, now I look back were very archaic.

Gunner Bob Foulds, 425 Bty

In many units such men would have been prime candidates for a commission. But the SNH were an élite unit and to be one of their officers required a little more than the application of intelligence to military efficiency. Bob Hingston was a young director with his family's lace manufacturing firm and as such was deemed worthy of a personal invitation from the Colonel of the South Notts Hussars himself.

Out of the blue, Colonel Holden wrote to me asking if I would care to join. I agonised over it, absolutely agonised... "God, this is the moment, I must do something, there's a war coming, I must get ready for it." And then "Oh my God, join that army, in the mud again, no I can't face it."

Second Lieutenant Bob Hingston, 426 Bty

Charles Laborde was from a comfortable background and had been educated at Harrow.

I thought of the Sherwood Foresters, having had some infantry training at school, but then I discovered that the South Notts had quite a Harrow following — the Birkin family of course were all at Harrow. So one drifted into the South Notts and I became a gunner!

Second Lieutenant Charles Laborde, 426 Bty

Charles Laborde had also been a rugby international forward for England and the Nottingham Rugby Club was regarded as a fertile source of potential officers for the SNH.

I was playing rugby regularly for Nottingham and the Captain of the Nottingham side was a very keen Territorial Army man — Peter Birkin. He was a born leader. They decided to double the Territorial Army and half the scrum all joined that night! We were told if we all joined together we would all get direct commissions. I came home and discussed it with my father and he said, "If you can get a commission you go and get it!" So I took his advice and went and joined. I nearly wasn't accepted because the Colonel at the interview said, "How many acres do you farm?" I said, "I don't know off hand!" This absolutely floored him — how anybody could farm and not know the acres they were farming. What I didn't know in those days was that you must never say you don't know in answer to an Army question!

Second Lieutenant William Pringle, 425 Bty

Thus the Nottingham High School boys found that their school, although 'good', did not have the same social cachet as the major public schools.

After I had joined I thought that I would like to have a commission but it was very much a 'County' situation. I got to know the officers of the regiment and it was very obvious that I was not in their pecuniary situation. I could not possibly afford to be an officer in those days, there was no question of it at all. The gentlemen were all gentlemen – the Birkins, the Barbers, the Seelys – they were there financially. That was the only deterrent – I didn't think I couldn't do it!

Gunner Ian Sinclair, 425 Bty

Being a territorial officer was indeed an expensive undertaking demanding substantial private means.

We got fifty pounds grant. The regiment required that we bought blues, sword, spurs – the lot. Did it hell last! At the end of it all I went to the bank and said, "How much money have I got?" They said, "About three and six!" I said, "I'd better have it and start square!" It cleaned me right out – very expensive.

Second Lieutenant William Pringle, 425 Bty

Yet the new recruits accepted the situation and took pride in the slightly archaic nature of the SNH, 'A yeomanry man was so proud of his yeomanry status. I think it probably goes back to the days when he was very much his own man, he was the freeman that joined the yeomanry and probably took along his own horse!'[6]

★ ★ ★ ★

Most new recruits joined as gunners – the equivalent of the infantry private. Their training started on the mid-week drill nights at the Derby Road Drill Hall in Nottingham. But, gunners or not, they still had to learn to march.

> You were taught which was your left leg and which was your right leg and it's surprising the number of people who didn't know, they seem to forget that marching is only walking in a smart exaggerated manner. Once they get on parade and they start to march they're all over the place – they don't know their left hand from their right. If you say, "Left, quick march!" They put their right foot forward instead of their left!
>
> ***Gunner Norman Tebbett,* 425 Bty**

If marching was problematical for some of the recruits, then their weapon of war was a nightmarishly complicated piece of equipment with a tangle of controls and parts whose function defied easy definition.

> When we got into the drill hall we were taken to an 18 pounder gun. A sergeant came along and there was a little group of us and he said, "this is the Mark IV 18 pounder gun, this is the trail, this the carriage and this is the breech". He went round the whole gun and gave the name for each part of which we remembered absolutely nothing. I don't think he was an expert teacher.
>
> ***Gunner Ray Ellis,* 425 Bty**

Each gun team consisted of six men, each with clearly defined duties.

> Number One was the sergeant, he was in charge of the gun. Number Two put on the range and operated the breech. Number Three was the gun layer, he adjusted the line of the gun and the angle of sight. Number Four was the loader and Five and Six brought the ammunition from the limbers and put on any corrections on the fuses.[25]
>
> ***Gunner Ray Ellis,* 425 Bty**

But every gunner had to learn how to perform all these tasks efficiently and quickly, 'Change round, change round, change round, change round forever! So that everybody knew every position on the gun.'[7]

At the weekends they would go out for more practise in the local parks.

> Sergeant Bennett used to start out about half past six in the

Officers of the South Notts Hussars: Tallest at the middle back row is Lieutenant Slinn; first left front row is Captain R. M. Bourne; second left front row, Major Peter Birkin; middle front row, Colonel William Seely.

morning to rattle the guns out there on their steel tyres. Then we would pick them up and do a bit of gun drill – coming into action. They were all man handled, there was no gun tower. Unhitching the gun from the limber and placing the limber beside the gun and pointing the gun left or right depending on whether it was "Halt, Action Left", "Halt, Action Front" or "Halt, Action Rear" occasionally, just to confuse the issue. Then we'd have Tiffy Smith's sandwiches and Hanson's beer!

Gunner John Whitehorn, 425 Bty

The weekend training sessions had another bonus for the eligible young gunners.

We were all very, very proud to be able to put on our uniform on Sunday mornings, you didn't wear it during the week for training drills. I used to love putting the uniform on and getting on the bus on a Sunday morning and going up. Beautifully turned out, polished boots, riding stick – everything. We were all very proud of being South Notts Hussars even before anything horrible started.

Lance Bombardier Ian Sinclair, 425 Bty

As the new gunners sweated away on their drills, they began to make the friends that would support them through the stresses and strains of the looming conflict.

On that first night Fred Lamb and I then went out to a pub at the top of Derby Road and had a drink. That was the beginning of our friendship. I did drink a lot. It was the 'in' thing – to be part of the scene you had to have your hair sleeked back with Brylcreem, baggy trousers, smoke with a nonchalant air and you had to drink.

Gunner Ray Ellis, **425 Bty**

At this stage in their training any kind of association with officers was rare, 'The officers were very distant and aloof – far removed from the gunner. He probably walked around and looked down at us but I don't remember meeting them as people.'[8] When they did meet, many of the gunners were unimpressed. 'They didn't enjoy the best physiques. Your first sight of them they weren't upright men, they didn't look strong – there were two or three with speech impediments'.[9] At this stage in their training the influence of the sergeants was paramount and above all ruled the awesome figure of the Regimental Sergeant Major.

We had an RSM Porter who was the epitome of every Regimental Sergeant Major you've ever seen, a regular soldier. He really was a sight to behold. On one night when he came in and he was going round the gun crews one unfortunate gunner saluted him. In his own words he said, "I'm not a So and So officer, I'm far more important! I am the RSM! When you see me you don't salute, you shiver!"

Gunner Ted Whittaker, **425 Bty**

The training of the recruits peaked in the annual summer camp which in June 1939 was at Redesdale in Northumberland. To men like Signaller Albert Parker, it was a welcome break from reality. 'The excitement of getting to camp and meeting people. I didn't have a good childhood and I didn't go to many places so it was an outlet – an adventure!'

The main body of the regiment travelled up by train.

I think we left at about 11 o' clock at night. We'd all met previously and I remember getting on the train worse the wear for drink – with more bottles! It must have been somewhere about one-o-clock when we all fell into a drunken sleep. We arrived at Redesdale on a cold, damp, misty morning at about 5 o' clock. We de-trained and got a lorry that took us up to the camp. It was wet and cold and misty and there were some bell tents. I thought, "Thank God – now for a lovely sleep!" The next thing we heard was, "ON PARADE!" We said, "Aren't we going to get a sleep?" "THE BLOODY DAY HASN'T STARTED YET!" To my horror

I realized I had to do a day's work and I had a hangover. It really was my initiation into soldiering!

Gunner Ray Ellis, **425 Bty**

The tired, hungover gunners then had one of their first encounters with the epicurean pleasures served up in the army.

We were all startlingly hungry so we were called into the mess hut and there were some pork pies, which looked very good indeed, and bread, three quarters of an inch deep, which was slightly different from the dainty bread and butter I normally took at home. But these pork pies, having cut through them, the outside of the meat was quite a bright green – entirely and absolutely uneatable. We just went away hungry!

Gunner Fred Langford, **425 Bty**

It was not the last discomfort the men were to face and some of them found the experience almost traumatic.

It rained pretty well for the whole fortnight, I'd never felt so miserable in all my life. The first time I'd left home and roughing it with the food and everything else was just about a disaster as far as I was concerned. Never been used to the boozing habits of the older members, who seemed to think it was wonderful to get away from the wife for a fortnight. All I could think of was my girlfriend, who I'd left in Nottingham, and I couldn't get back fast enough quite frankly. The lack of privacy was really shaking, to come away from a reasonable family background and it was shattering.

Gunner Harold Harper, **426 Bty**

Men who had considered a couple of pints after a drill night as a drinking session were introduced to a new scale of values! 'It absolutely staggered me when I saw what they were drinking – eight, ten pints – it absolutely staggered me, I couldn't believe it. It shows how naive I was!'[10] The crudity of the unabashedly male company was also initially a shock to those who had never heard the like!

It was quite an eye opener! I'd led a fairly sheltered life and I met some quite extraordinary people from the slums – some had been in prison! They used the 'F' word literally every other line, it was quite incredible and to some extent, I must confess that we rather slipped downwards, rather than bringing them up, and our language became worse and worse!

Gunner Charles Ward, **426 Bty**

Good intentions were inevitably eroded by the sheer ubiquity of swearing in the army.

I remember saying, "I am not going to use that particular swear word as long as I am in the Army!", and everybody else said the same thing. I remember coming home at the end of the war saying

24

to my particular friend, "How I can so and so stop saying this so and so word I have no so and so idea!"

Gunner John Walker, **425 Bty**

The differing social backgrounds of the gunners were sharply highlighted when they were thrown together at the Redesdale Camp. This was reflected most obviously at Battery level.

The 425 was considered the County battery and 426, on the other side of the river, that was the miners' battery. Never the twain shall meet, great rivalry always! You ignored them, they were a race apart, you only spoke to them to sneer or be rude. It was definitely class based and they disliked us probably more than we didn't like them. The rivalry made us what we were. If there had only been one battery I don't think we would have been anything like the regiment we were.

Lance Sergeant Ian Sinclair, **425 Bty**

Yet whatever the gunners of 425 Bty thought, the officers of 426 Bty valued their men highly.

In 426, which I call my battery, they were nearly all miners. They wanted to join – that was one of the things my father always said, "They make the best soldiers in the world". They're born fighters: they're always fighting against their employers for a start; they're almost always fighting against conditions.

Major William Barber, **426 Bty**

Second Lieutenant Charles Laborde, who had been posted to D Troop of 426 Bty, saw a less aggressive, more courteous side to his men.

They were a splendid crowd there's no doubt about it. Just nice people. They were friendly, they took you at your face value – I was incredibly ignorant – I'd had nothing to do with guns and these people were always anxious to help. If you started to do something wrong they very quickly put you right nicely.

Second Lieutenant Charles Laborde, **426 Bty**

This willingness to share knowledge with their 'superiors' was a welcome trait.

It always amazes me really that they did accept this young bloke coming in not knowing the first thing and being an officer. Some of them had been in the regiment for some years and knew quite a bit about gunnery and they had to take orders from me. I should have thought they would have resented me but I don't think they did. I think it was rather the accepted thing at that time. It's the only way I can account for it.

Lieutenant Bob Hingston, **426 Bty**

Class differences also emerged within the batteries themselves. Sinclair,

Walker and their friends were an identifiable grouping within 425 Bty and they were given a none too friendly nickname.

The 'cut glass boys' were the people who came from public school and the High School. The expression came from the like of Jack Brown who was a bombardier in those days – an extremely tough Nottinghamian – he had an endless fund of wisecracks and expressions. There wasn't hostility but there was an 'us and them' situation between the 'cut glass boys' and the remainder. They were fortunate enough to have had a better education than a lot of their contemporaries who had gone to the Council schools in Nottingham. You had to tough it out and stand up for yourself.

Gunner Bob Foulds, **425 Bty**

Some of the 'cut glass boys' saw a political reason for the unrest.

There were one or two members of the battery who had a distinct socialist outlook and they used to call us the 'cut glass boys' which didn't bother us one way or the other. They did resent the fact that we came from better backgrounds than they did. Albert Sadler was one of them, a tailor by trade, perfectly normal ordinary sort of a chap but he'd got this sort of a socialist kink. It was the way we spoke I think

Gunner Charles Westlake, **425 Bty**

Nevertheless some of the working class pre-war territorials had a perfectly legitimate grievance against the new arrivals.

They were High School people and well educated. Some of them were studying to be solicitors and that sort of things. They were in their own business, their fathers had owned their own firm. They'd either got to be called up for the militia or alternatively they could join the territorials. Of course most of them joined the territorials to avoid being called up. We got on well enough but what I found was that chances of promotion just went. You tried hard – I became a qualified layer. Well normally a qualified layer after a while was always given his first stripe – but that wasn't happening. We'd been in a couple of years then, in training, yet you got these new fellows who it didn't seem as though they'd been in five minutes and their promotion was quite rapid. They were taking over all the more senior jobs. At the time it seemed most unfair to us and there was a little bit of background grumbling but in retrospect I suppose it was only sensible because these better positions were the ones where you needed somebody with a bit of intelligence and they were ready made for it. So in retrospect the Regiment did the right thing, but from the gunners' point of view they didn't stand an earthly!

Gunner Norman Tebbett, **425 Bty**

As they all got to know each other, alternative priorities began to take precedence in deciding friendships.

It died away so rapidly that it's hard to remember there ever was such a thing. At one stage you used to think you were different from somebody because you'd been to a good school but very, very soon you decided that everybody was a friend or they weren't a friend depending on things that were entirely different from educational background.

Gunner John Walker, 425 Bty

At Redesdale Camp the drills so painstakingly learnt on drill nights and weekend training exercises were put into practice aided, rather than hindered, by the competitive rivalries which pervaded every level of the regiment.

You were vying for points awarded by onlookers who were nothing to do with the regiment. It was a question of getting into action, firing the guns, hitting the target and there was a Challenge Cup between the two batteries – I like to think that 426 won it in 1939! More than likely!! My pals in 425 used to think they'd got the intelligentsia so they thought they'd got a head start. But we'd got enough intelligentsia and we'd got these very strong mining lads who could really move things fast.

Bombardier Herbert Bonnello, 426 Bty

The great moment came when the nascent gunners fired their first live shells into the unprotesting Northumbrian hills.

I'd learnt to lay and I'd got my layer's badge, very proudly I wore an 'L' in a laurel wreath on my arm. It was exciting to actually take the fire orders – put the angles on the dial sight, the angle on the sight clinometer, to bring the graticule in line with the gun aiming point. Report, ready, and then fire. Then for the first time in your life you pulled back the firing lever and this terrific, CRACK! The gun bounces back – the smoke and the smell of cordite and you've become a gunner!

Gunner Ray Ellis, 425 Bty

The noise of the gun was stupefying.

I shall never forget that first round. Never! An awful CRACK and we just sort of sat there wondering what had happened – whether the world had come apart! Until Greensmith bawled in my ear, "Get that so and so round out and get re-loaded!" Then we sort of shook ourselves and got into action again.

Cunner John Whitehorn, 425 Bty

The gunners also learnt the routine of army camp life and the fact that senior NCOs are never, ever, satisfied!

I was left to do sentry duty on Saturday afternoon. I was a very smart soldier – at least I thought I was and marching up and down outside the guard room no guardsman was ever smarter than I. I was very proud of myself. I noticed RSM Porter coming down the road and he stopped to watch me for a while and I really put on my good show. Then he walked over, as I thought to congratulate me on my smartness, and I shall remember his words for ever, "Boy, do you know what you look like?" I said, "No, Sir!" He said, "You look like a bag of shit tied up ugly! SMARTEN YOURSELF UP!" With that he walked away. That was a salutary lesson – he obviously thought this boy needs taking down a peg or two and he did it. Good old Porter!

Gunner Ray Ellis, **425 Bty**

As has been observed, some of the brighter new recruits found themselves promoted sergeant within a year of joining. This elevation allowed them to enter for the first time the inner sanctum of the sergeants' mess.

We had our own mess tent and food was served by orderlies which was really something. You were a thing apart as much superior as the officers were to the sergeants. The sergeants' mess was sacrosanct. When we had a sergeants' mess night the officers came in – a real high jinks night – anything might happen – I've been up on chandeliers, climbing tent poles, scrummaging, any of the old army games.

Lance Sergeant Ian Sinclair, **425 Bty**

The officers mixed socially with the other territorial regiments at the camp including Captain Leonard Gibson[11] of the Elswick Bty, 72nd Field Regiment.

They had their guest night and most of us went to them. They were very open, a very wealthy lot of chaps I would think. More so than we were certainly. And they would come to ours and then plots would be hatched. We had the sort of normal mess games and you would have competitions – the first over the top of the big mess marquee and down the other side, and so on and so forth. Of course we raided each other – the naughtiest boy in each regiment laid on a raid at four or five in the morning when everyone would be sound asleep and would get the best trophy they could find in the opposing mess.

Captain Leonard Gibson, **72nd Field Regiment**

★ ★ ★ ★

On their return to Nottingham the pace of events quickened over the last two months of peace.

With Munich the year before I can remember being, lets face it, scared stiff – fear for myself – I don't think one ever envisaged defeat for the country. The relief when Chamberlain came back with his piece of paper was immense and yet it was tinged very strongly with shame. The thought in the back of my mind was, "Oh my God, what have we done now?" By the time 1939 came along I'd put in a lot of work on the Territorial Army and my attitude was, "Yes, its got to come, I'm as ready as I ever can be – let's get on with it!"

Lieutenant Bob Hingston, **426 Bty**

In these tense circumstances normal civilian life ceased to have any meaning.

Everybody knew there was a war coming and you were in a vacuum – waiting and waiting – your mind all the time was on the war. Week by week it got worse and worse because you realized it was only a matter of time. In the meantime you were trying to do a job and it was totally unreal.

Gunner Charles Ward, **426 Bty**

At last the key party were called up on 25 August and they worked hard to smooth the way before the SNH were finally mobilized en masse at 14.30 on 1 September 1939.

On the Friday afternoon we'd just got paid and an announcement came over the loudspeakers, 'All members of Territorial regiments are to report to their units as soon as possible'. We were due to leave work at five and this was a bit before four o clock. I think it left two men in the office. We packed up and said, "We're off!" The man in charge wailed rather despondently, "What am I going to do?" and I'm afraid that one of our number, probably Spud Baker, told him just what he was going to do – and we'd gone.

Gunner Ted Whittaker, **425 Bty**

For some of the men trapped in 'dead end jobs' even the call to participate in a war could seem like a welcome break.

I was on nights at work and I got a telegram and I thought, "Well that's a relief!" It was a job I was doing to earn money but I didn't like it. To think we'd be having a break from routine work – night and day and afternoons. I thought, "Now we're going to be out in the fresh air and breathe some clean air in for a change!"

Gunner Bill Adams, **426 Bty**

The moment had finally arrived, but, for their parents, it also meant the disruption and possible destruction of their family.

When you're young you say, "Oh, don't worry, I shall be all right!" At nineteen going off to war you don't realize the depth of their feelings, what's going through your parents' minds. Therefore you don't react to it because you can't, you're too young and immature.'

Gunner Ray Ellis, 425 Bty

Despite the lessons of the First World War, in which many of their parents had fought, many of the men retained the optimism of youth. 'I think one was young enough and brash enough to think it would be exciting. I don't think we looked too deeply on the horrors it would bring. I thought it was going to be exciting. My God it was too!'[12]. This is not to say that they were without natural apprehensions as to their future.

> We all had an element of fear – everybody does! If you're going into war you've a great chance of getting killed or wounded, as have milions more. I loved cricket, football, rowing – I would sooner have got killed, although that's not a very exciting prospect, than have my leg shot off so I couldn't pursue my normal sporting activities

Medical Orderly Harry Day, **Regimental Headquarters**

The men had to report to the Derby Road Drill Hall. There as a member of the key party Herbert Bonnello found himself in possession of uniquely interesting, but possibly dangerous, information about one of the toughest and most unruly men in the whole regiment.

> I had to fill a form in for him and his name was A C Ellis and I said, "Right, full name!" He said, "Albert Ellis", I said, "'C' – what's 'C'?" He said, "If you ever tell anybody, I'll knock your nose in!" "What is it then?" "Cornelius!" I said, "You're joking, Albert Cornelius...!" He said, "I'll have you!"

Bombardier Herbert Bonnello, **426 Bty**

The drill hall was a vortex of activity as the men went through the rite of passage which converted a civilian into a 'real' soldier. 'I think we began to realize how little we really knew about the job. Kit that wasn't there, who did what exactly when you were all having to live together rather than just joining up for a drill, shaking down and finding out what one did through the day not just in the evening.'[13] After all the excitements, the men faced their first night in the army proper. 'That particular night the piece of concrete on which I was attempting to sleep was the hardest piece of concrete that I have ever come across or am ever likely to come across. Instead of sleeping on a feather bed at home I had just two blankets and a greatcoat to lie on and cover myself up.'[14] The men got little sympathy, 'I was told by Major Teddy Batt, "You'll have far worse billets than this before the war's over!" I can truthfully say I never did because even the sands of the desert were warmer and softer than that concrete floor!'[15] The unit was divided up

Ready to put paid to Hitler, at the outbreak of war four South Notts lads. Standing left to right: *Berry Springthorpe, Albert Ward;* seated left to right: *Taffy Stanway, Nobby Clark.*

and billets were found for them at the drill hall itself, the Western Tennis Club, the Hollins Lace Factory on Garden Street, the Methodist Church Hall on Derby Road and local schools.

It was a tennis club and upstairs there was a small ballroom dance floor and we all slept on there. Colonel Holden came to say goodnight to us and there was three of us in the corner wearing pyjamas. He said in front of the whole room, "Ridiculous, I've never seen soldiers in pyjamas before!"

Gunner Bill Hutton, **425 Bty**

The tranquil sleep of the gunners could be rudely disturbed by drunks amongst them seeking relief for their over-stretched bladders.

I arrived a bit late and I had to take what was left and it was on the route to the loos. There were always a few people who had been out on the beer and you'd been in bed about quarter of an hour – just dropping off – when you heard some chap making his way unsteadily to the door in complete darkness. You could hear him getting nearer and nearer to you and you thought, "Oh, God, he's going to trip up over – or worse throw up over me!" So I used to find it difficult to get to sleep till this lot was over.

Gunner Dennis Middleton, **425 Bty**

The actual declaration of war came on 3 September, 1939.

We had a radio and we were just stood outside on the side road of the Drill Hall listening to this radio. Chamberlain was saying that he had no reply and therefore we were now at war with Germany. And of course, "Oooh heck, now what are we in for?"

Gunner Norman Tebbett, **425 Bty**

A spirit of determination motivated many who had found the uncertainties of war a relief after the years of appeasement and sabre rattling.

"We're going to have a war! No, we're not, yes we are, no we're not!" The strain was getting too much for the people of this country. Thank God it's come – now we can get on with the job and get it cleared up, we wanted rid of Hitler.

Second Lieutenant William Pringle, **425 Bty**

Any lingering hopes that war could be avoided had vanished and the reality of the situation struck home to the young men who would have to fight now that the politicians had failed. 'Chamberlain had been on the wireless – it was really upsetting, it really got down into your stomach in a way.'[16]

CHAPTER TWO

The Phoney War

Before the Second World War there had been widespread apprehension over the spectre of crushing air raids and indiscriminate gas attacks destroying the major population centres of Britain; fears which mirrored the subsequent post-war fears of a nuclear holocaust. The first air raid alert at 03.30 on 4 September 1939, brought all such fears sharply into focus, 'All these sirens went off and we all said, "Oh, here we go, H G Wells, 'War of the Worlds.'"'[17] Chaos resulted on a scale which would surely have brought joy to the German Luftwaffe. At Western Road they rushed blindly into action, 'There was an air raid alarm and we all went out and started to dig trenches! It was a bit late!'[18] At Derby Road it was no better.

> We were then at the back of the drill hall and the orderly sergeant came and rattled on the door panels with his cane and woke us all up. I'd worked it all out beforehand – I'd decided to put my boots on and be mobile; my greatcoat on and be warm; and put my trousers on and be decent! It didn't quite work out that way because I got my boots and greatcoat on, but my boots stuck halfway down the drainpipe trousers, and I was absolutely transfixed. I had to get Dave Tickle to pull my trousers off before I could move. So I arrived down in the air raid shelter, mobile and warm – but indecent!
>
> ***Sergeant John Whitehorn,*** **425 Bty**

The anti-aircraft precautions that had been established to protect the SNH from enemy bombing were laughable.

> The one piece of armoury we had was a Lewis Gun. I was put on to that with Taffy Stanway stationed on the Drill Hall roof. We had some ammo but we weren't called upon to fire the thing. Two sides of the parapet wall and we just rounded off with sandbags. We couldn't make too heavy a job of it because we were on a boarded roof anyway. I think if we had fired the Lewis gun we would have descended through it!
>
> ***Gunner Frank Knowles,*** **425 Bty**

Fortunately it was a false alarm and Bill Hutton had his own theories as to the cause of the alarms, 'It was pathetic it really was, there was an unidentified plane over Southampton! We all had to get out of bed and get our civilian gas-masks and go downstairs just like a lot of nervous school-kids!'

Hitler and his generals review their victorious troops as they parade through the Polish capital, Warsaw, 5 October 1939. Britain was at war and the South Notts began training in earnest to become an efficient fighting unit.

The war had begun with Hitler's invasion of Poland on 1 September 1939. Innovative German blitzkrieg tactics, combining thrusting armoured divisions with demoralizing air attacks, were successful in smashing all organized Polish resistance by the beginning of October. The British Expeditionary Force was, as in the First World War, deployed alongside their French allies on the Western Front where enormous faith was placed in the static fortifications of the Maginot Line, combined with the effects of the maritime blockade, to stop Hitler in his tracks. The Territorial Army units had a vital role to play and the process now began in earnest to convert the South Notts Hussars into a disciplined army unit who could take their place in the line in action and perform their tasks under fire without faltering.

Getting people on parade quicker, getting them better dressed, teaching blokes to march that couldn't. Having to exercise authority on things that yesterday didn't matter when you were still a free man whether it came from officers, sergeant majors or sergeants. Being told, "You must!" or "You will!" rather than "Will you?". That was the thing and some people didn't take kindly to it. Some NCOs didn't find it easy to give orders – they were good at their jobs – but found it very difficult to instil discipline because they weren't particularly disciplined themselves. As Physical Training Sergeant I was getting blokes out of bed, getting them on parade, going on a cross-country run and doing physical exercises before they had their breakfasts. I was the most unpopular man in the troop. The physical condition of many of the men was very poor, they'd been taught to be technical soldiers, that's all, not a fighting soldier. It made some of them wish they had never been born. To have to go on a three-hour route march killed them – they were falling out by the wayside. It began to sort out the men from the boys at a very early stage; as to those who really wanted to do it and those who had been doing it just for fun.

Lance Sergeant Ian Sinclair, **425 Bty**

It was not only the men who found it difficult to discipline themselves to the requirements of war and some officers unwisely sought to insulate themselves from the rigours of training.

We set off with our full kit and boots. At this period we were not accustomed to wearing army boots – we were used to wearing shoes and it's a big change, you've got to get your feet acclimatized. We had an officer marching smartly in front but he was not wearing boots – he was wearing a Sam Browne and a pair of light brogues and that was it. We had marched quite a long distance when we passed a parked car in which sat another officer and these two changed so that we now had a fresh young officer wearing shoes. We got back with our feet all bleeding and sore and they told us, "You have to be toughened up, you never know what might lie in store for you! We thought, "Isn't it going to lie in store for you as well? Surely you ought to be doing it!" It rankled.

Gunner Ray Ellis, **425 Bty**

As they got fitter the route march became a less dreaded and more joyous occasion.

One of our great characters was Max Miller, he used to march at the head of route marches and lead the singing. One of his favourites was a music hall turn who had this weird thing, when they came on the stage, he'd shout, "Are you ready girls?" and they'd shout in very falsetto voices, "The girls are ready!" And every now and then on the route march Max would shout at the top of his voice, "Are you ready girls?" and 425 Bty would all reply, "The girls are ready!" and then they'd break into 'Roll out the barrel'.

Gunner Ted Whittaker, **425 Bty**

35

Left: *'Are you ready girls?' Sergeant 'Max' Miller.*

Three weeks after the declaration of war the regiment was posted away from Nottingham to join the 5th Cavalry Brigade, 1st Cavalry Division in Yorkshire. The scenes as they moved off on 23 September illustrated that they still had a lot to learn.

> We had the band and we marched down from the Drill Hall down Derby Road. A very fine show it was! I don't know how smart we were, I should think half of us were out of step. We marched to Victoria Station and we all lined up. Lots of people had come to see us off – my parents had come – and they were all on the platform. The train came into the station and everyone got on. We put all our kit on the luggage racks and all sat down packed tight like sardines. That was getting on the train! Then we all had to get off the train! Why? Because the officers hadn't got enough room they wanted two compartments. So we all got on to the train again and moved down a bit so we were more squashed together. We all got nicely settled, "Get off the train!" We all got off the train again and they moved us up again – I think the officers wanted another compartment. My father said, "God, I hope the Germans are in just as big a muddle as we are!"
>
> *Gunner Bill Hutton,* 425 Bty

Or, as somebody else said, 'Thank God, we've got a Navy!'[19] The regiment was posted to Rillington in Yorkshire and took up a variety of billets in the village and the surrounding hamlets.

> We arrived in the very early hours of the morning and they'd just cleared the pigs out of the pigsty. We had to clean the pigsties up. I'd been used to an early morning wash and shave in a nice warm bathroom. Instead of which I was out in the open, a row of taps had been plumbed in, with a cold north eastern Yorkshire wind blowing. It rather shook one's faith in human nature.
>
> *Gunner Fred Langford,* 425 Bty

Most of the billets were as primitive as this, lacking even such basic amenities as toilets.

> We were upstairs in a barn. We had about one blanket each and by God it was cold! That's when they decided to put the pee buckets inside because it was too cold to go out. These pee buckets used to get so bloody full, they were like those big coal buckets with a handle on, and they were bloody heavy when they were full – they must have held four or five gallons of pee! It didn't half stink and about three of us objected but nobody else, so they stayed in. I don't know whether it was because we'd done the complaining but that next morning it was our job to empty them!
>
> *Gunner Bill Hutton,* 425 Bty

At Scampston, near Rillington, Yorkshire, where billets were primitive. Left to right: *Gunners Middleton, Collihole, Bush and Coup. Behind them is the 'pick up truck' for the battery and in the background a barn that served as a garage. They are wearing fatigues overalls and slung over their shoulders the compulsory gas masks.*

The conditions were insanitary and not surprisingly minor health problems began to multiply.

> We were living in such filthy conditions. The blankets were never ever washed. Where they came from or who'd had them before we never knew. There was no proper facilities for washing so not surprisingly we got impetigo. It was quite common. A nasty thing to have – disfiguring.
>
> *Gunner Ray Ellis,* 425 **Bty**

Many of the men were greatly dissatisfied with the quality of the food that was 'served' up to them.

> The food was obnoxious; it was terrible. We used to march up through the village to the hall and they'd bring this stuff. There was grease floating on top of the big Dixies they'd cooked it in. We got to the stage where we'd seldom go up for midday meal. There was a little pastry shop down the way where we spent all our money. Eventually they made us go up even if we didn't eat it!
>
> *Gunner Ted Whittaker,* 425 **Bty**

Most of the men blamed their cooks, 'It seemed to me that they picked the dirtiest, scruffiest man of the least intelligence to be the cook! He had no idea how to prepare food.'[20] To the uninitiated even the most elementary cooking skills of preparation and presentation seemed to be lacking, which meant that a simple necessity of life could take on a strangely daunting aspect.

Have you ever seen boiled sausages, still all joined together – they just looked raw as if they hadn't been cooked. Our cook, I suppose he said he'd been in the catering business, that's why they made him a cook sergeant. But all he'd been was an ice cream man with one of those tricycle things – stop me and buy one!'

Gunner Bill Hutton, 425 Bty

Some of the officers, with some justification, took an optimistic viewpoint of the situation.

We knew they grumbled but then people always do grumble don't they? People used to grumble at school, say the food wasn't any good – it was perfectly good really. I suppose the truth is that if you cook in an open dixie then it's not what mum cooked! Remember a lot of these chaps were young men and some had never been away from home – they would be bound to find it peculiar and rather difficult. Institution food is always difficult isn't it. We just ate in the pub you see!

Captain Charles Laborde, 426 Bty

Even officers who accepted that the food was below standard found themselves rendered helpless by their own inexperience.

It was bloody awful, but if someone told you to go and improve that food, what would you do, how would you start? You don't know whether its bad meat to start with – whether its rotten or tough – you don't know how to alter any of it.

Second Lieutenant William Pringle, 425 Bty

Nothing effective was done to improve the food and overall the men endured their lot with considerable fortitude.

I don't remember much complaint – there were a lot of jokes about the man who went on leave and his wife gave him stew – but I think the men were all new to the army too and I don't think they'd really got into their stride in the complaints business!

Captain Bob Hingston, 426 Bty

The men simply did not know what was the norm in the situation they found themselves in and were hence unwilling to draw attention to themselves by complaining to the authorities.

It was accepted because we thought at the time that this was soldiering and had to be accepted as such. It was absolutely unnecessary at the time, it shouldn't have been like that at all, it was ridiculous. The way we were treated as soldiers in 1939 was appalling. I think our officers had a lot to answer for – they didn't care. It didn't occur to them – there was a big gulf – we were not considered.

Gunner Ray Ellis, 425 Bty

Gradually they learned to distinguish between the sublime requirements of serving King and Country and the merely ridiculous.

> Lieutenant Neale put me in charge of a party to smooth down the mud in the farmyard so that the battery commander on his battery inspection had a path to go on. It didn't really make much difference because his boots sank into the smooth 'path' just as well as they did into the unsmoothed path. That rather coloured my attitude to bullshit for ever. I felt it was just too much – I didn't mind being smart and polishing things up but smoothing mud with the back of a shovel was a bit much!
>
> *Sergeant John Whitehorn,* 425 **Bty**

The officers had comfortable billets but even here there were problems.

> I think there were three of us in this house of this millionaire chap who was tied up with newspapers in Hull. He was as tight fisted as the Devil! We were forbidden to use the front door of the house and he rendered us a laundry bill at the end of the week although he was drawing billeting allowance. In the finish we dug the guns in on this bugger's lawn! There was a hell of an explosion but there was nothing he could do about it – the pits were dug, the guns were in them and that was it! Another thing we did was his car was a Lanchester – a fine engineering type of a car which requires good fuel. He couldn't understand how we could do so much running about and he couldn't. We said, "Well we put half paraffin in ours!" Well that was right but you wouldn't in a Lanchester! He put this paraffin in and it went great. Well of course it would because the carburetter and everything was full of petrol. He went down the bottom of the road and phut, phut, phut phut... He never got it to go again – the paraffin had ruined the engine.
>
> *Second Lieutenant William Pringle,* 425 **Bty**

It was perhaps as well for the three officers that on 6 November 1939, the regiment moved by rail to Wragby in Lincolnshire whilst the guns went by road. They had received their first news of the posting from the enemy! 'Lord Haw Haw was our great source of information and we heard from him that we were going to go down to Lincolnshire and sure enough about a week later the 1st Cavalry Division moved down to Lincolnshire.'[21] The orders caused the usual panic as, at this stage, the SNH needed all the warning they could get before a move. 'We'd been told that we had to move in two days! We said, "This is appalling – we can't possibly do it!" We always chuckled afterwards in later years when we got the order, "Be ready to move in an hour!"'[22] When they at last set off the drive was not without incident.

On the move from Rillington to Wragby we used coal lorries

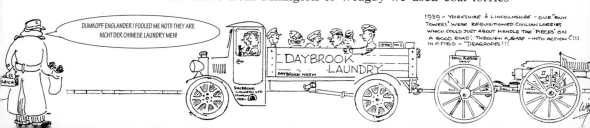

adapted with trailing eyes on them. I was to lead one little convoy of four guns and I was in the front in a pick-up truck with this officer. The drivers told me, "We don't want to go at ten miles an hour. When old Parsons is not looking just put your foot down Ted!" We set off from Scampston and we went through Malton. Official orders had been 15 miles an hour and I was knocking up 25 easily – and the officer said, "Pull to one side here!" We pulled to one side and watched the convoy go past. When it got to about the third the gun was missing – it had come off it. We had to stop them and turn back and it had gone through a shop window in Malton. I was disgraced then – they caught on I was trying to go fast and I was put in a 426 lorry as a spare driver and for the rest of the journey we went at a snail's pace that sent us all to sleep.

Driver Ted Coup, **425 Bty**

The regiment was billeted in another unsatisfactory set of billets in the Wragby area and the programme of training for war continued. One disappointment was the continued inadequacy of the guns.

The Old Mark IVs went away to be converted into 25 pounders so we were told and in their place we got a full complement of Mark IIs which were 1917 guns – they had 1917 marked on the breeches. The breeches were clumsier, they had a pole trail so that you got very little elevation and thus range without actually digging the trail in. Once you had dug it in of course you couldn't move it sideways. They were still steel tyred on wooden wheels. They had wooden bungs in the muzzles and 'For Drill Purposes only' marked quite clearly in white paint on the trails. So they really weren't very popular – they were useless we couldn't fire them!

Sergeant John Whitehorn, **425 Bty**

Preliminary preparations began for the regiment to go overseas and it was thus important to weed out all those who were too young, old, or just inadequate. Often men considered acceptable in the peacetime territorials were seen as potential liabilities on active service. Some of the replacements came from the newly formed 150th Field Regiment, SNH. 'I was transferred to 107th Regiment. They'd got some quite young boys, 18 year olds, 17 years old probably, in the 107th so they transferred those back to the second regiment and I at my advanced age of 23 was posted to the 107th in exchange for one of them.'[23] In addition drafts of militia men and recalled pre-war reservists from the regular army arrived to bring the complement up to full strength.

One of the good things the War Department did was include in the draft local people from Nottingham or South Derbyshire. Therefore they had a lot in common with people in the Regiment and there wasn't the resentment that there might have been. There were the odd Taffs and Jocks and Brummies but quite a few locals.

Gunner Frank Knowles, 425 Bty

The militia men were conscripts who had been called up on the outbreak of war. One of them was Ted Holmes who came from Chesterfield and had done his training with the Royal Artillery at Kinmel Park near Rhyl before being posted to join the SNH.

I liked the badge with the gun on it – the Royal Artillery badge. I thought, "An artillery regiment with an acorn badge, this seems funny." At first I didn't like giving the gun badge up, I wasn't ever so pleased at having to change it, but I got used to it and I wouldn't have any other. I took to it and I've been proud of it all these years.

Gunner Ted Holmes, 425 Bty

The more worldly-wise reservists were not pleased by the state of the billets they were occupying and were equally disgusted by the cooks' failings. They were a mixed group.

Some were real scroungers, caricatures of old soldiers who were there to get the maximum out of it whilst doing the least possible. There were others who became sergeants who were excellent soldiers and really taught us a lot.

Bombardier Charles Ward, 426 Bty

Depending on their own characters and ambitions the territorials picked on different aspects of the regulars' behaviour to emulate.

They were sharper as a soldier, smarter, the discipline was better. They couldn't understand why we were relaxed and too friendly. I liked it because they'd had this experience of being a soldier. Even the manner that they dressed – they were wearing a uniform – we weren't, we put it on and the uniform was wearing us instead of us wearing the uniform!

Gunner Norman Tebbett, 425 Bty

Other, less admirable regulars, were the role models for Bill Hutton. 'I think they were better at skiving than as soldiers but we didn't know how to skive when we got into the army. We soon learnt!' As the *ingenues* gained experience and the reservists made friends the unit began to mould together. 'They all started by being themselves – reservists or militia men – but it wasn't long before they became South Notts Hussars.'[24] Certainly one of the new militia men was more than capable of looking after himself in any kind of company.

In the first militia was a chap named Tom Foley who had been a professional boxer. He'd beaten a champion pre-war and he was contender for light-weight or middle-weight championship when war broke out. He was born at the wrong time – like Tommy Lawton. He couldn't compete in the army – I think there has got to be a six months' lull before a professional can drop his professional status and fight as an amateur. I'd done a bit of boxing in the Boys Brigade and I came under his wing a bit. We used to train at the Turnor's Arms where there was quite a big club room on the first floor and the landlord allowed us to use this free of charge. There were about half a dozen but mainly this Tom Foley used us as sparring partners to keep his fitness up.

Gunner Frank Knowles, 425 Bty

The local civilians made the gunners welcome, 'Everybody was good to soldiers then – they didn't know we weren't any good as soldiers!'[25] The approval of one section of the local community was naturally sought with particular interest by the men, 'The local girls were delighted to see the boys and the boys were delighted to see the local girls – there were quite a few romances started up!'[26] The local ales were also enthusiastically sampled when the men had the money, with occasionally amusing consequences.

This trumpeter used to come down into the middle of the square and blow lights out at ten o clock – nobody took any notice! One night I was in the office there on what was my bed and I heard these footsteps down the stairs, into the square and this trumpet started, UHHRRWEE! He was obviously stoned out of his bloody mind. He had a few attempts and went back upstairs – you could hear him faintly practising. He came down again and he had about three goes before he could blow 'Lights Out'!

Gunner Fred Brookes, 425 Bty

The regiment had been warned to complete their preparations for overseas service by 5 January 1940. As a result in the Christmas period most of the men were granted embarkation leave to allow the men a chance to see their loved ones before an indeterminate period of overseas service. The obvious corollary to this was that they may not return at all and emotions ran high.

I said goodbye to my mother, and I said, 'Now, don't expect me back soon, we shall be away a long time – at least two years...' And she burst into tears. I was merely trying not to raise false hopes.

Gunner Dennis Middleton, 425 Bty

In the days immediately preceding the embarkation the regiment were visited by a living link with the cavalry of the SNH who had served Queen Victoria in the Boer War.

We had a church parade and Colonel Sir Lancelot Rolleston

came. It was a bitterly cold day, one of those biting frosty mornings with a fog. After the church parade we stood on the school playground and old Rolleston, he must have been well in his eighties then, with no greatcoat he stood and addressed us. A great old man and that is where we first heard the words, "Once a hussar, always a hussar!"

Gunner Ray Ellis, 425 Bty

At last the time had come as the SNH set off as part of the 1st Cavalry Division to go to Palestine on 18 January 1940. The regiment was commanded by Lieutenant Colonel William Seely with his battery commanders Major Peter Birkin and Major William Barber.

We marched out of Wragby to catch the train about midnight. We were marching along this icy road and it was difficult to keep your feet with all your equipment – rifles, ammunition, field kit-bags – we were sliding about trying to march. Somewhere near the church I heard a woman say, "God help them, they don't know what they're going to". No we didn't!

Gunner Ray Ellis, 425 Bty

The Honarary Colonel, Colonel Rolleston bade
the Regiment Farewell at Wragby in January 1940
when I am SURE he told us to look after our
horses! He was a very old man, of course, to we
20 (ish) lads but a fine specimen of a South
Notts. Hussar. AND - who could forget his final
words? "ONCE AN HUSSAR - ALWAYS AN HUSSAR!"
(And We Are!!!)

CHAPTER THREE

Palestine Days

The Palestine Protectorate had been wrested from the Turks at the end of the First World War. It was not a war zone in January 1940, although there had been a substantial amount of trouble in the mid 1930s as tensions between the Arab population and the ever-increasing influx of Jewish settlers had boiled over in the 1936 Arab Revolt. These problems had by no means evaporated but simmered away, occasionally flaring up, as one side or the other took umbrage at real, or imagined, grievances. The 1st Cavalry Division were sent there as garrison troops, thus freeing regular units to move into the Western Desert to face the increasingly hostile Italians in Libya. The territorials would also be able to complete their training and to get used to the sort of desert conditions that they could expect to face in the event of full scale war breaking out in the Middle East if Mussolini brought Italy into the war on Hitler's side.

★ ★ ★ ★

The regiment embarked at Southampton on the SS *Amsterdam*. For many of the Midlanders this was literally the first time they had seen the sea.

> I'd never been very far previous, it was all like an adventure to me to be going down to the south coast. Southampton to me only existed on a map. Its not until you get down there and actually see it that you realize – you see all the ships and realize what the sea is like. I thought it was marvellous.
>
> ### *Gunner Ted Holmes,* 425 Bty

Many were not as cheerful as they may have outwardly appeared to their comrades in arms.

> I walked up the gang plank and I honestly thought I'd never see the shore of England again. I thought that – I don't know why. I was depressed, very depressed. When we were with one another we never showed signs of depression or anything – we were always laughing and joking. You kept these thoughts to yourself.
>
> ### *Driver Ernie Hurry,* 425 Bty

Although *en route* for the Middle East, they were sent across the Channel for the overland trip across France to the Mediterranean. The crossing did not take long and the regiment disembarked at Cherbourg.

> We stood on Cherbourg docks from early morning to late at

night in the most atrocious weather you can possibly imagine. It was absolutely bitterly cold. We were in field service marching order, weighted down. We'd stand for half an hour then they'd say, "Kits off!" So you lay down, unclipped the webbing and then you could sit up without the weight. You'd just get that done then, "Packs on!" You'd have to lie down again, clip it on, struggle to your feet again. Then you'd stand quarter of an hour, march about a hundred yards, halt, stand again, "Kits off!" This went on the whole day – there was no food, nothing to drink at all.

Gunner Ray Ellis, **425 Bty**

Although only passing through, the men were still keen to sample the delights of French hospitality.

They said we could go if there was six of you and you had to have a NCO in charge. Well Taffy Stanway was one of the regulars with a badge on his arm because he was a Lewis gunner. Taffy he says, "We're not having an NCO! I'll reckon to be the NCO when we go into Cherbourg". We sets off and we got to the gate and theres a guard of these French sailors. When he spotted them Taffy lines us up, and marched us off. When we got towards them he's going, "Left, Right", really regimental, we were all swinging away. These guards were so amazed they nearly came to attention as we went past. Anyway we had a good night, went to a café, had some egg and chips, dancing with these French lasses. It was really nice, they sort of put their arms round you and really hug you! None of us got too much beer or owt, just nice and merry!

Gunner Ted Holmes, **425 Bty**

Some of the men were innocent in the extreme.

We all got talking and exchanging stories of where we went. One said, "Did you go in such and such a place?" I said, "I think we walked in and walked out!" He said, "Did that girl come up to you making a fuss of you?" I said, "She did, why?" He said, "That was a brothel!" "Ooooh", I says, "I've never ever seen one of them before – I always wanted to see what one was like!" "Aye", he said, "She was after taking you upstairs!" "I missed me chance then!" Of course they pulled my leg and said, "You must have been dumb!" I said, "I must have been!"

Driver Ernie Hurry, **425 Bty**

Others seemed to have a sophisticated veneer, but Bombardier George Attewell gave a practical demonstration to Gunner Fred Brookes of the truth of the dictum that a little knowledge can be a dangerous thing.

George recommended, 'We ought to drink red wine and kirsch!' I hadn't been on the Continent before this don't forget – I was a home lad! We'd only got money for drink – hadn't got money for anything else! Red wine and kirsch! I got back to the train and sitting on this metal step I heaved my bloody heart out I really did! It tasted worse when it came back I'll tell you! I don't remember much of the journey!

Fred Brookes, 425 **Bty**

The next stage of their journey was by train right across France.

From Cherbourg to Marseilles was a nightmare of cold and misery and lack of food. The only thing that kept us going was that most of us had managed to buy somewhere in Cherbourg a fair amount of rather raw brandy and we kept our spirits warm in that sense. But it was a very cold ride.

Bombardier John Walker, 425 **Bty**

Everything seemed to conspire against them, 'The French driver kept stopping the train and I don't know whether the brakes weren't quite right but it used to stop suddenly with a lot of squealing of brakes. All your kit dropped off the rack straight down on to the floor.'[27] Occasionally, there was a silver lining, 'The next night we went over the Central Massif and it was beautiful. I stayed up all night, the scenes were spectacular, snow, mountains.'[28] But, by the end of the line, Ray Ellis was at the end of his tether, 'I was really ill, they carried me off the train on a stretcher. I lay there shivering on the quayside at Marseilles and eventually was carried on the *Devonshire.* I can remember saying, "I expected to come back on a stretcher, I didn't expect to go on one!"' As it was considered that the men could not be trusted to behave in Marseilles only the officers were allowed passes into town. This may have been a mistake!

We went round boozers, brothels, restaurants, cafés... Missed the boat! The boat had gone when we got down to the quay. We were told they wouldn't wait – they said that at five or six o clock they were moving – and they did! Mind they were a hell of a lot of officers short! We found a chap and they said that they had only moved so far out and anchored. They agreed to row us out for an enormous sum of money. There were two or three small rowing boats full. They knew who we all were because it was, "Name, rank and number", up the gang plank. It was all part of the game as far as I was concerned. You were going to make the best of it and get on with it. We were all very suitably dressed down the next day!

Lieutenant William Pringle, 425 **Bty**

The reunited SNH finally sailed aboard HMT *Devonshire* from Marseilles on 22 January 1940.

The moon rose just after we had sailed. Perfect Mediterranean night. The following morning there was a howling storm, the ship was pitching and rolling – there were two of us went to breakfast and I was one of them! We ate till we couldn't eat any more! All

46

Aboard HMT Devonshire *sailing from Marseilles to Haifa.* Left to right: *Gunners Collihole, Middleton, Bush and Coup relaxing on the promenade deck.*

the others were in these hammocks and one or two of us were doing the classic, going round, "Anyone for bacon and eggs!"

Gunner Ted Whittaker, 425 Bty

For many the rough weather created a physical torment of repetitive, gut wrenching vomiting.

The boat was pitching and tossing all over the place and everyone was seasick. Somebody had been to fetch the food and they were coming down the steps and the boat lurched and they fell. All the way down the steps was rice pudding and bully beef all slopping down among the sea sick. It was really miserable!

Gunner Ray Ellis, 425 Bty

In these circumstances it was difficult to imagine that things could have been worse but according to German propaganda they were! 'Half way across the Med we were listening to Lord Haw Haw and he said that they'd sunk His Majesty's Troopship *Devonshire*! And we were on it – load of old tosh! But they knew we were on our way, they knew all about us.'[29] Gradually however things began to improve, 'As we got further out the sun gained in strength and things looked a bit brighter, the sea calmed down a bit and we were able to go and sit on the deck.'[30] To the men fresh from a harsh European winter the warmer temperatures

47

seemed bliss but they soon realized that everything was relative. 'As we were approaching Palestine although it was their winter we were beginning to undo our collars because it was a bit warm. Yet the army fellows on the side of the docks, they had balaclavas and coats on!'[31] Disembarking at Haifa on 29 January the men were made what seemed to be a tempting offer by local entrepreneurs. 'Young Arab lads selling us oranges for which we were highly delighted to get about four for a penny. Later we found that all you had to do was go to the nearest orange grove and they'd fill a truck for you!'[32] The regiment was directed to the nearby Sarafand Camp which was still under construction as they had arrived two days earlier than expected. Here they were placed in quarantine due to two cases of meningitis which had caused fears of a full scale epidemic.

> The tents had been pitched on rather sticky clay soil on a bit of a slope. Fortunately there were some contractors there who were making concrete bricks and they'd got some wooden pallets. We managed to scrounge a few pallets to lay our bedding out on. It was very fortunate we had done this because, when we woke up in the middle of the night, it was absolutely pouring with rain and water was running through the tents, mostly underneath the pallets, but there was quite a lot of kit swilling about in it.
>
> **WO3 John Whitehorn, 425 Bty**

This quarantine period placed rather a strain on the men.

> We had a period of really low morale, "Please, Sir, I want a transfer!" "I'm sorry to hear that, where do you want to go to?" "I don't mind where, anywhere!" That was the general approach to life. They were all thoroughly fed up. They'd left home quite excited and here we were settled down in this foreign place which they instinctively disliked and there was nothing else to do except square bashing. It was a very nasty period.
>
> **Captain Bob Hingston, 426 Bty**

Entertainment opportunities were perforce limited but the camp cinema was running an intriguing special promotion for hard up gunners wishing to sup at the well of popular culture.

> If you save a tin of flies, a fifty cigarette tin, you were allowed to go to the cinema free. Instead of taking money you took a tin of flies and they'd tip these out and give you a ticket to go in. That was to encourage you to swat flies. It was very easy to get a tin of flies – you just sat there swatting for half an hour there were so many!
>
> **Gunner Ray Ellis, 425 Bty**

Film watching was indeed a communal experience, 'If a couple started to look like kissing on the screen people would shout all sorts of very lewd advice as to what they should do. It was quite amusing to sit at the back listening to the advice rather than watching the film!'[33] The cinematographic equipment was often fairly primitive and the audience was not always tolerant when things went wrong, 'It was always breaking down and we used to throw oranges at the screen.'[34]

★ ★ ★ ★

On 12 February they were moved to Gedera Camp which their advance party had helped to erect. 'Our job was to put up a lot of EP/IP tents. Swinging big mallets, knocking in pegs – putting up lines of camps and in fact building an army camp. When the regiment arrived all the lines in the camp were given Nottingham names like 'Long Row' and 'Clumber Street''.[35] Now out of quarantine the men soon became aware of the conflicts raging on and below the surface in the 'Holy Land'. Modern values such as racism cannot easily be transplanted back in time and in 1940 it is evident that most British people considered themselves part of a 'superior' race. As such they were regrettably intolerant of other nationalities, 'Arab dockers unloaded the boat and we decided that Arabs were quite nice chaps, just as good as we were. It wasn't very long before we decided they weren't. We soon found they were scrounging, thieving sods!'[36] The prevailing view seems to have been that, 'The Arab had a knife in your back and the Jews had got both hands in your pockets – so watch it.'[37] Naturally the priapic urges of

Under quarantine after arriving in Palestine the South Notts are quartered in tents, during the rainy season, and have to cope with water running through the tent lines.

49

A group of fairly typical Arabs in front of their village, which the South Notts lads were delighted to learn was called Bash Shit!

many men were not affected by such prejudices, 'We used to have to come back past these kibbutz's. They were in tents and you would see them getting undressed by candlelight and what have you! It was a bit frustrating!'[38] Such yearnings were often repelled when even the most innocent of contacts was sought.

> You could sense a lot of hostility in their looks. One afternoon I was walking along a street in Gedera and passing two Jewish young ladies. I said, "Good afternoon" to them and they spat at my face! That was rather a shock because I'd always been brought up to believe that everyone thought that the British were marvellous people.
>
> ***Gunner Ray Ellis, 425 Bty***

Commercial arrangements were however still available to those unable to resist the pleasures of the flesh with the consequent inevitable risk of venereal disease.

> Lectures were given by Doctor Finnegan and Major Batt, the adjutant. Major Batt suggested that a man should work off his surplus energy by indulging in sport and as much physical hard work as he could. Finnegan advised that the men should have prophylactic treatment by carrying and using a condom and using the prophylactic centres afterwards.
>
> ***Medical Orderly Harry Day, Regimental Headquarters***

Without the guns which had been left in England, training could not properly start, but there was still much that could be done to get the regiment ready for war.

> All our heavy baggage had gone off to South America they said! We were there for several weeks with no equipment of any sort at all. The result is we spent our time going on route marches. The

whole battery, and we marched and marched and marched and marched all over the place. The usual thing – ten minute halt – at the end of the hour. The ten minutes was a bit elastic but it was very nearly always up against an orange grove and as soon as the people fell out they all disappeared and came out looking like Mae West! Bulging with oranges!

Captain Charles Laborde, **426 Bty**

On 29 March the regiment moved to Hadera Camp where the heavy equipment arrived and training began again. Some, like Bill Hutton, had learnt a thing or two from the regulars by now and had secured a plum job, 'I became a 'Don R' – despatch rider – and that's a job that suited me down to the ground – "Excused all duties!" It got you from under the sergeant major's wing. Every time he looked at you, you said, "Oh, I've got to go up to RHQ!" A good job despatch rider was!'

Thankfully the cooks had begun to improve and perhaps one crucial reason was the arrival of a new cook, ex-Savoy Chef Ted Hayward, just before they left England. He was commencing a career which would over the years take him to the rank of Brigadier in command of the whole Army Catering Corps! His first reaction to army food was not untypical.

There was a big dixie of stew which was hard to decipher what it really was. There were some stewed apricots and some custard. You had a plate and they seemed to use the same spoon for dishing out the stew as they did the apricots and custard. The taste of it was quite abysmal.

Cook Ted Hayward, **425 Bty**

In a few months he had risen to the rank of Cook Sergeant and gained, through personal experience, a greater understanding of the awful

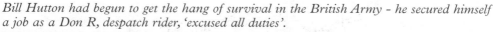

Bill Hutton had begun to get the hang of survival in the British Army - he secured himself a job as a Don R, despatch rider, 'excused all duties'.

problems faced by all army cooks. Even his culinary imagination failed him at times!

> Nobody gave any thought to linking the main element of the meal, the meat such as it was, with any vegetables that were issued. For instance I've seen frozen rabbits issued and the only veg issued were raw beetroots. Now I defy any chef to produce a meal from that!
>
> ***Cook Sergeant Ted Hayward, 425 Bty***

In the end one solution nearly always beckoned for the main mid-day meal.

> Stew – there was no other way. If you're feeding three people you can get three fillet steaks, but when you're feeding that number you had only a small proportion which is fit for roasting or frying. So therefore it all has to be stewed – shove it all in the pot and brown it!
>
> ***Cook Sergeant Ted Hayward, 425 Bty***

The pink boiled sausages, so feared by Bill Hutton, also had a perfectly rational explanation.

> When you were issued with sausages they arrived in reasonably good condition. But you couldn't keep them because there was no refrigeration, so the only thing you could do was to boil them in water, which didn't make them terribly attractive quite honestly. But it was either that or have rotten sausages. You could keep them cooked for a day or so but they wouldn't keep for a day if they weren't. There is no other item of food that is so liable to

An orange bonaza for the South Notts during a break in one of their many time consuming route marches.

contamination than the average sausage – that's under ideal conditions but under these conditions... We served them as soon as we possibly could. The whole regiment literally could have gone down!

Cook Sergeant Ted Hayward, 425 Bty

Even Hayward, who had been taught by some of the world's strictest chefs, could not keep clean as an army cook. 'You were clean to the best of your ability. It wasn't possible, you were dealing with a dirty stove handling dirty fuel all the time – they were doing their own stoking.' Even such a simple job as making a mug of tea wasn't easy when it was for the whole battery rather than a couple of chums in a bivouac.

It takes a lot of boiling water to make tea for 600 people and they did like tea! You couldn't get that amount of boiling water so what one did was make an infusion with boiling water and then added hot water to the infusion to make it up to the required amount. Probably that accounts for army tea – some liked it!

Cook Sergeant Ted Hayward, 425 Bty

And as the cooks struggled they were only too aware that only one thing really mattered in the army.

The important thing is that at a given time of a day a soldier has got to sit down and be fed – nothing else is taken into consideration. How the supplies come, how you can manage to keep it and cook it – that is not important. A great crime is not serving bad food but not having it there on time!

Cook Sergeant Ted Hayward, 425 Bty

All these improvements and remaining problems were as nothing to the crueller humourists in the regiment, 'We used to say to people from another unit, "We have a fantastic cook in the troop at the moment – he's a classical scholar!" "Really?" "Yes, in fact he has a Latin motto!" "Really, what's that?" "Fucum! Givum stew!"'[39]

★ ★ ★ ★

At both Gedera and Hadera Camps they were close to the sea and many of the men went on the regular bathing parades, 'There were no women about so you could swim with no costume on. Its surprising what a difference it makes, it seemed to sort of give you more freedom, you can't express it really.'[40] While their bodies browned in the sunshine memories of pre-war English seaside resorts paled in comparison to the Mediterranean! 'We did a lot of swimming there. I enjoyed it – you could see the bottom of the sea, nice and clear, lovely sands – Blackpool wasn't in it!'[41]

Local Arabs failed to appreciate the finer art of the British national game and wandered at will across the pitch during the game, oblivious of the stinging potential of the 'corky'.

Sport provided another form of recreation and a cricket match was played between the officers and sergeants at El Mughar during the period at Gedera, 'We played a cricket match and our quartermaster sergeant a chappie called Len Craven said, "In the First World War I charged over there on a horse with a sabre!"'[42] Captain Bob Hingston had played a little pre-war cricket as a fallible but straight hitting batsman and he thoroughly enjoyed the game.

A hilarious afternoon. The locals were accustomed to walking across the village green whenever they wanted to. The idea of having to stop doing that for a cricket match never entered their heads. Two women walked across being very careful with all these men about to veil their faces so they nearly fell over the stumps on the way through. Donkeys wandered across too. It was a grass wicket, pretty rough, I don't remember there being any fast bowlers so there was no danger – they might have caused havoc! I played, Joe Comber was our Captain, he'd kept wicket for Cambridge, and he said, "Bob, you bowl at that end", I said, "I can't bowl!" "You can, you can bowl!" So I proceeded to turn down some very slow tweaky slow balls, one of which immediately got a wicket! "There you are, Bob, I said you could bowl!!" About the only time in my life I bowled. I didn't get many runs, double figures possibly. The officers won almost entirely owing to Bill Barber. He came in and hit it all over the place and made a lot of runs.

Captain Bob Hingston, **426 Bty**

A joint officers and NCOs team from 426 Battery also played against the Palestine Police and Charles Ward[43] showed some of the gritty determination he would expect from the players of Nottinghamshire County Cricket Club of which he became president in later life.

It was against Lydda Police and we played on a matting wicket. Some of the officers had whites, we other ranks – I had a pair of grey flannel trousers and I played in those. I was a bowler and on this matting wicket it was very difficult to turn the ball so the batsman had a big advantage. Nevertheless I didn't do too badly and I got a couple of wickets. They put me in Number 9 and I'd scored eight – got a couple of boundaries – and the last man was in, the other two had lost their wickets. We'd got a chance of playing for a draw but the idiot at the other end ran half way down the wicket to a slow bowler, missed it of course and was stumped. I was furious because I felt absolutely certain we could have held out for a draw!

Lance Sergeant Charles Ward, **426 Bty**

The officers normally spent their evenings in their mess.

The mess was tented and we got very browned off with having to wear blue patrols in the evening. Our mess dress was tight blue trousers with a double yellow stripe down the side, a blue jacket with chain mail on the shoulders and it was rather thick blue serge and it was very hot. After a time a deputation was sent to the Colonel to say, "Please may we not wear this, please can we wear our dinner jackets!" That was agreed and of course it was much cooler with a white shirt and no waistcoat just the jacket.

Captain Charles Laborde, **426 Bty**

At first the mess was fairly formal with a 'high' and 'low' table which caused a little resentment amongst the junior officers. The Colonel again showed a flexible outlook.

Bill Seely had the tables re-organized and he himself did not have a Colonel's seat – he sat anywhere and he mixed with everybody else. The other senior officers got the idea and the whole thing was mixed up. It was a very good move on Bill's part it really brought the whole lot together. He believed in the army principle that there should be no rank in the mess. You called the Colonel 'Bill' in the mess, if you met him outside you called him, 'Sir', and saluted him.

Captain Bob Hingston, **426 Bty**

At this stage the SNH officers do not appear to have been a very hard drinking mess.

By then, as so often happens with Englishmen, we all drank beer at home but as we got to a hotter climate we rather tended to turn to whisky. For some reason or other whisky produced in a rather cold chilly climate in Scotland is a very good drink in hot weather. But the actual drinking of alcoholic beverages declined and we drank an awful lot of soft drinks. The general heat encouraged one to drink and most of us realized that if we were going to knock back whisky when we were thirsty we would be in trouble because we would drink too much.

Captain Bob Hingston, **426 Bty**

Many of the officers were being taught to ride which illustrates the continuing strength of the horse culture within the 1st Cavalry Division even in 1940.

> While a lot of the officers were fairly accomplished horsemen there were a great number like myself who had never ridden and so Major Batt instituted an officers' riding school which used to take place at 2.15 in the afternoon, when it was very hot. The horses were all fairly splendid, high spirited and what have you, and we used to ride round in circles and it must have been a fairly comic sight to watch – because we used to fall off like nine pins. It was terribly hot and we did in the end persuade Teddy Batt that it was too hot to do it in the middle of the day and we started in the morning at six fifteen, which was very much more attractive. It was cool and pleasant – and not so many other ranks looking on laughing either. It's always fun to see your officers making fools of themselves isn't it? We got to the stage where we could go round the circle without falling off then we started riding without any stirrups. That was very difficult to start with when you came to the sharper corners one tended to go straight on while the horse went off to the left! We got reasonably proficient at that and then we started to ride the horse with just a blanket – no saddle at all. That was a fairly hazardous affair to begin with and I fell off so many times I lost count! Then we did some bareback riding and all sorts of exercise. We had to run alongside the horse holding on to the saddle and then leap into the saddle. The first time I did it I gave a great leap as I used to when I jumped for the ball in the line-out at rugger and I went right over the horse and landed flat on my back on the other side which caused a great deal of mirth! Not mine!

Captain Charles Laborde, 426 Bty

On Easter Monday a boxing competition was organized throughout the whole of the 1st Cavalry Division and the tougher members of the SNH initially fancied their chances.

> Tommy Foley persuaded me to go in for it because I'd done a bit when I was younger. Frank Knowles said, "Well if you do, I will!" When they have these tournaments the winner gets a voucher to go and spend in the canteen, the loser got less. I said to Frank just before, "Look, we'll share what we get. If you win and I lose, we share and vice versa."

Driver Harold Thompson, 425 Bty

Frank Knowles was confident that whatever happened no-one could take too severe a beating.

> One of our officers, a 426 Bty officer named Clarke, he'd done a bit of boxing at university and he was our fight manager. He had

set himself up to check that no-one was mismatched. That was supposed to be his function. But some of the regiments that had boxers taking part, they didn't let them out, they brought them in a 30 cwt vehicle with tarpaulins over the back and let them out one at a time. They got more and more like Rocky Marciano! Frightened you to death – they shouted professional!

Gunner Frank Knowles, 425 Bty

It is perhaps not strange that even fifty years later Frank Knowles did not wish to recall exactly what happened to him that day in Palestine. Harold Thompson was due to fight shortly after him and after seeing the rather messy results he seems to have lost much of his enthusiasm for boxing.

Frank was first and oooh, he got caught. I looked at him and I said, "I'm not sharing that lot with you!" Because all his face and eye was cut, blood all over the place. Anyway I came to my turn to go in and this youth came in with boxing shorts and shoes on and I thought, "Aye, Aye, he's not going to hurt me!" I went straight across and hit him Whhoof! He sort of shook his head and then he got going. He hit me on top of the head and I thought, "Aaaah, I'd better go down!" I went down, then I realized he hadn't hit me hard enough! I lasted three rounds but he hardly laid a glove on me because I was getting out of the road all the time! If I'd have won I'd got to fight this bloke that Frank had lost to and I wasn't wearing that!

Driver Harold Thompson, 425 Bty

Of course the SNH had their own professional but, rather naively, he had not been entered for the competition. 'Tom Foley was quite put out to put it mildly. He was throwing challenges out left, right and centre because we had abided by the rules – he could have been included as one of the team.'[44] However, Albert Swinton was skilful and strong enough to avenge his comrades in one of the title fights.

I was light heavyweight and I'd had two bouts before, I won easily. I watched this semi-final and this Scots Grey bloke had taken advantage of one of our blokes, an older bloke, mid-thirties which was old to me. He gave him a rough time, he kept going at our chap, he was inflicting punishment on him that was absolutely unnecessary. He'd already won but he was really going mad and that to me was wrong. I thought to myself, "Now if I come up against you I'm going to give you a hell of a tawsing!" I met him in the final – it was set up for three two minute rounds. We started off and he landed one on me – right in me bread-basket – and I thought, "My God, you've got to watch yourself, Swinton, or you're going to get panned out here!" Because it hurt! I back-peddled a bit and sort of got me breath back and then I hit him about three times and I cut him each time with the force of the blow. He finished up hanging on the ropes with blood pouring from his face and with everybody shouting, "Finish him! Finish him!" Well I'm afraid I couldn't I hadn't got that killer instinct – I'd won and that was it finished as far as I'm concerned.

Lance Bombardier Albert Swinton, **426 Bty**

Bombadier Albert Swinton about to land the knock-out blow during the Light Heavyweight Boxing Final during sports day.

★ ★ ★ ★

At Hadera 425 Bty were re-equipped with Mark II 18 pounders – a case of back to the future – whilst 426 Bty got 4.5 howitzers. Intensive gun drill training commenced in readiness for attending the firing camp at Asluj near Beersheba.

We used to go down the road towards the South and then we would drop into action on the left or right hand side of the road. What I remember mostly about it is of course the wild flowers which in Palestine at that time of the year are famous. We would drive off the road into a field flaming with colour – lupins about 18 inches high, lilies of the valley – it was really rather sad driving over these and crushing them, putting the guns into action. The drill orders were all the same – dropping into action, paralleling the guns, firing them off just clicking the trigger.

Captain Charles Laborde, **426 Bty**

One major handicap was the shortage of basic equipment, 'For instance we only had one dial sight to the troop so that when the troop went into action the dial sight had to be taken from Number One gun, to Number Two, Three and Four, so that the guns could be laid out.'[45] A training programme had commenced to train suitable candidates to become 'specialist' gunners to assist the officers in the mathematical side of gunnery.

> To start with you were teaching educationally matric level people. There was no problem you could tell them how to work logs – they knew how to work logarithms! You then got down to the nitty gritty of miners, brickies, labourers – who couldn't care less about logs, or slide rules or directors. Well it was a bit of a thankless job.
>
> *Lieutenant William Pringle,* **425 Bty**

One of the NCOs who took over running the courses had not appreciated the necessity for a back to basics approach.

> George Attewell had got to run a specialists' course and he had these lads, about ten of them. He was going through what was involved, how many degrees there are and all this sort of stuff. He'd been talking for about quarter of an hour and he said, "Would anybody like to ask a question?" One lad at the front said, "Yes, Sarge, what's a degree?" He said, "Right! We'll start again!"
>
> *Gunner Fred Brookes,* **425 Bty**

The regiment slowly worked up to full efficiency and their progress was monitored by the inspection of various senior officers.

> The Brigadier, Royal Artillery, he was a demon. The first instance he came to inspect us and we were all drawn up. Instead of coming to inspect the troops he went to the lorry park. He found something wrong with a lorry because he crawled underneath it which of course Brigadiers don't do! He called off the whole thing and said, "I'll come back when you're ready!"
>
> *Signaller Ted Whittaker,* **425 Bty**

Brigadier Keith Dunn was obviously a man of strong views which he was by no means reticent in expressing.

> Brigadier Dunn came and gave us the most God awful roasting of all time. For the first time I was afraid of a man – his steely blue eyes. We were sloppy, we didn't know our drill, we were no bloody good. There was nothing really wrong but there was no way they were going to let you think that you were God's gift. He didn't say that one troop or battery was any better than any other – we were all bloody awful. No-one ever forgot him, or forgave him for that matter, because we were trying so hard!
>
> *Lance Sergeant Ian Sinclair,* **425 Bty**

On 15 April the SNH were inspected by General Sir Archibald Wavell, the General Officer Commanding, Palestine.

> He walked along the line as Generals do and picked up some odd man to speak to. He stopped in front of me and said, "Do you feel ready to go out and meet the enemy?" To which I replied, "Yes, Sir!" "Good man!", he said and walked on. Had Hitler known I was ready to go and meet the enemy the Third Reich would have trembled!

Gunner Ray Ellis, 425 Bty

At last they went to the Asluj firing camp on 1 May. The strenuous drive through open desert was a training exercise in itself as, before the regiment could function properly in the desert, they had to learn the skills of driving on sandy, rough terrain.

> You learned eventually to change gear without using your clutch for quickness. In them vehicles you double de-clutched. Instead of just putting your clutch in and going into gear, you had to put your clutch in, take it out of gear, put your clutch in again and put it into your next gear. Without the clutch you listened to your revs and then put it into gear. Its something you've got to learn how to do. You've got to know exactly when to do it otherwise you get a KKKKRRH!!

Driver Harold Thompson, 425 Bty

On arrival they began a vigorous programme of practice shoots. But the desert conditions were quite extreme, with sandstorms and the extreme heat of around 95 degrees in the shade, making life a misery. 'When we got down to Asluj it really was like the last place God made – the most awful desert!'[46] The men had been warned about the dangers of heat stroke and sunburn but, as Harry Day recalled, 'There was one particular case because a stupid fool had laid in the sun and went to sleep – and that was the medical orderly himself – me! I had a temperature of 104, I treated myself with calamine lotion!' In that climate there was a real danger from rotting food.

> It was so bad that if there was any cooked food left from one day you could not keep it in the camp overnight because the next day it would be riddled by maggots. We had no means of cooling left over food and the temperature at which the food was kept naturally by the climate was ideal for the breeding of all types of germ, maggots and rot! We had swill contractors who used to come and if by five o clock in the evening they had not arrived we had to dig pits and bury the left over food.

Cook Sergeant Ted Hayward, 425 Bty

Another extreme was the presence of Australian troops at the camp! 'There was some Australians with us that were pretty lively. It was the

Gunner Ray Ellis with one of the 18 pounder MkIIs at Gedera Camp.

first time we'd come across people like them. Provided you could swear more than they did, you got on fine. You had to stand up to them, they thought you were a bunch of pansies if you didn't swear and drink.'[47]While the regiment were at Asluj they suffered their first casualty in circumstances which, even today, arouse considerable ill feeling and controversy. A group of gunners had already developed a lack of faith in their Medical Officer Lieutenant J E Finnegan.

> When you went to him you didn't seem to get any compassion at all. His main purpose seemed to be to get you back on duty with the minimum of fuss. You always had the feeling that he considered that you were malingering and you were brushed off. Harry Day was his orderly, he was very keen and took the job very seriously and it was to Harry we went rather than to the doctor. We had more faith in Harry Day.
>
> **Gunner Ray Ellis,** 425 **Bty**

In fairness to Finnegan it could be said that his *raison d'etre* as a doctor was indeed to get people back on duty without fuss and that diagnosis is never a foolproof affair especially when a proportion of the patients undoubtedly were malingering. 'The MO started off being what I would call a civilian Doctor. Then he became more hardened – he had to because there were so many people going to him so anxious to get a few days sick!'[48] The regimental history also refers to him as 'the ideal active service Medical Officer.[49] Nevertheless some felt that the first casualty could have been avoided.

Bob Paulson was in a little bivouac tent and he developed this illness that Harry Day knew was appendicitis but the Doctor said he'd just got stomach ache. We'd go out on the range and come back and see poor old Bob writhing in pain on the floor of this stinking little tent in the desert. He was in absolute agony, sweat was pouring off him. But still the Doctor wouldn't do anything about it until in the end after three days he had to realize he was seriously ill. He was sent away but he had peritonitis – a burst appendix – and he died. Being one of his closest friends I was sent as one of the burial party. We set off across the desert to follow the same track that poor old Bob had made. It was an appalling journey, it was so bad the bouncing in the back of this 15cwt that I hit my head on the stanchions that hold the canvas in place and my nose was pouring with blood. I thought, "Poor old Bob, coming along a thing like this with a burst appendix." We saw the sister at the hospital who said that she had never known anyone fight so hard for his life but he died. We buried him in Ramleh cemetery and he remains there. He shouldn't have died. Had Bob lived he would possibly have been killed at some later stage, but that's beside the point. He was so young, you don't expect nineteen year olds to die. The first one.

Gunner Ray Ellis, 425 Bty

The regiment returned to Hadera on 18 May. It was as well that they were approaching the end of their training because the 'Phoney War' was at an end. Hitler had been biding his time preparing for his spring offensives. These at last commenced with the landing of German troops in Norway on 9 April 1940, which was vigorously, but ultimately futilely, countered by a British landing on 15 April. This though was a mere curtain raiser to the devastating *Blitzkrieg* offensive launched by Hitler on the Western Front on 10 May 1940. A thrust through Holland and Belgium, drew the BEF forward into Belgium, only to be followed by a brilliant armoured lunge through the Ardennes area which hopelessly split the British and French armies and flung them into a scrambling retreat. Long lines of demoralized troops and terrified civilians were mercilessly harried by the screaming Stukas as they fell back with all pockets of resistance being surrounded and ultimately

Observation post established by D Troop, 426 Bty during training at Hadera Camp, Palestine. Left to right: *Gunner Isherwood, Battery Sergeant Major Wigley, Gunners Monteith, Widdowson and Lynch. All the real action was taking place in Belgium and France.*

swallowed. Relief only came with the humiliating evacuation of most of the BEF from Dunkirk in late May and early June. These staggering events – so different from the popular perception of endless stalemate left by the First World War – had a marked effect on morale viewed from the side lines in Palestine.

> While we were there the balloon went up in Europe. We all wanted to know what was happening especially when the disasters began – the Germans' breakthrough. One of the first things we used to do when we got back to camp was to put the Eleven Sets on to the news in London. We had these special 'end fed' aerials which vastly increased the range. We could hear this terrible news coming through night, after night after night. That was a constant source of conversation in the evening. The news was simply awful if you can imagine being stuck down in a God-forsaken part of Palestine with everything going wrong at home. The one thing that never for one moment entered into our minds was that we should lose the war but it was then that one realized that the war was going to last for a long time.
>
> *Captain Charles Laborde, 426 Bty*

Many felt that they were in the wrong place entirely at this crucial moment in the war.

> There was a lot of discontent, we were out in Palestine where nothing was happening doing meaningless drill, when we knew that all our people at home — mothers, wives and sweethearts — were at great risk. We thought they were going to be bombed to hell and naturally you thought of the people at home. People were suffering like that in France and at home and you felt rather guilty about it. You felt, "Why aren't we back there?"
>
> *Lance Sergeant Charles Ward, 426 Bty*

The catastrophe in France also began to raise concern among the men about what would happen when they actually had to face the German juggernaut. 'We were armed with the old 18 pounders, the most modern bit of which was the tyres – and we heard about the *Blitzkrieg* and the German Air Force! Quite frankly I really wondered if I should ever get home again.'[50] They now knew that the war was going to be far from easy, 'After the fall of France it became quite apparent, as Charles Laborde used to say, "this war will go on for six years. It's going to take us four before we can do any attacking!"'[51]

With the German invasion of the Low Countries in May 1940, and the immediate success of their army, the Phoney War came to an end. The South Notts felt left out of it as the panzers rolled towards the Channel ports.

Chapter Four

Mersa Matruh: Hell Spot of the East!

Benito Mussolini had led his fascist party to power in Italy during the years of post-war political and economic chaos. He formed the government in 1922 and shortly afterwards assumed dictatorial powers as Il Duce. As such he had predated Hitler in his rise to power in Germany in 1933, but the two were natural Allies and formed the Axis Alliance in 1936. Mussolini's long term aims were to establish a new 'Roman' empire in the Mediterranean and North Africa which naturally brought him into conflict with the existing colonial powers. The strategic importance of the area was absolute to the British Empire guarding as it did the Suez Canal – the gateway to India – and the Middle Eastern oil fields. Initially cautious on the outbreak of war, Mussolini was tempted by the prospects of rich pickings from the vulnerable British and French African empires, if Hitler should win, as indeed appeared likely after the fall of France. Overcoming his fears he formally led his country into the war on 11 June 1940. The Italians immediately moved their armies right up to the Libyan/Egyptian border where they unaccountably paused, despite a considerable superiority in numbers over the British forces in the area. In these circumstance the SNH were chosen to move up into the Western Desert to take over defensive positions at Mersa Matruh, approximately 250 miles west of Cairo. This would allow the regulars of the 1st Field Regiment, Royal Artillery to move up into the front line facing Mussolini's somewhat hesitant legions. As the first unit of the Cavalry Division to move up into the desert they faced the symbolic departure of the horses as they were brought up to war readiness.

Suddenly we got this seven days' notice that we were moving. Then of course things began to happen. First of all the horses were to go which was very sad and the day before the Colonel organized a so called 'hunt'. There were no hounds and no quarry but all the officers went out and we had a tremendous gallop about. Then of course the equipment started to arrive. The poor 104th, The Essex Yeomanry and the Lancashire 106th – they were completely denuded of everything. All their guns, their dial sights, their trucks – suddenly we were absolutely smothered with equipment. I must say I didn't envy the quartermaster who had to take it all on and sign for it all! It was a fairly hectic seven days.

Captain Charles Laborde, **426 Bty**

Group of South Notts men, bound for Mersa Matruh, waiting transport across the Suez Canal at El Kantara.

They set off on 23 June 1940.

> We knew we were going into action and we got some chalk and wrote on the side of the train, "Mussolini, here we come!" How green we were. There was no fear, exhilaration – at last we were going into action – we were really going to show these Italians what was what! The South Notts Hussars were coming!
>
> **Gunner Ray Ellis,** 425 Bty

Now that the war had moved thousands of miles closer a traditional 'spy' scare occurred.

> A man we called 'Palestine Post' he was a little Jewish man who followed us around in Palestine. He sold newspapers and had a little stall which he had permission to set up in our camp. The main paper was called the *Palestine Post* and so he was christened. He went with us but when he got to the border somebody saw he was there and there was some talk of him being a spy and he was sent away.
>
> **Gunner Ray Ellis,** 425 Bty

As they moved into Egypt they became aware of one of the traditional features of rail travel in that country.

> Sitting on this Egyptian State Railways train we first saw the men who used to wait at little wayside stations with trays hanging round their necks carrying pieces of bread and eggs. They used to say, "Eggs y bread, eggs y bread!" Which in fact were quite tasty and we used to buy them. These men used to stay on the train to the very last moment and then jump from the train doing probably

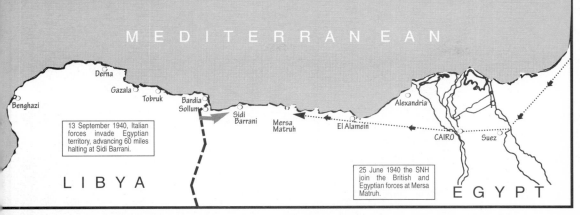

MEDITERRANEAN

Derna

Gazala

Tobruk

Bardia
Sollum

Benghazi

Sidi
Barrani

Mersa
Matruh

El Alamein

Alexandria

CAIRO

Suez

13 September 1940, Italian
forces invade Egyptian
territory, advancing 60 miles
halting at Sidi Barrani.

25 June 1940 the SNH
join the British and
Egyptian forces at Mersa
Matruh.

LIBYA

EGYPT

25 or 30 miles an hour, with bare feet onto the sharp granite
chippings at the side of the railway and without spilling their
precious eggs and bread.

Gunner Ray Ellis, **425 Bty**

Many of the men were only too happy to buy their wares.

Anything for a change from bully beef and biscuits and I leaned
out and said to this lad, "Give me some eggs and bread!" I gave
him a ten piastre note and that was the last I saw of him! He was
off. What I'd got was worth about fifty cents and he was off with
my ten piastre note. Someone said, "That'll teach you won't it!"
That was my first lesson in Egypt!

Lance Bombardier Albert Swinton, **426 Bty**

Their destination, Mersa Matruh, was still intended as the final bastion
to stop any attack on the Nile Delta from the west. It was a slightly
incongruous fortress.

Mersa Matruh had been a seaside resort and had a lot of very
attractive villas and what was supposed to have been a nice hotel
called the Lido where it was said that the Prince of Wales and Mrs
Wallis Simpson had stayed. But it didn't strike me as being very
splendid – of course it had been heavily bombed then, all the
windows had been blown out and it didn't retain much of its
peacetime glory.

Captain Charles Laborde, **426 Bty**

On 25 June the SNH joined the garrison which consisted of the 22nd
Infantry Brigade dug in along the western perimeter with elements of
the Egyptian Army continuing round to the east. They took over gunpits
and half completed dugouts from the 1st Field Regiment, Royal
Artillery but there was much digging still to be done. The urgent need
to complete it soon became apparent as Italian aircraft began making
regular high level air raids. 'They came in from the sea and they were
there before you knew it – you didn't hear them!'[52] The surprise could

67

Road into Mersa Matruh, a pre war holiday resort for the rich and famous, being steadily bombed to ruin by high flying Italian bombers.

be terrible for inexperienced troops.

> I heard a screaming sound and the next thing there was this vicious explosion and I hurled myself to the ground. It was a stick of bombs falling but I didn't know at the time. I hadn't heard any aircraft and there had been no air raid warning. There was this devastating flashing, crashing and blast – then it went quiet. Then there was another scream and a soldier came out into the street. He was holding his guts in and all his stomach had been torn open and his entrails were trickling through his fingers. He was screaming and then he sank to his knees and his screaming changed to a gurgle and he just sort of dropped almost at my feet. He was the first man I saw die.
>
> ***Gunner Ray Ellis, 425 Bty***

This was the beginning of a real bombing offensive against Mersa Matruh by the Italians 'The bombing was simply terrible, it went on for most of the day, every day, on and on and on – we reckoned we were the most bombed place on the surface of the earth.'[53] Although the high altitude bombers could not be heard they could just be seen by those with good eyesight. 'If you looked up in the clear blue sky in the sunshine they were just like teeny wee little silver fish. The Italians used to get somewhere near Mersa Matruh and then just shovel the bombs out and get away as quick as they could.'[54] One of the first casualties was Major Edward Batt who was hit on 18 July.

> Major Batt was lying in a shallow trench dug out under a Bell tent with Colonel Seely. He was a very tall man – about six foot three – and inadvertently he lifted his leg and a piece of shrapnel

A Cant Z1007bis Alcione, of the Regia Aeronautica, one of the types used for high altitude bombing of Mersa Matruh which provided the baptism of fire for the SNH.

Major Edward Batt

took his foot almost off. He was put on a stretcher and I supported the foot. Finnegan told him that artificial limbs would mean that he could still partake in his favourite sport of riding. He was evacuated to the Casualty Clearing Station and then removed to the 15th Scottish Hospital in Cairo. The amputation proved a success but some time afterwards a piece of shrapnel was belatedly found in the other foot which caused gangrene. The other foot was amputated and he died.

Medical Orderly Harry Day, **Regimental Headquarters**

It was obvious that a system of slit trenches was required to minimize the effects of this awful random threat from the sky. These were dug so that wherever a man happened to be, he was only a few yards from cover.

You were for ever on the alert. Listening all the time to see if you could hear a drone, looking up all the time – especially if you had to go somewhere. Say I had to go from the gun position to

Photograph taken during a raid on Mersa Matruh in June 1940. The Italian bombers were too high to aim accurately.

headquarters, before I set off I would be looking all around, then run like the clappers to a slit trench, get down and have another look and so on till I got there. That's how it affected me.

Driver Harold Thompson, **425 Bty**

This form of reaction was not uncommon in the early days at Mersah Matruh for it was, after all, how most people react under fire for the first time.

I felt a bit jittery, nervous... To me these people who say they were never scared, I just can't believe them – it can't be true. Yes you accept it, you're there and there's nothing you can do about it. But I'm blowed if I can accept that anyone who's being bombed is not scared! You know full well the next one could land against you and kill or badly injure you. You do your job because you're there to do it and you've got to do it. People used to go a bit bomb happy – it's bound to affect you I don't see how anyone can possibly say that they weren't afraid – of course they were afraid! But you've got the courage to carry on.

Gunner Norman Tebbett, **425 Bty**

Some men found great difficulty in controlling their inner fears.

Some people just spent all their time near a slit trench. They had to be kicked to be moved. Even though they'd got good sleeping accommodation they'd go and sleep in a slit trench. People who were bomb happy couldn't get in a truck and drive –

Medical Orderly Harry Day attending a minor injury to Lieutenant Clark in the Medical Tent.

Left and above right: *Officers Bob Hingston and Charles Laborde engaged in digging slit trenches at Mersa Matruh.*

you had to make yourself keep going because once you said, "Oooh, I can't go out", you'd had it. You had to carry on as far as possible normally.

Sergeant Charles Ward, 426 Bty

Under the strain their nerve could crack altogether. This appears to have been especially apparent amongst the older men who perhaps had been tested to their limits in the First World War and could not stand the return of such traumas late in life.

The Sergeant Major who signed me on, he literally gave up. He went all to pieces. He became an alcoholic, went down to hospital and we never saw him again and apparently he died only a couple or so years after. I was very disappointed to think that a man of his calibre, who told us what to do and what not to do and then we suddenly find he wasn't much of an example. I had very little time for anybody who swafted around like that when there was bombs flying because I thought people should have a little more common sense.

Lance Bombardier Harold Harper, 426 Bty

Another man resorted to an old army trick. 'We had a regular soldier with us who eventually got out by tapping his knee with a wet towel and a spoon – making his knee come out. We watched him. You wouldn't have dreamed of doing it yourself, we were a bit scornful really but nobody thought of reporting him.'[55] In a tense atmosphere like this, the slightest alarm could set off a dangerous panic, which the officers and NCOs had to contain before it spread from a few individuals to infect the whole unit. 'We got so bomb happy. If you saw a man running to the latrine everybody would take cover! So there was a garrison order given that no one must run in Mersa Matruh.'[56] For a while many remained sceptical.

Freddie Porter was a very professional soldier – it had been his life. He was a great disciplinarian, "There's no need to run for a

71

slit trench, you'll get there safer if you walk!" That was his feeling but quite a lot of the chaps said, "Aye, but I shall get there a damn sight quicker if I run!"

Bombardier Herbert Bonnello, 426 Bty

Gradually most of the men realized the point of the order as their experience grew.

> You get far too dependent on dugouts and trenches when there are air raids about. I was thankful to Captain Porter because when there was an air raid on we all used to run and jump into a trench. That was absolutely the wrong thing to do because you did more damage to yourself jumping into the trench than anything that would have happened if you'd taken your time in quietly walking. He issued an order that anybody seen running to take cover would be put on a charge. That was one of the first basic drills we learnt.

Gunner David Tickle, 425 Bty

But Captain Hingston tested the inner calm of his men to the limit!

> I was inspecting C Troop when the signaller poked his head out of the dugout and said, "Air raid red!" One or two men swayed a bit and I heard one of the Sergeants say, "You haven't been given any orders to move yet!" I carried on the inspection and trying to keep as calm a voice as I could I said, "Sergeant, will you let me know if you can hear any enemy aeroplanes?" "Yes, I can hear one now, Sir!" So I said, "Right, well we'd better take cover then!" They broke off and there was a shout from one of the NCOs, "WALK!" And everybody walked calmly to their slit trenches!

Captain Bob Hingston, 426 Bty

It did not help that their enemy was out of reach, 'We were all strained by this continual bombardment from the air and we couldn't fight back. Had we been anti-aircraft gunners we wouldn't have been afraid – we'd have been doing something but it was the fact of just sitting there.'[57] What anti-aircraft guns they had were considered to be useless, 'There were two three-inch guns which were manned by the Egyptian Army. We used to say that just before a raid they would knock hell out of the sky, then whilst the planes were over they were very quiet and as soon as the planes had gone they knocked hell out of the sky again.'[58] Another grievance was the suspicion that indirectly their fellow countrymen in the arms industry were the authors of their misfortunes. 'It aggravated the point that these bombs were made by Cammell Lairds – what we didn't call them was nobody's business. We found a nose cap and it was stamped on it.'[59]

The men began to discern a pattern in the bombing which alleviated the terror generated by its formerly apparently random nature.

They would come over at a great height – mere specks in the sky – in arrow head formation. They would drop bombs – centre; right left; right left – five in the arrow head. They came over in absolutely straight lines and you could see exactly where they were going and hopefully take avoiding action in time.

Warrant Officer 3 John Whitehorn, 425 **Bty**

With such experience many came to terms with the scale of the threat and were able to rationalize their fears.

I've never been a brave man and I must admit that I took cover as quick as the next person when an air raid started. But you became more selective if you could get some indication of where the bombs were coming. You didn't used to worry if you knew darn well that they weren't going to land on you. You could tell by the sound whether they were or not. But nobody could say that it was a pleasant experience. One treated them with complete contempt after one had experienced it because they were quite useless. The thousands of bombs that were dropped on Mersa and although it was regrettable for the individuals concerned there were probably no more than half a dozen people killed. They were so frightened they flew so high. One never saw Italian planes coming over, they were like little dots in the sky and they were more keen to drop their bombs and go. This may be a slur on Italian aeronautics but this was the feeling we all had.

Bombardier John Walker, 425 **Bty**

The men became aware that even 'direct hits' on the gun positions did not necessarily cause casualties.

There was a raid came over and we were watching Troop HQ from the dugout entrance. We saw the figure of George Pearson walking across, he made a dash for a slit trench and disappeared into it. The raid came over and when it had gone we saw that where the slit trench had been there was just a black mark and we said, "Alas, poor George!" But George got up out of the black circle, walked away in the wrong direction to start with, then turned round and went in the direction he was going originally. It gave us all some confidence that you could get that close to a bomb and not get knocked out.

Warrant Officer 3 John Whitehorn, 425 **Bty**

George Pearson had his own perspective on this closest of shaves.

There was this very loud bang and I won't say I was knocked senseless but very badly shaken. When I got up I found I was on the black rim that just surrounded the bomb hole but not even touched by a bit of shrapnel – it must have just gone straight over me because I was lying so close. It certainly perforated my eardrums, I didn't hear reasonably well for two or three days.

Sergeant George Pearson, **425 Bty**

Captain Charles Laborde had studied geography at Cambridge University and he attributed geological rather than supernatural reasons for the seemingly amazing lack of casualties suffered by the SNH.

The desert itself is stony and very dusty. Whenever there is a duststorm, sandstorm or what have you, all the fine material on the stony parts is blown away and it settles in the hollows. There it forms the soil which is technically known as loess. This is packed earth or sand. You can dig in it very easily, trenches with straight sides, sandbagged round the top, you don't have to revet it. To give you some idea of the resistance and strength of this soil – in the position we dug forward of our main position we had an anti-aircraft pit which was five feet across and about six feet deep. One day when we were all on this gun position we had a fairly hairy bombing attack and the bombs fell all over the position. The nearest one was to that Bren gun anti-aircraft pit. The edge of the bomb crater which was about five feet deep and six or seven across was about five feet from the side of the pit and the wall was only just cracked – amazing the resistance and hardness of the soil. It meant that the digging was not too bad and when you had dug a trench you were pretty safe in it.

Captain Charles Laborde, **426 Bty**

There was even a rather good joke circulating about the bombing!

They had a dummy airfield and railhead nearby. The camouflage people used to shift dummies on the latrines each day, they had oil fires which they set off when the Italians came over bombing in the hope that they'd bomb the dummies rather than Matruh. There were a lot of dummy aeroplanes made out of painted mess tables. It was said that they came over and bombed them with wooden practice bombs!

Warrant Officer 3 John Whitehorn, **425 Bty**

Finally the RAF provided a more practical and satisfying solution to the problem.

In the autumn reinforcements were arriving and – *mirablu dictu* – some Hurricanes. That was the biggest excitement, they got among these bombers and I think they shot down several. The men were standing up and cheering like mad at the sight of these bombers being chased off. They didn't come again.

Bob Hingston, **426 Bty**

However they had reacted, every one of them had

Digging in was to be become second nature in the desert.

74

faced death, and their perspective on life had almost inevitably changed, 'There were huge spiders almost as big as your hand with big jaws. They dug holes and you could hear their jaws clumping as they picked up sand – they were fascinating things. I used to find pleasure in bombing them – throwing things at them – but after Mersa and being bombed I stopped!'[60]

* * * *

The men spent a great deal of time digging and given the presence of so many miners it is not surprising that some remarkable creations were constructed in the guise of gunpits and dugouts, although one officer was a little unwise in offering his advice, 'At Mersa Matruh Charles Laborde told George Smith, "That's not how you use a shovel and spade – you should dig this way!" Major Barber said quite politely to Charles, "I shouldn't tell him how to use a shovel and spade, he just happens to make his living that way!"'[61] The men worked with a will to improve not only their safety but their comfort.

We first dug the ordinary gun pit. Then we decided to put a roof on the gun pit. This was done with wooden beams and corrugated iron. We stole it from dumps – we'd go off and steal equipment from the Royal Engineers. It wasn't bomb-proof it was just under cover. At the back we built a high wall of sandbags to protect the rear. We left a huge recess about two foot wide the whole width of the front of the gun pit. The gun was in an enclosed pit like a home made turret. Whilst this was going on the Royal Engineers were busy building a concrete pillbox for the machine gunners. They worked during the day and at about six o' clock they packed up and went back to their camp. As soon as they disappeared over the horizon we started up the concrete mixers again and set to work. First we built a flash apron in front of the muzzle of the gun so that when we fired we wouldn't give ourselves away with a big cloud of dust. We built a concrete semi-circle for the trail of the gun so that when you dragged the gun round it ran in this concrete gully. Then we set to work to build our own dugout. We dug a hole with shovels and picks about eight or nine feet deep and about the size of an ordinary living room. Then we lined the sides with corrugated iron supported by posts, all stolen. We decided to make the top as bomb proof as we possibly could. We had seen near an RE dump some long iron girders. Under Smedley's leadership we planned an assault, we set off in the gun tower, fetched these back to the site, put them in position, covered them with corrugated iron and then worked through the night until we had put a layer of concrete a good nine inches thick over the whole rest room and it was done. We'd also stolen from the long suffering Royal

Officers' Mess and dugout of 426 Battery at Mersa Matruh.

Engineers a big water tank complete with tap and we buried this in the sand at the side filled this with water. So we had our rest room with bunks made with posts and Hessian and water on tap. It was grand. Having described these marvellous strongpoints, looking back with the experience of later fighting, they were absolutely stupid – the very last thing we should have built. Had there been an attack they would have been virtually useless. For a start if there was a tank attack you need to have a clear field of 360 degrees. We had put ourselves in a turret: I should think we hadn't got more than 100 degrees in the arc. We would have been powerless to engage any target coming from behind our position. If a bomb or shell had landed anywhere near that roof it would have fallen in and put the gun out of action. They were silly things really, we were very proud of them but I would dread to think of facing a Panzer Division sitting in such an emplacement!

Bombardier Ray Ellis, 425 Bty

Life at Mersa Matruh was fairly hard even without the bombs, 'Tansy Lee used to go through a little parody of what he would say to his grandchildren, "And there I was, Mersa Matruh – hell spot of the East! And you sit there and talk about hard lines you bastards, you don't know what hard lines are!"'[62] The food was still awful but this time the cooks were largely blameless, 'Corned beef: you had it boiled, you had it fried, you had it made into pastry, you had it cold – or what they called cold, you opened the tin and poured the corned beef out and that was considered cold because it hadn't been cooked again. So the menu was limited!'[63] The lack of vitamins led to desert sores caused by any form of abrasion to the skin, 'Opening a tin and my hand slipped and I just banged my knuckles on the edge of the tin. It didn't even draw blood or take any skin off but the bruise turned septic.'[64] From such small beginnings grew the classic desert sore which was:

> In some cases almost the size of a small orange, an open area suppurating with pus. The treatment was various, some men yielded to one treatment and another man yielded to another. First we tried aquaflavine ointment then we'd try something else – eusol, M and B powder, sulphonamide powder, hot fomentations, zinc ointment – there was a lot of them. In some cases they had to be evacuated if they got secondary infections and the lymph glands were affected and they had a prolonged temperature.

> *Medical Orderly Harry Day,* **Regimental Headquarters**

Various types of fleas, bedbugs and sandflies swarmed in the dugouts causing considerable physical discomfort.

> The sand fleas used to bite me. Other people used to have them and they would itch, but I'd be covered in great big weals as big as a half crown after a bad night, which used to stay for several hours before they would go down again. I used to take my bed to bits, shake everything and put DDT powder in it, but I lost hours of sleep on account of them.

> *Lance Sergeant Ian Sinclair,* **425 Bty**

Bill Hutton really suffered, 'I just couldn't stand the dugouts. They were so full of fleas. If there was a flea on you and I stood next to you it would jump off you on to me! They love me fleas do! I used to sleep outside – I was more terrified of fleas than I was of bombs.' Captain Laborde was one of the lucky ones but still abhorred the omnipresent bedbugs.

> Some of the wretched men would run out of the dugouts in the middle of the night beating these brutes off them. I discovered to my great pleasure that they don't like me, they would walk about all over me but they wouldn't actually bite me, I was never bitten by them, I don't know why! But of course the revolting thing about them is that when they walk on your face and you put up a hand and squash them, they stink! They have the most awful stink!

> *Captain Charles Laborde,* **426 Bty**

Different things of course irritated different personalities. The desert was not a place for the fashionable.

> Hair was a great problem because you sweat and your hair becomes greasy. Then the sand blows, gets into your hair and matts it. You can't get your comb through it. My brother said, "I

think the best thing we can do is to cut the whole lot off!" We discussed this and thought this was a good idea so I sat on a petrol tin and George cut off all my hair. Then, when they saw what it looked like, everyone changed their mind and I was the only one with all his hair cut off!

Bombardier Ray Ellis, **425 Bty**

Stuck out in the desert as they were, there was not a great deal for the men to do and there was some stress resulting from the uneasy combination of boredom and danger. Occasionally this spilled out into minor violence.

There would always be somebody wanting to fight for no good reason. You'd find that so and so had been at it again. Somebody would say something stupid, somebody would take objection to what they wouldn't even have thought about under other circumstances. People would say, "Say that again, you bastard!" – and he'd say it again! That would provoke a fight

Lance Sergeant Ian Sinclair, **425 Bty**

The example of some of the officers and senior NCOs helped give the men a sense of purpose and self respect.

I personally was a stickler with my men. I shaved every day and I insisted that they did. They didn't like it to start with but I think they appreciated how much better they felt once they'd shaved as opposed to being scruffy with a couple of days' growth and always rubbing their chins. It didn't take them very long to shave and

William Barber and Lieutenant Peal catching up with the news at the mess table inside the officers' mess of 426 Battery.

once we'd got the facts of life established there wasn't any problem.

Captain William Pringle, **425 Bty**

One rather amusing incident summed up the enduring spirit of most of the SNH.

We used to keep beer in the gun barrel to keep it cool. You closed the breech and dropped them down. We had a general officer come to examine the position and by this time we were all black – because we worked naked virtually, just a pair of shorts is all we wore – and he said to someone, "Is it wise to have native troops so near the front?" The Colonel said, "Bwworrr! These are the South Notts Hussars!" The General was most apologetic! Having said this he went to the gun and opened the breech and – plonk, plonk, plonk – out came the bottles of beer as they slid down the breech and dropped on the ground. He just looked around, closed the breech silently, nothing was said! He had called us native troops so he owed us that, didn't he!

Bombardier Ray Ellis, **425 Bty**

Small scale concert parties were held where Sammy Hall gave impressions and recited scurrilous rhymes, impersonated certain officers and NCOs with their pet sayings – Peter Birkin's stammer, Shakespear's loping walk and his hesitant delivery.

Much pleasure was to be had down by the sea in a boat which had been left as part of 'battery stores' by the previous occupants of Mersa Matruh.

I was the NCO in charge of the battery 'yacht' and I used to spend quite a bit of my day teaching people to sail in the sea, lagoon and salt lake of Mersa. This was a particularly pleasant way of spending time. It was a felucca rigged sailing boat, it had a single main sail and a jib. We used to wear no clothes whatsoever.

Bombardier John Walker, **425 Bty**

Nude bathing parties formed another part of men's recreation.

We'd all gone down to have a bathe at the lagoon. A raid came over and we'd been warned that it wasn't a very good idea to be in the water when the bombs dropped nearby. So we scuttled out of it and I remembered seeing a slit trench on the other side of the road by the lagoon. I dashed out of the water, picked up my steel helmet on the way, went over the road, through the wire, cutting a strip out of my backside, landed on the other side and there wasn't a slit trench there at all! I stood there absolutely naked except for my steel helmet and I've never felt so naked in all my life. Everybody else had a jolly good laugh out of it!

Warrant Officer 3 John Whitehorn, **425 Bty**

Officers enjoy the warm Mediterranean aboard the recreational boat at Mersa Matruh. Note the steel helmet worn with nothing else - air raids were usually a surprise.

Albert Swinton was actually in the water when a bomb exploded during an air raid. 'It's the queerest sensation, you feel as if all your body's being squashed. It was the other side of the harbour but the waves coming through the water sort of squeezed you!'[65]

★ ★ ★ ★

The best form of relaxation was offered by the chance of leave in that honeypot of pleasure – Cairo. On one occasion when it was available two unscrupulous rogues took advantage of the remaining vestiges of innocence that remained amongst their comrades. Fifty years after the event Harold Thompson confessed his crimes!

We all had a leave to go down to Cairo and Sam and I wanted to go together. What they did was put all the names in a bag and draw two out as to who would go together. Me and Sam, we were the ones who organized the draw. There was only our names went into the hat. Pringle picked them out!

Driver Harold Thompson, **425 Bty**

On the journey into Cairo the more sensitive became aware that it was not only their heroic aura which marked them out as desert veterans.

There were civilians in the train with me all very cool and smart and I was not very cool nor was I very smart. After a while I discovered to my horror that I really didn't smell very nice! It must have been rather embarrassing for the other people in the compartment. I hope they thought, "Poor wretched soldier!"

Captain Charles Laborde, **426 Bty**

On arrival they cleaned themselves up and plunged into the Cairo nightlife.

What did I do in Cairo? You shouldn't ask questions like that! I stayed in the Continental. The first night on leave I had a Turkish bath and it was fascinating watching the dust run out of one's pores. You realized how much got in when you got terribly hot and sweaty and the pores opened – with the sand blowing it gets into your body. I can just see it running down in yellow streams. Not much to do except see the sights and booze. You had all your ready money, I hadn't been able to spend a penny for months so there was a lot of money – far more money than I'd ever had. Oh it was lovely – four wild days! The 'flesh pots' of Cairo were really rather pleasant.

Captain Charles Laborde,
426 Bty

Drinking was an obvious attraction after the choking desert sands of Mersa Matruh.

I went with John Shakespear and my God we knocked it back! We used to amble out of the hotel about mid-morning, wander

John Walker and Ken Tew on leave in Cairo, 1940.

round for a bit and about half past twelve he would say, "Bob, I think its time for our morning beer!" Then the session started! We drank a good deal, ate a good lunch and then went and lay down. Woke up with a bit of a hangover and he'd say, "Well the only way to deal with a hangover is the hair of the dog that bit you!" And so it started up again – that was a highly alcoholic leave!

Captain Bob Hingston, **426 Bty**

Many visited the traditional 'tourist' attraction of the Pyramids. 'Well you know, "Bin there, seen it, done it all, and that's it!" Some wog there said, "Do you want a ride on a camel, for ten piastres I'll make it run!" I gave it a kick and said, "I'll make it run myself!" I nearly fell off the damn thing!'[66] Like a magnet many were also drawn to the very thing that their mothers and the medical officer had warned them against.

We went to the Birkar a whole street of brothels. You go in an open doorway on the ground floor a sort of stone hallway entrance with an open urinal opposite. Up the stairs on the first floor is all the action! By the time you got half way up the stairs there was a great queue of men and girls coming out of their rooms and calling for the Condes – an old woman went in with the Condes fluid for disinfectant purposes. But by golly! The girls looked rough and the thing was so grim. Phil Collihole was a married man and he wasn't going to have anything to do with it but I must say one felt that you'd need to be pretty desperate to take advantage – but of course lots of chaps did.

Gunner Dennis Middleton, **425 Bty**

This seems to have been a typical reaction from the younger soldier exposed to the reality of brothel sex for the first time. It did not however persist as natural urges warred with morality.

We saw the girls – peeped through keyholes and saw men having intercourse with girls. Quite honestly I was absolutely horrified, I thought it was terrible. But there is a saying that when you're abroad black girls grow a shade whiter every day and by the time I next went to Cairo all that sort of priggish horror had gone and I looked at it with different eyes altogether!

Bombardier Ray Ellis, **425 Bty**

So it was that on his next visit to Cairo, Ellis fell into conversation with an Egyptian dancing girl in a bar.

She paused and looked at me and said. "Are you asking to take me to bed?" I was flustered and managed to stammer out that it would be a very nice thing to do but what would it cost? She laughed and said, "Far more than you can afford!" I think it was five hundred piastres which was about two months salary for me at the time. Yes, it was far beyond my pocket so we just talked and

On leave in Egypt, Ted Whittaker stands atop the Cheops Pyramid - a long way from Nottingham.

had a drink. I looked up and saw Frank Birkenshaw, he saw me and waved. I excused myself and went over and he said, "Where did you pick up that dreamboat?" I said, "I think dream is the operative word she's five hundred piastres!" He laughed and went away! I was thoroughly enjoying myself when I caught sight of Frank again at the door waving to me. I went over and said, "What's the matter?" He said, "Here you are, the lads have had a whip round – five hundred piastres!" That was the type of comradeship we had – it was fantastic really! I went beaming back to the table!

Bombardier Ray Ellis, **425 Bty**

This feeling of comradeship was now at the centre of their lives. People they barely recognized on the street had become first acquaintances, then friends and now bosom mates. 'We each shared our letters with the rest of the gun teams even the most intimate letters from wives and sweethearts were all shared.'[67] Another source of ordinary conversation between them was the thorny problem of what would happen next. Bill Hutton was always willing to oblige with the latest news! 'I was the rumour spreader, I used to get round the troops and if there was a rumour going around that we were all going to China I would be the one that would spread it around. There wasn't a deal else to do was there?'[68] They also talked to the men from other units.

83

The Cheshire Regiment were there and they had water cooled Vickers machine guns. We had a lot of friendly rivalry with them, we were always pulling their legs and saying they weren't very competent. If the enemy got through our lines who was going to protect us because we were pretty sure the Cheshires wouldn't be able to. One day we said, "Do you know how to take your gun to pieces and put it together again?" To prove themselves they said they could do this in no time. They did, and in doing it so quickly, they forgot some little part and when they put the water in it all trickled through the bottom and we were able to walk away shaking our heads in despair!

Bombardier Ray Ellis, **425 Bty**

It was as well that such feelings of manly comradeship in shared adversity were blossoming, as their former romantic relationships left behind in England, were coming under severe and often terminal strain.

She wrote a horrible letter accusing me of being out of the way. You must remember that we'd just had Dunkirk. I was out in the Middle East in the sunshine enjoying myself, out of the way and couldn't care less about people back home. I wrote and tried to put things right, but she didn't want to know. Next thing I knew, I was told by my parents, that she was going out with all and sundry and had gone right off the rails and I thought to myself, "Well fair enough, perhaps it's just as well I'm out of the way!"

Bombardier Albert Swinton, **426 Bty**

All in all, life at Mersa Matruh was pithily summarised by Lieutenant Tony McCraith in a letter home, 'Life might be described as bathing, boating, bombed and bored!'[69]

★ ★ ★ ★

In August and September parties of officers, NCOs and men were sent for temporary attachment to the regulars of the 4th Regiment, Royal Horse Artillery in the Sidi Barrani area immediately facing the Italians to gain yet more experience. Whilst they were there the Italians launched their long awaited offensive on 10 September and the detachments quickly found themselves in the middle of the battle. They soon discovered that their training may have taught them gun drill but there was still much to learn about war in the desert.

If shell fire opened, up don't panic and run like hell – walk and get on with whatever you are doing. If you were travelling by vehicles in the desert, because of the overwhelming air superiority of the Italians, vehicles travelled 400, 500 even 600 yards apart, really spread across the desert. You didn't go fast, unless there was

Gun team and 18pdr during practice tank shoot at Mersa Matruh. Shortly after this some officers, NCOs and men were sent for temporary attachment to the RHA facing the Italians at Sidi Barrani.

any need to, because dust would blow up and you became easily spotted from the air. Simple things. If a bombing raid came, the vehicles stopped and you dived out – you didn't all run together in a bunch, you spread out away from the vehicle, found yourself a hole if you could and lay down. If you stopped and you were going to be there for a couple of hours, every man got down to it and dug himself a slit trench – that was automatic. In our own unit the sergeants would be going round saying, "Get stuck in and dig yourselves a slit trench" but these fellows had been at it so long that they did these things automatically.

Sergeant George Pearson, 425 Bty

The commanding officer of 4th RHA was a man who became legendary in the Western Desert.

The name 'Jock' column came from the name of the commander of 4th RHA who was Colonel Campbell, known affectionately as 'Jock'. Jock Campbell thought out the idea of taking a troop of 25 pounders with an escort of a couple of light tanks and two lorry loads of infantry as escort. You would go south into the desert and then west behind the enemy lines. An Auster aircraft or one of your own vehicles 'reccied' ahead of you and endeavoured to find a worthy target. On one of the columns we went on we actually found a concentration of about 400 Italian vehicles. We shadowed them during the day and then at night, when they put themselves in a laager, we quietly moved up to the ridge about 5000 yards away, laid out about 40 rounds a gun behind the 25 pounders and opened up. Up went ammunition vehicles, petrol waggons – the lot. Then we hooked up and scuttled off into the night with the intention of getting back to our own lines as quickly as we could. The next day Italians would be sending bombers out to find you and you would get bombed and machine gunned from the air as you made your way back.

Sergeant George Pearson, **425 Bty**

As they pulled back Pearson saw an example of Campbell's inspirational leadership.

One day we were withdrawing and I was riding in the gun tower with the rest of the gun crew and Colonel Campbell swept alongside in his vehicle. He shouted to his regular Number One, "Come on Sergeant, get a move on, there's a tank battle raging four miles ahead!" Well that seemed at the time, both to me and I'm quite sure to the others, "What the hell do we want to hurry for if there's a tank battle – we'll take our time and let them get it over and done with!"

Sergeant George Pearson, **425 Bty**

Back at Mersa Matruh the anti-tank defences were strengthened in case the Italians broke through.

When the Italians pushed down to Sidi Barrani and everybody thought they were going to come down into Egypt, we abandoned all our gun positions and we dug the guns in as anti-tank guns. The Cheshires who were machine gunners were at the back of us. An Engineer came round to the gun, the traditional 18 pounder which was being registered and worked out as an anti-tank gun. He said, "Now then, can you see the dragons teeth - the dull ones are wood. So if they get on to those they'll get through – so watch it!" We were registered from 600 – 1000 yards and the Brigadier came and said, "They'll be on you in 48 hours, they will outnumber you at twenty to one in men guns and tanks". I didn't hold much for my chances on that job – but they never came!

Bombardier Herbert Bonnello, **426 Bty**

The Italian advance in fact stumbled to a halt just east of Sidi Barrani, where they set up a series of fortified camps and the waiting game began once more. As a result the SNH remained at Mersa until December 1940. The initiative had now passed to General Wavell, who planned a sweep forward into Libya, confident in the superiority of his force in everything but crude numbers. The plan was developed mainly by Lieutenant General Sir Richard O'Connor, the commander of the Western Desert Force. In essence the 4th Indian Division and the 7th

Elements of Marshal Graziani's motorized forces during the Italian 60 mile advance from Sollum to Sidi Barrani. The Italians dug in and faced the British 7th Armoured Division.

Royal Tank Regiment were to pass through a gap in the line of Italian camps; wheel to the north to attack from the rear the camps of Nibeiwa, Tummar West, Tummar East and Point 90; whilst their rear would be protected by the 7th Armoured Division. A force drawn from the Mersa Matruh garrison under the command of Brigadier A R Selby, hence imaginatively known as Selby Force, were to pin down the 1st Italian Division at Maktila Fortified Camp.

The idea was that we should act as a decoy unit against the nearest of the Italian Forts by the coast road whilst the Indian Division carried out the main attack on the group of camps around Sidi Barrani. We were just there really to make a nuisance of ourselves. I don't think we were ever intended to do any more than that.

Warrant Officer 3 John Whitehorn, 425 **Bty**

General Wavell and General O'Connor.

Selby Force was made up of various units including makeshift elements drawn in part from the SNH. A 'Composite Battery' armed with 18/25 pounders was created in co-operation with the 8th Field Regiment, Royal Artillery. It was under the command of one of their officers, a long standing regular soldier who had served in India, Major Robert Daniell. The SNH provided F Troop drawn largely from 426 Bty and under the command of Captain Bob Hingston. More remarkable was a 'dummy Battery' under the command of Captain Gerry Birkin[70] made up of one gun and eight dummy guns.

He had an OP party from 425 Bty, the Gun Position officer was Lieutenant Slinn. The gun itself came from the 8th Field Regiment and the Sergeant in charge was Sergeant Mallett who was known as 'Ammer and was so addressed by all his gun crew. They were an efficient lot. The gun itself was a 25 pounder, very well worn and we'd been warned that it was liable to be grossly inaccurate and not to fire supercharge in case it fell to pieces. It had originally been an 18 pounder Mark V with a split trail.

Warrant Officer 3 John Whitehorn, 425 Bty

John Whitehorn was with the 'real' gun of the 'dummy Battery'. They moved off into the desert on 7 December 1940.

> We were collected together and we went out in a south easterly direction, not in the direction of Sidi Barrani at all. Once we'd got out of the sight of Matruh, we then turned westward and went along out of sight of the main coast road up towards Sidi Barrani. The dummy troop were with us in the sense that they were part of the decoy arrangement, but personally, I never saw them during the whole operation. Neither did I see Daniell's Battery. We went up and as we approached the camps we went in at dusk – it was just turning dark. We put the gun in position and fixed aiming posts. I remember having great difficulty in persuading one of the drivers to give up his rifle because it was wanted by the OP party. We were on the extreme right, nearest the coast, the Dummies were on our left and Daniell's battery was further round to the south.

Warrant Officer 3 John Whitehorn, 425 Bty

The men had not been briefed and had no idea what they were doing, or going to do, even as they approached the Italian Fort Maktila on the night of 8th/9th December.

> I thought this was part of some training scheme. Then we were told that we had to be very quiet and still because we were close to the enemy. Again I though it was the pretend enemy. Then I realized from the whole solemnity of the occasion that we really were close to the enemy, that we were going into action. We went into an observation position and I was lying at the side of the OP officer with the signaller at the side of me. Looking over the ridge adjusting the field glasses I found myself looking into one of these huge camps that the Italians had built. Most astounding! They had built big stone sangars round the camp. The next thing we were sending down fire orders. Almost simultaneously there was more firing from the Royal Navy out at sea off the coast. These naval shells were huge things and had much more effect than our own fire. We were looking into this huge camp and these shells were just crashing into vehicles and guns – it must have been causing great carnage.

Bombardier Ray Ellis, 425 Bty

The naval bombardment was coming from the monitor HMS *Terror* and the First World War super dreadnought HMS *Warspite*, both armed with 15-inch guns.

> Just after we got there they shelled the fort from HMS *Warspite*. Oh my goodness, I felt sorry for them. It sounded just like a tube

HMS Warspite *shelled the Italian positions at Maktila causing great damage among the entrenched Italians – to the delight of the SNH men working with their own 25 pdrs.*

train when it comes out of a tunnel, WHHHORRRR. These things coming over the top. They gave them an hour or two of that and then it was quiet till morning.

Signaller Ted Whittaker, 425 Bty

That morning, on 9 December, Daniell's Battery and Birkin's sole real gun shelled the camp intermittently to help prevent the garrison from interfering with the real assault on the neighbouring Italian camps by the 4th Indian Division. It was their first real experience of the Italian Army.

The Italians were utterly lamentable! We were pretty green but they were... God Almighty! They were appalling soldiers! The first thing I saw four of their guns perched right out in the open, not dug in! Why they'd put them there, when there was quite a bit of cover round about, I simply cannot imagine. They started firing and so I managed to range onto them and gave them a good plastering and that was the end of them – they weren't manned again for the rest of the day.

Captain Bob Hingston, Daniell's Composite Bty

Hingston's guns were real enough but from the Italian perspective they were the tip of a threatening iceberg.

There was a period when we were between the Italian lines and our own lines. Looking back on our own lines in the distance you could see all these tanks going across the front making a lot of

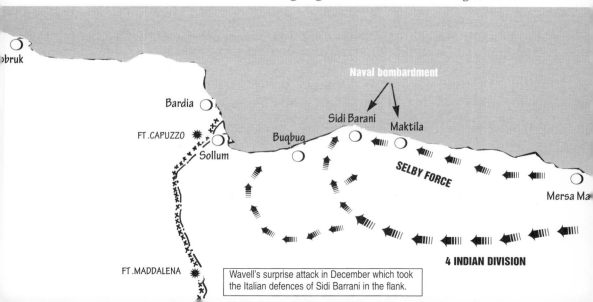

Wavell's surprise attack in December which took the Italian defences of Sidi Barrani in the flank.

dust. Well we knew of course that they weren't, they were three ton trucks! Also these 25 pounder plywood guns with their thunder flashes exploding giving the impression of a great long line of guns! It looked most realistic if you hadn't known and the Italians looking at this must have been quite afraid that they were facing some formidable foe.

Bombardier Ray Ellis, 425 Bty

The dummy gun battery was not sophisticated but it served its purpose reasonably well, 'They had plywood gun shields and a telegraph pole type thing for the barrel. You didn't need anything else because you couldn't see over the shield. It looked just as much a real gun as a real gun!'[71] The illusion was assisted by, 'Flash bombs made from rolls of tarred roofing felt, with ammonal and magnesium powder mixture rolled in them, with a fuse made of a stick of cordite.'[72] When they were set up in a position they proceeded to 'fire', 'One of the gunners was in a trench just in front of it and when the real gun fired he threw a flash bomb forward, so it looked like that fired as well.'[73]

★ ★ ★ ★

Meanwhile the outflanking attack by the 4th Indian Division was progressing exceptionally well with the capture of the camps at Nibeiwa, Tummar West and Tummar East during 9 December. From his forward observation post Hingston heard the Maktila garrison start to withdraw on the night of 9/10 December but he was helpless to interfere.

The Italians had very noisy lorries which were quite easily distinguishable and during the night I could hear them moving east to west – withdrawing. Our radio didn't work and I hadn't got a line so I could't get this information back to anybody.

Captain Bob Hingston, **Daniell's Composite Bty**

When news finally got through, an effort was made to block the western exit from Maktila Camp, but they were too late and the Italians successfully evacuated the camp. On 10 December Hingston moved forward with his OP team and managed to re-establish contact.

Daylight was coming and I managed to find an OP, rather an obvious one – it wasn't ideal by any manner of means – but I could see things. There were the Italians stretched out along the coast. They'd had a hell of a time, poor devils, bumped into our tanks and not got very far away. They were spread out and hopelessly vulnerable. I'd got my signal truck and he started to lay a line just as they opened up with every gun on our OP. The signal truck got away in time, the rest of us were pinned down pretty badly. They

90

were using very small guns and they weren't frightfully terrifying, but it wasn't very nice and we crawled out.

Captain Bob Hingston, **Daniell's Composite Bty**

That night Hingston, who was not a physically strong man, was beginning to feel the strain a little.

I was bloody cold and there was a cook-house there manned by the 8th Field. They had a priceless chap, he had last war ribbons up and had reached the proud rank of lance bombardier. He saw me and he said, "You look starved, Sir!" I said, "Well its been a bit cold out there all day I must admit". He said, "I've got just the thing for you!" He handed me a mug of tea and it had a hell of a slug of rum in it – it certainly did warm me up nicely!

Captain Bob Hingston, **Daniell's Composite Bty**

Next day, 11 December, Hingston ran straight into the Italians who were making their far from heroic last stand.

The next morning I set off again and set off up a sloping hill and there I saw the whole Italian formation spread out down below me. A most ludicrous arrangement all out in the open, a sort of square they'd made with a gun at each corner, almost Napoleonic style. I'd just ranged on to that when the tanks arrived and Colonel Harland said, "Would we put down a smoke-screen to cover his tanks advance?". I think it was completely unnecessary and can't think it did any good at all. I was very annoyed about this because I'd just ranged this beautiful target. So eventually I compromised. We had to get two guns to give them their smoke screen but the third gun proceeded to pound away at this target and sent all the Eyeties under cover. It was a thoroughly disorganized battle and these tanks appeared behind me and came charging line abreast up the hill and over the top. I was sitting out in the open on the ground and as they came over every Italian gun opened up on them. It was quite hectic for a bit. Then there was silence as the tanks disappeared into a dip. A message came from battery headquarters, "You've fired all the shells you're going to have on that target, what's happening?" I said, "I don't know, nothing seems to be happening!" Then I saw a whole lot of Italians appearing out of their holes and stand around. I thought, "This doesn't seem quite right!", so I landed another shell amongst them

Italian field guns and towing tractors caught in retreat on the road to Sollum.

A lone soldier leads a hundreds of Italian prisoners – a familiar sight after the highly successful British attack.

which sent them scuttling again. The poor devils – I'm sorry I did because they were only surrendering to our tanks, who shortly afterwards appeared on the scene and took over.

Captain Bob Hingston, Daniell's Composite Bty

Captain Gerry Birkin's Dummy Battery ran into another group of the Italians and they opened up with their sole real gun.

We parked the gun behind a small mound that didn't really cover it but there was nothing else. We banged off a lot of rounds from there and we got fairly well shelled. The Italian guns were obviously ranging on us – they dropped one in front and one behind and we were on the line in between which didn't look a particularly healthy place to be. They landed quite a few shells, including one right beside the gun position officer's truck. A splinter came in through the engine compartment, pretty well severed the steering column and went out the other side of the truck.

Sergeant John Whitehorn, 425 Bty

Birkin took position in an observation post from where he could clearly see the Italian positions.

The message came down from Captain Birkin that he thought he'd spotted the General's dugout and that he wanted to "Knock at his front door!" That was the exact message. He wanted the gun to lay as accurately as it could. Shortly after that the Italians surrendered! I saw what I thought at first was a row of stakes forming a palisade, but it turned out to be a row of Italians giving themselves up. That turned out to be it! I think the Guards had about six casualties, we got away without any. It had come over the telephone that 'some' Italians had surrendered to Captain Birkin and I thought half a dozen maybe.

Sergeant John Whitehorn, **425 Bty**

Birkin had gone forward to receive his prisoners in some trepidation accompanied only by an infantry officer and some 20 men.

> When we got to the ridge, hundreds and hundreds of Eyeties and Libyans appeared and threw down their arms. I was a bit frightened, but I brandished my revolver in the general's face, and he said, "No ammunition left!" Which was a lie, as I found 2,000 rounds on one gun. However, everything seemed peaceful and our 20 men with bayonets controlled the party all right. I disobeyed orders and took the General's epaulettes and hat – just like Musso's – also I got two pistols and an Italian flag.

Captain Gerry Birkin, **425 Bty**

The gunners went forward and met an incredible sight for they had taken no less than 5,248 POWs!

> We all went up to this fort and they were still all there. There was a general and we were in time to hear him declaim, which an interpreter told our people, that they'd never have surrendered if they'd had enough ammunition. And they were standing in front of piles of ammunition boxes! I found out later that Captain Birkin had pinched the General's epaulettes, because they are in the regimental museum.

Signaller Ted Whittaker, **425 Bty**

It was quite a surrealistic experience as the few gunners were surrounded by their erstwhile enemies.

> When we got there something over five thousand were all gathered together in a hollow by a road and Lieutenant Slinn went off to find Birkin to get orders as to what to do with them. They were completely disarmed but I was just left in charge of the whole party with about a platoon of the South Staffords. They were there with fixed bayonets at about 200 yard intervals round this enormous group. Slinn simply gave me the instruction, "Look after them!" So we dropped the gun into action about 50 yards away, put a round up the spout, made a lot of clanking noises and hoped we were being fairly fearsome and that the Italians wouldn't turn nasty. There were so many of them – it was absolutely ridiculous we couldn't have done anything if they'd decided to turn on us.

WO3 John Whitehorn, **425 Bty**

Captured Italian ammuntion and stores giving lie to the claim made by their surrendering commander: 'No ammunition left'!

Lone gunners took sole charge of hundreds of Italians.

They came streaming out in thousands – it was the most amazing sight. There were so many that there weren't enough infantrymen to look after them. I was given the job of taking, it must have been a hundred men, and all I'd got was a rifle. But there was no danger – they were just slouching along demoralized. I couldn't speak to them because I couldn't speak Italian. It was the first time I'd ever seen any enemy. They just came docilely along in a long column. I handed them over and they all filed into a barbed wire compound.

Bombardier Ray Ellis, 425 **Bty**

The demeanour of the Italian POWs did not impress their captors.

They were hopeless, shattered – the last thing they had expected, I think was to be attacked. I don't know what they thought they were there for, quite frankly! They certainly didn't give the appearance that they'd come to fight! They were so dishevelled, so dirty.

Lance Sergeant Ian Sinclair, 425 **Bty**

The captured camps gave an almost unrivalled opportunity for looting before the more legitimate activity of salvage began.

There was kit all laid out in rows and we systematically went through it. I got a dagger with a beautifully enamelled coat of arms on the handle. The thing you were looking for was the Berettas – a little tiny automatic. We found a large store of tinned food and condensed milk. My mother and father had always stopped me eating condensed milk with a spoon and there was nobody to stop us there!

Signaller Ted Whittaker, 425 **Bty**

Older and more experienced soldiers were looking for something a little stronger than condensed milk.

I was disturbed by one of the South Staffords who had got very drunk on stuff that had been found in the camp and was persistently trying to get on a stray mule. He was getting on one side and falling off the other and this went on pretty well through the night at intervals.

Warrant Officer 3 John Whitehorn, 425 **Bty**

The aftermath of any battle is grim and Ray Ellis was brought face to face with the reality of war.

For the next two or three days I was trying to organize a burial party which is a horrible job. We attempted to dig graves, but it was impossible, because it was all rock and there were too many – hundreds and hundreds of them. We hit on the idea of dragging them into any hole we could find and then kicked the rocks and

The SNH experience the spoils of war for the first time and help themselves to various items among the abandoned kit, trying out the Italian equipment.

sand in on top of them. After the first day or so, these corpses were beginning to swell and smell. We found some big meat hooks in a cookhouse so we used those. You stuck it under the shoulder and dragged them. We made no attempt at all to identify anybody, we were treating them like carcasses. We put up a sign, with scratched on it, "Five Eyeties or six Libyans or ten Eyeties", we didn't even call them Italians. There was no reverence or respect at all. The main thing was to get them under the ground.

Bombardier Ray Ellis, **425 Bty**

Throughout December, the salvage teams roamed the erstwhile battlefields collecting abandoned Italian artillery, transport and infantry equipment. Finally, to the relief of all, the regiment left Mersa Matruh on 8 February 1941 and moved back into the Egyptian Delta.

To some members of the SNH fell the grim task of locating and burying the Italian dead.

CHAPTER FIVE

Watching the Canal

The Italian offensive had catastrophically failed to cut through Egypt, but German modern technology was nevertheless beginning to deny the British the benefits of the Suez Canal route to India. The Luftwaffe had begun a programme of dropping mines into the canal at night and as a result some 250, 000 tons of urgently needed shipping was being held up. These mines were of the acoustic and magnetic type which were extremely difficult to sweep clear without having first pin-pointed their exact location. The SNH were called in to help.

> We were put in little posts of four men every quarter of a mile along the banks of the canal. I found myself in charge of a little party and we quickly got ourselves established, we dug a few slit trenches and made a little gun pit. We had a Bren gun, four rifles and a stick to point with!
>
> ***Bombardier Ray Ellis,*** **425 Bty**

As a technologically unsophisticated operation it was more than a little reminiscent of the Boy Scouts.

> The Germans were using Junkers 88s and were dropping these mines from low level and they had a parachute to steady them. If they dropped one you rushed out and stuck a post in and someone else rushed at the back of you and put them in line where this thing had gone down. If two posts got them you'd got a mine spotted.
>
> ***Signaller Ted Whittaker,*** **425 Bty**

Junkers 88 of the type that dropped mines into the Suez Canal in an attempt to block that important waterway. The SNH had the job of spotting where the mines fell and then marking them from the bank.

Mines of the type dropped into the Suez Canal.

The German aircraft flew considerably lower than the Italians had managed at Mersa Matruh.

> One night the air raid warning was on so we were standing to, alert, when we suddenly heard a sort of PHHEWWW! Tiny Williams said, "Look at the cheeky devil!" It was so low you couldn't believe it. Everything we'd got was going at it and we must have been close because the rear gunner got a bit fed up and started firing back again, so we dived for cover.
>
> ***Bombardier Herbert Bonnello,* 426 Bty**

It appeared impossible to miss the German bombers at that range, but the SNH revealed that anti-aircraft fire was definitely not their *forte*.

> These planes were flying very low and I was firing a Bren gun into them absolutely convinced that I was riddling them with fire but they just flew through. It was very difficult to hit a flying aircraft.
>
> ***Bombardier Ray Ellis,* 425 Bty**

All along the bank the gunners tried to shoot the planes down, whilst straining to see and mark where they had dropped their mines.

> We saw a big German plane, really low. Sergeant Staniforth let go at it with the Bren gun. Unfortunately it had been blowing sand all day and it wouldn't fire automatic and he only got five shots in as it went past, like. A light appeared and I says, "I think you've got it!". Next thing there's a big mine coming down, swinging down on a parachute, seemingly just above our head, but it landed towards the other side of the canal. We got some bits of stick and

we were putting these sticks to point where it had dropped to let
the Navy know – when it blew up! It bowled us over.

Gunner Ted Holmes, 425 Bty

Even when mines were observed it was no guarantee that the Navy
would subsequently be able to sweep them up.

Jock Reid was absolutely certain that he heard a splash so the
two markers were put out there. Well, they sent divers, mine-
sweepers, depth charges, a plane with a magnetic hoop and they
came to the conclusion he must have been mistaken – there was
no mine. One day a naval patrol boat came whizzing down the
canal at great speed. It turned round and came up the canal again
and WWHHUUMP up he goes. The theory was that the noise of
the engine would set off the mine but by the time it went off it was
going at such speed that it would be out of harm's way. That wasn't
so! There was nobody killed but one or two ribs had been broken
with the blast. It drifted down and we pulled it in at my particular
section. Albert Ellis was on board like lightning and once they had
got all the wounded off all the food was gone before they knew
what had happened.

Bombardier Herbert Bonnello, 426 Bty

After a while the situation had eased and the Canal was re-opened for
traffic.

A squadron came through headed by the aircraft carrier
Indomitable and in trying to get past a wreck she ran aground and
was stuck there for a bit. That was a most amusing effort. They
kept bringing ropes ashore and various groups of sailors seized
them and pulled them around. One time an Egyptian boat came
ashore with a rope and there was nobody else there so I said to
some of our chaps who were standing around looking on, "Come
along, lets pull on this!" and we started pulling the rope ashore.
This was of course a frightful insult to the Navy and the next thing
I knew a burly matelot got his shoulder on to me and sent me
flying. That must have made his day being able to bowl an officer
over like that. He seized the rope from us and pulled it ashore. But
just as he did that she came off the mud – so we always claimed
afterwards that we had refloated her!

Captain Bob Hingston, 426 Bty

During this period Albert Ellis maintained his well merited reputation
for toughness – even if his middle name was Cornelius!

Albert Ellis was in his thirties, he quite often got drunk and was
abusive. He was the first one to go down to Port Tewfik and I said
to him, "Look Albert, promise you'll behave yourself, we all want
to go and if you do anything that damages it...!" But by the time
11 o' clock came he was under arrest! When he came out next

morning I said, "Well you promised!" He said, "I did nothing! It was that Geordie he was going to knock hell out of young Cousins and I just said to him, "If you hit him you hit me!" and when we got off the truck I said, "Right if you're going to hit him I'll hit you first!" There was a commotion and I wasn't to know it was straight outside the officers' mess was I? All these chaps came out and I said, "Right, I'll have you one at a time!" So they arrested me!"

Bombardier Herbert Bonnello, **426 Bty**

He was not the only gunner to misbehave and Ray Ellis was witness to an awful demonstration of drunkenness from three other members of the regiment in Port Suez.

We got to Port Suez to see two soldiers walking up the road dragging a third man by his ankles with his head in the gutter. He was so drunk he couldn't walk. I remember saying to Bob Foulds, "This is disgusting! Its just the type of thing that gets the British Army a bad name abroad". While we were looking with disgust at these three, I realized that one was Fred Lamb and the other was Wag Harris. I said to Bob, "That's Fred and Wag – the other must be my brother – the one with his head in the gutter must be my brother!" It was! These disgraceful British soldiers were my best pals and brother.

Bombardier Ray Ellis, **425 Bty**

The real thing - a gun that was up-to-date, the 25 pounder issued to the SNH at Kabrit Camp, Egypt March 1941. On the left is the limber.

On 9 March the regiment moved to nearby Tahag Camp where, as part of a complete re-equipment, they received a full set of 25 pounders. At last they had a gun that did not date from the First World War.

The 25 pounder was a gun/howitzer. A howitzer is an artillery piece which can fire at a very close target by firing almost vertically lobbing the shell high in the air to drop very close. They used to be short barrelled guns. The 25 pounder could elevate to that extent and firing a low charge it could become a gun howitzer. The 25 pounder had a different loading procedure from the 18 pounder because the cartridge and the shell were separate whereas, on the 18 pounder it is one thing – rather like an enlarged .303 bullet. Therefore on the 25 pounder it is possible to alter the charge. Inside the cartridge there were different coloured bags of cordite: red white and blue. You could have Charge One, Two, Three or even a super-charge. When the shell landed the fragmentation was very tiny. A big shell may shatter into no more than 20 splinters which could hit or miss – but the 25 pounder fragmented into tiny little pieces which never got much above knee high as it spread. So it was a great killer and as an artilleryman looking for something that will kill it was an efficient projectile. Picking up the new drill on the 25 pounder was simple – we didn't need a lot of conversion as trained gunners.

Bombardier Ray Ellis, **425 Bty**

They were also issued with new gun towers called 'Quads' to replace the lorries which had previously pulled the guns.

The Quads were a curious stubby little vehicle purpose built for towing a gun. Four wheel drive so that it could get out of difficult situations. It had a flap in the roof so you could put your head out and you could see where you were going and direct the driver. There was room inside for the gun crew, kit and gear. It had the unfortunate impression that it looked like an armoured vehicle because it had flat slabby sort of sides. I think it gave people a feeling of security that was totally false – but it wasn't armoured at all.

Sergeant Bob Foulds, **425 Bty**

Between the Quad and the gun came the limber.

The limber is the towed trailer which carries ammunition. It was attached to the back of the Quad and had two pneumatic tyres. At the back were two doors which opened and inside were trays of ammunition for emergency. The ammunition supply came up in the trucks separately and the ammunition in the limbers was very rarely used. When dropping into action, you first unhooked the gun and swung it in the direction which you had been told. Then you unhitched the limber and pushed that onto the left hand

101

side of the gun looking from the rear. Then the Quad would be taken away to waggon lines.

Bombardier Ray Ellis, 425 Bty

The old guns had been handed in earlier and Quarter Master Sergeant Fred Brookes had grasped a chance to improve his technical stores.

I took all the guns and gunsights, field clinos, everything like that, with all the vouchers made out for the battery. We drove in and said, "Where do you want them?" "Oh throw them on a heap there!" That was it – so I took a few dial sights, field clinos – things like that. Keep some stuff in hand, you could need it, you never knew when someone was going to lose one. No problem at all!

Quartermaster Sergeant Fred Brookes, 425 Bty

New signal equipment arrived and Sergeant Jack Gore of the Signal Section invented a gadget designed to increase greatly efficiency in action.

Jack had invented a thing to save using several telephones at the command post. A sort of thing with knife switches so that you could switch over, A Troop, B Troop all the lot. The first was such a disaster we called it the 'Bollock Dropper'. It was a massive box and we put on it 'BD'. The second one was a huge success, the Royal Corps of Signals made one for us, nicely made up. But Jack had a sardonic sense of humour and it said on this one 'BD Mark II'. We were using this one day out on a manoeuvre and this Major came along. He said, "That's not an authorized piece of equipment is it Sergeant Gore?", "No, Sir!" "What's it for?", and he told him. "Why do you think it's needed?" Jack said this, that and the other. Then he said, "And what does 'BD' stand for?" Jack had to confess, "Bollock Dropper, Sir!"

Signaller Ted Whittaker, 425 Bty

Whilst at Tahag the SNH were ordered to begin special combined operations training with 16th Infantry Brigade in preparation for the proposed invasion of the Greek island of Rhodes. The assault craft loading and landing exercises were carried out at the Salt Lake in the Canal zone.

103

Officers of 425 Battery having lunch next to their truck during firing exercise. Left to right, Angus Carr, Anthony Corbett Thompson, Freddie Porter, Charles Bennett and John Shakespear.

We practised these assault landings with the landing craft. They were very small and we had to get the gun, the wagon and the gun tower on to it. Well they wouldn't fit, the only way they could be fitted was the gun was put on first with the trail facing forward and slewed round to one side, the trailer was run over the top of that and then the gun tower was backed on. In order to get off the ramp had to be let down, the Quad had to be driven forward a little, the trailer hooked on, the Quad driven forward a little bit further and then the gun hooked on. By that time we reckoned everybody would be dead and the gun destroyed if there was anybody trying to stop us from landing! So the rank and file were not over enthusiastic about any great success.

Captain Charles Laborde, 426 Bty

They were also not enthusiastic about any prospect of getting wet!

> The pilot took us so far out in the canal and then he'd say, "Right, we'll come back again to land". When we came into land we used to say, "Get closer in – we'll get bloody wet!" "I can't", he said, "this is an invasion. You might be in nine foot of water! You've got to be prepared for it!" We kept saying, "Bring us in a bit more, come on." We used to find the shelf – in the canal you could walk out a yard or two and then if you took another step... We'd bring it in to there and then when we came ashore we were only paddling. Then our Sergeant Major Jim Hardy said, "That's no bloody good, don't forget you're going to invade Rhodes – you'll see a lot of water over there! Take it round again and I'll show you how its done!" He did – he didn't find that shelf – he disappeared. Funny thing – he'd got a tin hat on and it started to float on the water and then disappeared. He was down below – he'd gone! When they pulled him out we all said, "Like that, Sergeant Major?"

Signaller Albert Parker, 425 Bty

A further refinement to the training made life even more difficult.

> The powers that be decided that if we did invade Rhodes Island we may not get all our gun towing vehicles ashore, so that it would be a good idea if you got 10-12 men with drag ropes and they went on marches pulling along 25 pounders and their ammunition trailers. Man-handling the guns going off on virtually route marches. They expressed themselves in typically Nottingham terms on what they thought of the chap who thought up this idea!

Sergeant George Pearson,

The signallers, who normally lead a reasonably civilized existence, were selected for special treatment.

> All the signalling equipment had to be carried. Some of them put the stuff in packs, but we invented a stretcher with straps over your shoulders and two of you put the set in between and trotted or marched with it. We did route marches to get us fit. We passed the Durham Light Infantry one day – we passed them! Their officers had some very sharp things to say, they said we were trying to make fools of them! I was fitter than I had ever been.

Signaller Ted Whittaker, 425 Bty

As the men trained, unaware of their exact fate, the usual optimistic rumours circulated.

> We went abroad thinking that we'd probably be abroad for six months. Then a year passed and we thought, "Well we must be getting towards the end of our time now!" Then two years had gone and, "Well, surely now we must be getting near!" It seemed

a long way from home, England was farther away than the moon! We were always thinking about coming home. It's a sort of hope soldiers have, "I've heard a rumour!" or "Next month we're going home, there's a ship already packed in the harbour to take us!" You live on this hope that very soon you'll be going home again.

Bombardier Ray Ellis, **425 Bty**

Unfortunately for the dreams of Ellis and his friends, the war in the Western Desert had taken a lurch for the worse.

INVASION' TRAINING ON [?] THE BITTER LAKE, SUEZ CANAL MARCH 1941

There was a deadly secret plan to invade an
un-named Greek Island with a minimum of equipment.
To this end some practice was carried out on the
Suez Canal with not always great success!
[EVERYONE – particularly in Cairo – knew the secret and
the island concerned – RHODES! There, but for the grace ..

CHAPTER SIX

The Rats of Tobruk

Whilst the SNH had been otherwise engaged on the Suez Canal, Wavell's forces had advanced in a series of thrusts across Libyan Cyrenaica, culminating in the successful Battle of Beda Fomm on 7 February 1941, which resulted in the final destruction of the Italian Tenth Army. Yet this very success sowed the seeds of trouble. Hitler realized that he could not allow his Italian allies to collapse and he therefore decided to send the first German troops into North Africa. Initially the 5th Light Division and 15th Panzer Division joined the

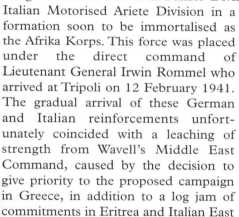

Italian Motorised Ariete Division in a formation soon to be immortalised as the Afrika Korps. This force was placed under the direct command of Lieutenant General Irwin Rommel who arrived at Tripoli on 12 February 1941. The gradual arrival of these German and Italian reinforcements unfortunately coincided with a leaching of strength from Wavell's Middle East Command, caused by the decision to give priority to the proposed campaign in Greece, in addition to a log jam of commitments in Eritrea and Italian East

Africa. This dissipation of the limited British resources meant that the forces remaining in Cyrenaica were given a purely defensive role and consequently Wavell sensibly impressed upon his diminished command the importance of safeguarding the integrity of fighting units rather than in defending relatively useless empty miles of desert.

At the end of March Rommel cautiously began to move forward and as planned the British fell back avoiding contact. The Afrika Korps accelerated the pace as they advanced through Cyrenaica in a mirror image of Wavell's triumph just a few weeks earlier. Wavell realized that unless something was done quickly Rommel might not wait courteously at the borders of Egypt, as the diffident Italians had done, but would probably burst through to the Nile Delta and the Suez Canal – the strategic jugular of the British Empire. The situation called for resolute action and it was decided to hold the crucial port of Tobruk with the intention of diverting Rommel from an attack on Egypt and to give time

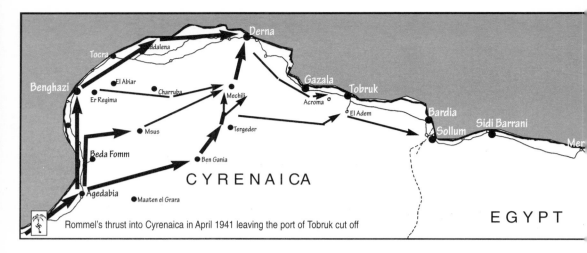

Rommel's thrust into Cyrenaica in April 1941 leaving the port of Tobruk cut off

for British reinforcements to arrive. The only troops available to defend Tobruk were the 9th Australian Division, the newly re-formed 3rd Armoured Brigade, three 25 pounder artillery regiments, two anti-tank regiments and one anti-aircraft brigade. The positions they were to occupy were a double ring of concrete posts and dugouts on a perimeter frontage of some thirty miles which surrounded Tobruk in a half circle about nine miles from the harbour. The core strength of these defences lay in a series of minefields. The final addition to these deployments was a further regiment of 25 pounders to be sent post-haste from Egypt.

* * * *

So it was that the SNH were chosen to join the defenders of Tobruk! 'One day a fearful panic stations – everybody had to be recalled – and I

B Troop, 425 Battery ready to leave Kabrit Camp, Egypt on the 300 mile desert drive to help man the defences at Tobruk against the Afrika Korps.

remember the absolute chaos. One detachment was out on the lake and they couldn't be got hold of. It was such a whirl!'[74] For the 'Q' staff back at the camp there was a real challenge to be met.

I was back in camp, having a quiet sip of ale and smoking a cigarette with one or two mates around. This damned staff car came tearing across the camp and pulled up and out jumped a Brigadier who said, "Your regiment will be back here in about an hour and you'll be moving out at first light tomorrow morning. Draw ammunition, stores, anything you're short of, rob who you like within the area, get fully equipped and be ready to move out." I said, "Yes, Sir!" Saluted smartly and went on a predatory mission with two or three trucks.

Quartermaster Sergeant Fred Brookes, **425 Bty**

Bombardier Albert Swinton was acting as a quartermaster's assistant.

I was booking stores in and out. Each unit has got what they call a G1098 stores which covers everything that a regiment needs to perform its duties. That covers a multitude of items from first field dressings to guns and ammunition – everything that you want. They were taking stores from other regiments to get us to our G10/98 strength. Within hours we were ready for action and up the desert.

Bombardier Albert Swinton, **426 Bty**

They set off on their 700 mile journey for Tobruk at 07.30 on 5 April. 'We were escorted through Cairo with sirens sounding, we went through like a streak of salt. "Pull the traffic over to one side and make way!"'[75] The first overnight stop at Mena Camp near Alexandria was marked by a series of splendid parties.

Peter Birkin said before we went in, "I've arranged with MPs to treat the South Notts gently tonight because we're going up the desert tomorrow. I spent that night at the Casino Bardia which was kept by Madame Bardia. Her daughter aged 17 was the most beautiful girl – a smashing belly dancer. That night I did drink a lot of beer and I got on to the stage trying to get at one of the girls and was very politely ushered off the stage by an MP.

Lance Sergeant Dennis Middleton, **425 Bty**

Ted Whittaker witnessed Middleton's daring foray into the world of belly dancing.

We had what can only be described as a riotous night out. I can remember Dennis being gently but firmly moved from the stage of the cabaret where he was attempting to accompany one of the belly dancers. They had candles in candlesticks but Dennis insisted in putting these in a bottle and proclaiming it was some sort of tribute to our predecessors in World War One on the eve of battle. He was quite a lad! Getting home was a bit of a problem – I'm afraid several of us finished up on our hands and knees crawling through the flower bed. I halfway stopped the taxi and was heartily sick on the road, the driver was most alarmed. We got back to camp – I don't know how late it was – but Peter Birkin was walking up and down through the camp making sure everybody was safely in. I can remember him telling me that I would be on that so and so truck in the morning even if it killed me. In the morning I can remember getting into the truck and the Major saying to me, "Have you got a headache?" When I said, "Yes!", he said, "Serves you bloody well right!" It was all the sympathy we deserved!

Signaller Ted Whittaker, 425 Bty

The journey was resumed with several of the gunners considerably under the weather. Convoy discipline was maintained, 'You had to remain 50 yards behind the vehicle in front. That was not always easy. You had to discipline yourself considerably to make sure you didn't get within that distance. Very tedious. I travelled in a 15cwt truck and we took turns in driving – I remember falling asleep driving and bumping into the vehicle in front.'[76] Once they had passed Mersa Matruh it became obvious that all was not well.

There were signs of panic: troops coming back at great speed; more and more troops; everything was going east; then we passed rear aerodromes of the RAF where we could see crates being set

Afrika Korps Panzer units, newly arrived in Africa, driving towards the front along the Libyan coast road. The British fell back without giving fight but planned to hold the port of Tobruk as a thorn in Rommel's side.

Rear party of 425 Battery halted for lunch between Amariyah and Daba during the drive to Tobruk. They could only look on as, what appeared to be the entire British army drove in the opposite direction before the advancing Germans – they seemed to be the only ones going west.

on fire which we knew contained aircraft engines; then we met convoys of ambulances coming back. It all grew a bit sombre. This trickle developed into a mass exodus of troops – it seemed that everyone in the Army of the Nile was doing their level best to put the greatest distance they could between themselves and the enemy – everyone was rushing headlong back into Egypt. The only troops moving west were the South Notts Hussars!

Bombardier Ray Ellis, **425 Bty**

Not all the Hussars were enamoured with the prospect of attempting to reverse the fortunes of war.

We had some nasty bits of information coming back to us, "We're going into the retreat!" "Bloody hell! Well what are we going up there for then if we're going into retreat?" "Somebody says we're going to take over!" "F*** that!" The usual army reaction.

Signaller Erik Morley, **425 Bty**

The situation became increasingly tense.

We got to Sollum near the escarpment when suddenly, somebody pressed the panic button. We were to get to Tobruk as fast as we possibly could. We had to get up that sensational road zig zagging up the steep escarpment. I was standing up in the front of my truck looking back and there was my troop – beautifully spaced out, all driving skilfully – no trouble at all. I really felt, "By Jove, we've done a lot of work, but we have got the results in the end". We got to the top and shortly afterwards there was a huge

notice held up in front of us, "CLOSE RIGHT UP!" We who were at the back of the convoy had to sprint a hell of a way to close up all these gaps. There was a rare old panic on – everybody got what rifles we had ready. I remember thinking to myself, "Well if we're attacked when we're spread right out along the road like this we simply haven't got an earthly!"
Captain Bob Hingston, 426 Bty

The drive was relentless, 'We were going into the setting sun, and it was gradually getting darker and darker. The drivers were changing over without stopping – they used to get out one door, nip over the bonnet and back in the other door. We just kept going.'[77] It was touch and go whether the SNH would get into Tobruk before the rampaging Germans swirled round the perimeter to close the gate.

My gun tower was tail end Charlie of the regiment and my Battery Commander Peter Birkin, who stuttered a little, came up to me and said, "Nnnnow, wwwhen we get on the top, if we get atatatacked by tanks, your truck, ammunition trailer and gun tower will go on and you will hold them off as long as you can." So we went on to the top of the escarpment – I praying that there would be no German tanks anywhere! By the middle of the afternoon a few tanks appeared on the escarpment side. I was watching them, they were German tanks, and they kept pace with us, following along and I was shaking in my shoes thinking, "Oh my God, please, please, don't make me have to drop off"! Luckily they didn't attack but I had a distinct looseness of the bowels when I thought of what might have happened.
Sergeant George Pearson, 425 Bty

The SNH entered Tobruk at midnight on 9 April and as the last trucks entered the defence perimeter the Royal Engineers laid the final rows of mines and pulled the barbed wire across the road.

★ ★ ★ ★

The siege of Tobruk had begun – and it began in almost total chaos.

We got to a junction in the road in the dark, Eagle crossroads. There three artillery regiments got mixed up in the dark, there was confusion everywhere, there were guns that were not ours, there were cap badges that were not ours – everyone was milling about. Had the Luftwaffe come and dropped a few flares they could have wiped out the whole of the artillery power which was to defeat them in a few days time.
Bombardier Ray Ellis, 425 Bty

The common perception of the desert as miles and miles of soft shifting sands was contradicted by the ground conditions in many areas of the Tobruk perimeter.

They said, "Dig in!" Well I got out and got a pick and a shovel and it was just like rock. I hit the ground and sparks flew up from the pick. I thought, "To hell with it!" and I made my bed and went to bed. I woke up next morning and some cocky chap came along and said, "We're the last in, Rommel's out there with his Panzers!" I said, "Who's Rommel and what's a Panzer?"

Driver Bill Hutton, 425 Bty

Colonel William Seely

As the regiment took up their first positions on the morning of 10 April their Colonel acted to calm any jangling nerves amongst his men as they collectively prepared to face the Afrika Korps for the first time.

Colonel Seely made a point of walking in front of the guns pacing up and down carrying a rifle. A gesture – he couldn't have done anything with a rifle. We knew what he was doing. He was saying, "You're here and I'm in front of you!" No sense of heroics, he wasn't strutting, he might have been walking round his estate in Nottingham with a twelve bore, that was his attitude.

Bombardier Ray Ellis, 425 Bty

As one less respectful said, 'Its nice to see the Colonel's on our side!'[78] Later in the day the Regiment moved a couple of miles south into gun positions about 5, 000 yards from the wire.

Battery positions were situated on the top of the second escarpment, where there was an excellent field for anti-tank fire, (considered to be one of our most important roles) 425 Bty moved into the area just south of PALESTRIMO more or less alongside B/O Bty of 1 RHA and 426 Bty came into action on the left of A/E Bty in the angle of the fork where the main road from TOBRUK bears left and a track leads straight on for El Adem. There were 8, 000 yards between Btys.[79]

SNH War Diary, 10 April 1941

The SNH were intermingled with the guns of the regular 1st Regiment, Royal Horse Artillery. The 425 Bty was covering the 2/17th Australian Infantry Battalion and 426 Bty the 2/13th Australian Infantry Battalion, both of the 20th Australian Brigade, who were holding the outer perimeter defences thoughtfully provided by the former Italian garrison of Tobruk. Observation posts were established and Captain Bob Hingston, who by then was in command of D Troop, picked a spot just to the west of the El Adem road as it passed out through the perimeter.

Everybody was a bit tense. I was sleeping just by the telephone on the surface and I told the sentries, "Wake me up if anything happens". There was no hesitation. During the day whoever it was on sentry go said, "Captain Hingston, Sir, there's something there,

I don't see what it is!" He drew my attention, quite correctly in the way he'd been trained, to this lump, a very small lump, right out in the desert. I got my glasses on it and I said, "No, I don't think it's anything to worry about..." Then suddenly it put its head up – it was a camel!

Captain Bob Hingston, **426 Bty**

On Good Friday, 11 April, the German tanks marked the Easter festivities by launching their attack on Tobruk.

A number of German tanks appeared on my right heading very rapidly down towards the perimeter. We got on to them and things really warmed up. Then they stopped and ran across our front and we had a fairly good shoot at them – there were several left behind damaged. I always claimed that I'd hit them but I think the 1st RHA claimed they had too! They got to the El Adem road and then they withdrew a bit. They were firing light signals, I don't know why. Suddenly they charged down the hill, most impressive, down on either side of the El Adem road going flat out. Our tanks had arrived and they pulled them up and a real slugging match started between the two tank units. Then the trouble set in – the tanks had cut our line and we could not get through by radio.

Captain Bob Hingston, **426 Bty**

Back at the gun positions D Troop faced the Panzers over open sights under the command of Lieutenant Ivor Birkin with his gun position assistant Harold Harper.

There was an escarpment and these tanks came over the ridge, probably about 6,000 yards away. We were firing at between 5 and 6,000 which rather shook us as on exercise we had been used to firing at 8, 9s and 10s. They didn't attack in great strength, probably about 14 or 15 tanks altogether. I was responsible for relaying the instructions to the guns, shouting out all the different angles using the megaphone. The firing was almost incessant. It was rather like going to a cup tie – when you knocked a tank out everybody cheered. I think we managed to knock out three or four tanks before they retired.

Lance Sergeant Harold Harper, **426 Bty**

During the fighting an incident occurred which perhaps provided a skimpy basis in fact for some stirring nationalistic propaganda for the people back home.

We had a very illiterate, loud mouthed man as cook, certainly not a brave man. Our guns were firing over open sights at German tanks who had broken through and this idiot, who I am quite certain didn't realize what was happening, suddenly came out with his serving spoons and shouted, "Come on, come and get it!" He hadn't been in action before and he hadn't realized what was

A German casualty of their first offensive against Tobruk. This PanzerKampfwagen *MkIV was knocked out by a 25 pdr after it had broken through the outer perimeter.*

happening! There was a BBC man there and he said, "The morale of the troops there was indescribable. Amidst all this battle I saw a cook waving his spoons and shouting, 'Come and get it!' as though nothing was happening".
Sergeant Charles Ward, 426 Bty

After the first German assault had been parried the situation temporarily calmed down. During this lull Ray Ellis was sent up as a relief specialist observation post assistant to Captain Charlie Bennett. They were installed in the front line trenches alongside the Australian troops. At around 02.00 on Easter Monday, 14 April, a real attack was launched and their OP was right in the path.

First there was a lot of shell fire landing upon us. Then looking through the binoculars I could see these men creeping towards us, running from cover to cover, diving into holes in the ground as they approached. I realized I was really watching German troops advancing towards me in the front line. It was quite a sensation – a game I had played as a boy – it was actually happening!
Bombardier Ray Ellis, 425 Bty

115

The observation post team had to direct their troop or battery fire onto targets that were invisible from the gun positions. The infantry attack was repelled by a combination of artillery fire and the vigorous small arms fire of the Australians. Then a more dangerous attacking force began to rumble across No-Man's-Land straight towards the OP.

There was mortar fire, shell fire and machine-gun fire. You had to stick your head over and look over to observe – that was our job – and it wasn't a very pleasant sensation watching this lot come towards you. Bennett gave the orders, I was just helping him really. We were two men together in a very tight situation and you're passing information to each other, "Have you seen this, there's one over there!" The signaller would be on the telephone and you're passing the orders. As the tanks advanced so we were reducing the range of the guns, so that our own shells were beginning to fall nearer and nearer. The tanks made short work of the anti-tank ditch and no problem at all in coming through the barbed wire defences. Eventually the tanks actually passed through us so that our gunfire was falling on our own position – they passed straight over us, some people must have been killed, they were either side a matter of a few yards away. Following the tanks were the German infantry with their bayonets fixed.

Bombardier Ray Ellis, **425 Bty**

Bennett with considerable courage continued to direct fire on to the German tanks even as they passed over his OP position.

Captain Bennett was at the OP and he'd been over-run. The call came down the telephone line, "Target me!" We thought, "Crikey what's happening?" He kept shouting, "Target me!" Then it dawned on us what had happened.

Gunner David Tickle, **425 Bty**

As the guns responded the whole essence of the British tactics was to separate the German infantry from their tanks. Together they were a potent force, but they could be dealt with separately as tanks could not permanently occupy ground without infantry support.

My role was to try and concentrate the fire of all the guns I possibly could on the gap in the wire that the Germans had cut and through which their tanks were coming. The effect of that was that when they tried to bring their infantry through they were wiped out. The lorries were blown up and set on fire. At all costs we were to keep out every single infantryman we could.

Major Robert Daniell, **Regimental Headquarters**

The front line infantry had to deal with those that escaped the artillery fire.

Australian infantry employed the tactic of waiting for the panzers to pass through their positions before taking on the supporting German infantry.

Then the Australian infantry went into action against them – bayonet fighting in fact. Men paired off and fought individual battles. I was absolutely petrified of this. I hadn't even got a bayonet and if I had it wouldn't have done the slightest bit of good to me because I wasn't trained and to take on a German infantryman would have been suicide. All I could do was pray! No German came towards me and fortunately the Australians overcame the German infantry who started to retire and took cover in the anti-tank ditch. We switched our fire to the ditch and we did great carnage there, we dropped our shells right into the trench and there were hundreds of them there – and I mean hundreds.

Bombardier Ray Ellis, 425 Bty

As the German tanks manoeuvred around behind the Australian front line the SNH gun positions took precautions which were less than effective.

Sergeant Major Hardy says, "There's some tanks broke through, they're wandering round anywhere". He took me out somewhere into the desert in this truck. I'd got a Boyes rifle, it was only like a bullet it fired but it had got a lot of velocity, it's supposed to penetrate tanks. He left me a tin of bully beef, packet of biscuits and a bottle of water. I was in this here hole for about twelve hours. His instructions were, "If you see any tanks not flying a blue pennant on the aerial, mow them down!"

Gunner Ted Holmes, 425 **Bty**

Holmes did not realize how well armed he was in comparison to another group of signallers ordered to fight to the death.

I was stood with the signal section wondering what we were doing next when Lieutenant Newman said to me, "Hurry, grab a bar or pick shaft to wrench off the tracks of the German tanks as they're going by!" I've never heard anything so ridiculous in all my life! We'd heard that much about the German tanks advancing in Europe. Imagine going up to a German and saying, "Hey mister, can I knock your tracks off?"

Driver Ernie Hurry, 425 **Bty**

As the tanks blundered around they passed close to Captain Colin Barber's OP team and so a Hussar legend was born.

Suddenly there was a tremendous roar behind them and out of a cloud of dust came a dozen German tanks driving straight at the OP pole. Somehow they managed to get down and into their trucks before the tanks charged straight past and up to the wire. There they turned right handed and back to the gap through which they had entered. Captain Barber was after them in his wireless truck, but more German tanks were coming up from behind, and he decided to hide his truck and to watch them from the ground. Back at his OP, with his wireless set some distance away and his telephone line cut in 40 places, he contented himself with shooting with his revolver at the infantry hanging on to the sides of the last few tanks. Range was only 7 yards, but in the best Gunner traditions he missed them all. The story that went the rounds of the bars of Cairo months later when people talked of the horrors of Tobruk was of the South Notts Hussars, in desperation, using their revolvers to repel tanks.[80]

History of the South Notts Hussars

Albert Swinton was acting as Captain Colin Barber's OP assistant during the flurry of action.

They were surrounding us, "Get out and get out quick!" A lot

*Captain Colin
Barber*

of sand and tanks milling about. A case of get in the truck and get the hell out of it and hope for the best. I was in the back of the truck, he was in the front. He was a right mad bloke – not mad stupid – but he'd have a go at anything.

Lance Bombardier Albert Swinton, 426 Bty

Unsupported as they were there was little the German tanks could achieve.

The tanks were marauding around in the rear somewhere not doing anything in particular, pointless manoeuvring in the dead ground behind us. When they realized the infantry were not following up they eventually came back and again came through us and back across No Man's Land. They never got as far again.

Bombardier Ray Ellis, 425 Bty

Throughout the whole of the Easter period the guns had responded to the fire orders of their various OPs. But the gunners soon found the demand for continuous fire on constantly changing targets to be physically exhausting. Ray Ellis saw both sides as, when not forward at the OP, he was a member of a gun team.

On the end of the gun trail is a sharp piece of metal called a spade. When the gun fires and recoils this drives the spade into the ground and so anchors the gun so that between rounds it needs

Shallow gunpit at Tobruk. The 25 pdrs were brought to bear on any threatened breakthrough on the perimeter.

only a minimum of operation of elevation and line wheels. When you change the target it means you've got to get that spade out of the ground. To do that you go through an operation called running up. Everyone took up position on the gun wheels and on the command from the sergeant, "Heave!" you all put your shoulder to the wheel, that's where the saying comes from. Sometimes you need drag-ropes to get it out. Then the gun can be moved, it fires and re-anchors itself again. When you're working a gun in action it is extremely tiring. You don't fire at the same target all the time so you're swinging a gun from place to place and every time you change line the gun has got to be run up.

Bombardier Ray Ellis, **425 Bty**

The supply of ammunition stored in the gun pits was soon exhausted and a number of men were pressed into service to ensure a constant flow of shells.

I was sent for to be an ammunition number. You carried a box with two 25 pounder shells in a box. Somebody else carried the box of high explosive – that wasn't as heavy as the shells. You had to get them out of the three tonner and carry it about 100 yards to the nearest gun. They were very awkward things to carry – they banged against you – they were very hard and sharp. There were ropes round the box and your hands got all sore, then you started carrying them on your shoulder and your shoulder got sore. You were being sworn at because you weren't bringing the stuff fast enough. I hadn't got a clue what was going on and we were being shelled and dive bombed. Running around with high explosive in your hand – not a very glamorous job I'll tell you, but it was a job that had got to be done. I carried ammunition till I dropped.

Driver Bill Hutton, **425 Bty**

At one point the guns ran short of ammunition and Ted Whittaker was sent with Lieutenant John Newman to the ammunition dump.

There was a sergeant on the gate who refused to let him in, he said, "I must have authority." To everybody's delight, Mr Newman replied, "My authority's coming over that bloody hill in Mark IIIs and IVs – German tanks!" This chap let us in and we loaded up. When we left this chap in charge was still bemoaning the fact he hadn't got the paperwork and he didn't know how much we'd taken!

Signaller Ted Whittaker, **425 Bty**

At the culmination of the German attacks the pace was absolutely frenetic.

We had to keep ramming them up the spout on the line we were on without any movement, told to keep on firing. One of the troop guns seized up because it got so hot. Eventually we stopped firing in turn to let the guns cool down. I reckon that my gun alone fired something like 1, 200 rounds. We loved it, that's why we'd come, that's what we had expected or hoped to do from when we were called up in 1939. Everybody was exhilarated.

Sergeant Ian Sinclair, **425 Bty**

It was not only the guns that suffered from the constant firing. The noise also took a terrible toll on the hearing of the gunners, which is reflected by the number drawing pensions fifty years later for partial deafness.

The shield in front of the gun is not to shield the gun crew from shrapnel or shells because its not really strong enough for that. It is to protect them from the blast coming back from their own gun. But you'd catch one! You'd happen to have your head turned as the gun fired and if you were standing up you'd get the blast back from the muzzle and it would hit you rather like someone boxing your ears – a pain in your ear drum – and you would be distinctly deafened for a few minutes afterwards and then an hour or two before you would get back to normal hearing.

Sergeant George Pearson, **425 Bty**

The Germans finally gave up and fatigue took over as the dominant force. By then Ray Ellis had returned to his gun team.

Between Friday and Monday we never slept at all, never closed our eyes. We were sitting on the gun and everyone's face was one mass of sand. The sand adhered to the sweat on the face. The eyes were little red slits, everyone looked grotesque. The guns had been so hot that all the yellow paint had gone. They were bringing round bully sandwiches and handing them to us as we went on firing. Then it got to the point where at the end of that battle I remember whisky bottles being passed and we were drinking it from the bottle, gulping and passing it on. Things gradually quietened down and it was obvious that the battle was over. We were absolutely exhausted. Everyone fell on the desert where they were, anywhere, rolled themselves in their blankets and just went into a dead sleep.

Bombardier Ray Ellis, **425 Bty**

Taking it easy after the German attack was beaten off, John Walker in 425 Battery Command Post.

The aftermath of battle, as ever, was grim.

> After the attack had ceased in the evening the Reverend Parry, myself, Doctor Finnegan and a couple of men for carrying water went up to the gap in the wire where the German tanks had come through. We found that the anti-tank ditch, which was about nine feet deep, was absolutely crammed with German wounded who had crawled in there from the vehicles that our shells had set on fire. They were lying in the ditch. We started giving them water but, while the Doctor was attending one of the soldiers who was badly wounded, I saw a German rise up on his feet and have a shot at him with a revolver. I shouted to the Doctor and the Reverend Parry to withdraw. I left the water with the wounded and I said –a lot could speak English – to them, "If you shoot at my efforts to alleviate your wounded then you can fend for yourselves".

Major Robert Daniell, Regimental Headquarters

As the opening battle ended the siege proper began.

> We realized that the Germans were a totally different cup of tea from the Italians that we'd known all about from the previous campaign. We went to look at these damaged tanks and there was this great big 75 millimetre gun. The tank gun we were used to was the 2 pounder sticking out in front! In May we heard about German paratroop troops taking Crete and we thought, "Well, if

they can take a great Greek island, what about Tobruk – are they going to drop on us next?" We felt very isolated and very cut off. It was a very different enemy and we began to wonder whether in fact we were going to be able to hold out in Tobruk.

Sergeant Bob Foulds, 425 Bty

In the face of such enemies it was as well that the gunners were given the occasional proof of their own burgeoning powers.

Just as it was getting dark two German staff cars came careering down the El Adem road – they must have lost themselves completely. Colin Barber engaged them very correctly in best Larkhill fashion with ranging rounds of gunfire. He did it brilliantly. The two cars were standing together not very far outside our perimeter defences, when he landed a round of gunfire right on them and they both burst into flames. It was most spectacular because it was dusk and the sight of these flames shooting up – there were a number of Australians around us and they were cheering wildly at this. One of them rushed up and smote me heavily on the shoulder and said, "You're the best bloody battery in the British Army!" It was very good for morale!

Captain Bob Hingston, 426 Bty

★ ★ ★ ★

When the battle had finished and they had time the guns were protected as much as possible by gunpits; but these differed radically from the grandiose and impractical creations of Mersa Matruh.

You dug yourself a gunpit, digging down maybe a foot and a half, couple of feet if you could. Then you put a sandbag wall, two or three sandbags high round the front so that you had a certain amount of protection for the gun crew and the ammunition which you piled in the gunpit. They were set out not four guns in a line, but two forward and the wing guns back a little bit, so that if you were attacked by tanks you could always bring two guns to bear even if it was attacking from the flank.

Sergeant George Pearson, 425 Bty

During the opening battle, the German Stukas had made their first attacks, but had barely been noticed amongst the general mayhem. 'We were involved in this full scale battle and the Stukas were part of the general crescendo of noise, smoke, screaming engines, bombs and shells. It just sort of fitted into the general chaos.'[81] As the siege developed there were some tremendous Stuka attacks on the vital port facilities of Tobruk of which the SNH had a grandstand view.

It was a great spectacle because the defences of Tobruk were very good. So you got these clouds and clouds, streams of red,

An oil tanker on fire in Tobruk harbour after an air attack. The Stukas were about to extend their target to the troops on the ground.

blue, green and white tracer going up into the sky a tremendous barrage they put up. Above it the higher shells bursting and then the great flashes of the bombs as they landed on the ground – it was a splendid sight a real sort of enormous fireworks display.

Captain Charles Laborde, **426 Bty**

Yet it was soon clear that the regiment's role in repelling the German tank attacks had not gone unnoticed.

We'd seen these Stukas incessantly bombing the harbour. But, having had their tanks knocked out by these gun troops, they decided to turn their attention to the guns. They sent up one or two recce planes, then the next minute we saw these boys curling round in the air and there we were. When you found out it was your troop that was being attacked it was not a very happy moment.

Lance Sergeant Harold Harper, **426 Bty**

The aggressive might of the Luftwaffe was a very different experience from the high level Italian raids. 'The first dive bomb attack I made the mistake – I laid down flat and I would have been glad enough to get under a piece of newspaper. It's just as though they are picking you out personally. I'd never really bothered about the Italian stuff'.[82] There was an extra dimension to the Stuka raid that rattled almost all of the men. 'It was frightening, the WHHEEIAOUW was worse than the noise of the bomb when it dropped. You never got used to it. The Stuka would not have been nearly as frightening if they hadn't screamed and if it had a different shape – it looked like an eagle coming to pick you up.'[83] It was

A formation of Junkers 87B dive bombers over the Western Desert. The Stuka's siren, activated by the rush of air during the bombing dive, caused nerves to be severely rattled.

more than most people could physically cope with. 'People were scared to death – I was more than scared. If people weren't loose before, they'd be loose after a Stuka raid.'[84] However, despite their fear, a grudging admiration was born amongst the gunners for the sheer skill and courage of the German pilots, especially after the lack-lustre performance of their Italian air force counterparts at Mersa Matruh.

> They were really good. They came so low they nearly scraped the floor by the time they pulled out of the dive. They aimed the Stuka at the target, just let the bomb go at the last minute and machine gunned you as well. With this fixed undercarriage there used to be a saying that you don't know you've been 'Stukad' till you've got tread marks on your back!
>
> **Gunner Ted Holmes, 425 Bty**

The gunners could not hit back at the Stukas but at least they could strike back at the Germans.

> The main thing after every bombing, immediately as the last plane was disappearing, was to man the guns and fire some shots at the German lines. A, it would keep the morale of the men up and B, to let the Germans know that, "If you shoot at me I'll shoot you back!"
>
> **Captain William Pringle, 425 Bty**

The first line of defence against the Luftwaffe was of course the Royal Air Force but, although they did their best, they were totally outnumbered.

Ken Tew beside the grave of Flying Officer Lamb the last RAF pilot in Tobruk. Lamb took on three Me110s and their combined fire power proved too much. The SNH lads could only look on with heavy hearts as the Hurricane ripped into the desert.

One early afternoon there were three 110s, twin engined Messerschmitts, and this Hurricane dived on them from a patchy faint wisp of cloud. You could see the tracer from these three straight on him. He kept coming all the way, his dive continued almost vertical, straight into the ground, Oooh Dear! By the time I went to look they'd put a rough wooden cross with his name and dogtags, Flying Officer Lamb. All that was left was a big smoking hole nearby where the Hurricane had gone deep into the ground.

Lance Bombardier Signaller Ted Whittaker, **425 Bty**

The gunners had appreciated the efforts of the RAF pilots and some were roused to fury at their fate.

We saw a German pilot shot down and he took off in his parachute and started to come down apparently very near to us. We were feeling very cross after Lamb had been shot down and we said, "Let's jump in a vehicle and go over there and get him!" And we intended to shoot him! He landed rather further away than we thought and as we tore over the desert one calmed down a bit and we thought, "This is not a good idea" But that is the kind of feeling that you can get – I can understand atrocities committed in hot blood – in anger.

Lance Sergeant Dennis Middleton, **425 Bty**

As the raids proliferated it was essential to hide the regiment's position. One particular problem that had to be overcome was the fact that from the air any tracks in the desert 'shone' out like beacons. In an effort to reduce this effect strict discipline was imposed on the drivers.

We would have a track plan so that any vehicle coming on to that site must follow the diversion from a main track going round in an arc and rejoining that track rather than being just a diversion from a main road finishing like a 'T' junction which is obviously going to be a position of some sort.

Sergeant George Pearson, **425 Bty**

Nevertheless it remained almost impossible to hide a battery position from serious air reconnaissance. They brought us these reconnaissance photos taken by a high flying Hurricane. There were our positions beautifully visible. Four little black dots, white lines leading to the command post which wasn't quite as visible, lines leading up to the latrines. It stood out like a sore thumb. We went to work with bits of scrub thorn and tried to obliterate the tracks and the pattern.

Lance Bombardier Ted Whittaker, **425 Bty**

Such efforts were still unsatisfactory.

That part of the desert is dotted by a little tiny shrub called camel thorn about 18 inches high, a scrubby thorny thing. With the trucks continually bringing things onto the position and the blast of the guns the camel thorn got blown away and we thought it was a good thing to fetch more, dig little holes and plant it so that aircraft wouldn't spot the position. It didn't work of course!

Bombardier Ray Ellis, 425 Bty

Gradually the gunners learnt the requirements of life under the constant threat of a Stuka attack.

You saw the bombs leave the plane – it did seem so near to you, you could count the bombs and see them coming at you through the air. We began to learn that if the bombs appeared to be coming straight at you, then they were going to go overhead, and hit something behind you. But if they appeared to be coming down in front of you, then they were going to drop on you or very, very close to you which wasn't a very nice sensation. It's the most naked feeling in the world and really all we did was to get as far into the ground as we possibly could.

Sergeant Bob Foulds, 425 Bty

There could, however, be a touch of complacency about a gunner's reaction once he considered he had secured relative personal safety, 'You learn to sit and watch it. If you could get into a little slit trench and you could see they weren't comng for you it was rather a wonderful sight!'[85] Such a raid could appear awe-inspiringly destructive.

I remember approaching B Troop and they'd just fired and the firing had given away their position. They were given such a hammering with dive bombers that I thought, "There can't possibly be anyone still alive there".

Battery Clerk Ted Coup, 425 Bty Headquarters

George Pearson was on the B Troop gun position as the Stukas screamed down.

I dived into a slit trench and another young chappie called Phil Collihole dived on top of me. When the bombs had finished exploding and the aircraft were going away I said, "Come on, get up, Phil!" He didn't move and I got up and he sort of flopped over on his back. I said, "What's the matter, are you hit?" I couldn't see a mark on him, but he was obviously out and he was in fact dead. A small piece of shrapnel as big as would cover a thumb nail had gone into the back of his neck and must have severed the spinal column and killed him just like that.

Sergeant George Pearson, 425 Bty

In fact there had been one other casualty – the popular NCO who had been Number One of Ray Ellis's gun team.

Cliff Smedley was a very big chap and when a dive bombing raid came he dived into the Boyes anti-tank rifle pit. He and the

500 pounder had a race for it and the 500 pound bomb won. He was not mutilated as such – I think it was blast that killed him –because when we picked him up it was rather like picking a fish up he was all floppy. It must have broken every bone in his body.

Sergeant George Pearson, 425 Bty

These Stuka raids marked a second attempt by Rommel to remove the Tobruk garrison from the flank of the Afrika Korps so that he could concentrate on his true objective of the Nile Delta. On 30 April a massed infantry attack supported by artillery was launched and despite the attentions of the SNH who fired a 'prodigious amount'[86] the Germans managed to break through the Australian lines to form a salient protruding into the perimeter area. A counter-attack improved the situation but the salient remained. In due course the front line stabilized and once again the siege resumed its course. As the focus of Rommel's attention moved away he began to replace German units with Italian units – but the Tobruk garrison remained a thorn in his side.

★ ★ ★ ★

The role of the SNH within the garrison forces was to be ever vigilant at the gun positions, ready to bring down fire on any German movements visible from the observation posts, which threatened the safety of the infantry in their front line trenches. The infantry in turn held back the Germans from breaking through to the guns. The OP team would liaise closely with the local Australian officers and would even occasionally accompany Australian patrols into No Man's Land ready to bring down fire on various targets or, if necessary, to cover a hasty withdrawal.

Clouds of dust used to move up and down this valley into which we couldn't see into below the escarpment. I kept reporting this dust and I got various rude comments coming back, "Don't you realize there's quite a bit of dust around!" I said, "These are distinct clouds of dust and I think they are vehicles moving up and down that valley". Eventually it was decided we'd better investigate it. I went out with a patrol of Australian infantry. Just out of sight of our OP was a very aged ruined village. We got there in the darkness and bedded down in amongst these ruins so that we were tolerably invisible. Then things happened – it was the regular German supply route to their forward troops that came down this valley. I had a section forward and we began to shoot at them and very soon we'd stopped them. I thought, "This is grand – now we'll get at them!" Then one driver with more guts decided to charge straight through – the risk of being hit is very little. He rushed right through from the back of the jam, went right past us and he got away with it. Then of course the others in a rather sheep like way followed him so we didn't get as many vehicles as we'd hoped. But we did knock out several. After a week or so of this they packed it in and they eventually built their Axis highway right out beyond El Adem airport which must have given them a rather longer journey.

Captain Bob Hingston, **426 Bty**

Such excursions into No Man's Land could be nerve wracking for artillerymen.

We used to go forward with the infantry. It was hell! I was terrified! It is a funny thing you notice that each arm of the services is not frightened by being shot at by its own arm. Machine guns and rifles don't worry infantry anything like as much as they worry me. And shells don't worry me anywhere as much as they worried the infantryman. It was a pretty eerie sort of task, I'm not an infantryman at all and I certainly didn't like night patrols, but you had to do it and that was it. As an officer you had to set an example and not show that you were terrified to death.

Captain William Pringle, **425 Bty**

The signallers would lay out telephone lines to the temporary OP set up in No Man's Land.

One night me and the signallers laid a cable out to Captain Slinn, and I think Whittaker, who went out at dawn to a little funk hole in No Man's Land. They used a periscope for observation, whilst the Australians put in an attack to capture Medwa, to give them artillery support. We had a steel bar through the drum cable and we wrapped the bar with plenty of insulating tape. As we walked forward there was a signaller pulling it off and every so often the other three signallers would stop and put a ladder from one cable to another, so that should it get shelled there's a way of communication getting through. The job was complete at about ten o'clock at night when one of the signallers getting out of the hole tripped over one of the spare drums and clanged it with another. Of course everything went wild as Jerry opened up with everything he'd got. He sent these flares up and they machine-gunned us. I lay on my stomach and incendiary bullets were going over my head – I could hear them and see them. Every time the flares went up I looked for a worm hole I could crawl down. I think it took hours to crawl over the next hill out of range. I crawled a bit, stopped a bit, crawled a bit, waited a bit – if blood had have been brown I should have bled to death! I was scared, oh dear!

Driver Ernie Hurry, **425 Bty**

It was not only the Germans who were life threatening to men operating in No Man's Land at night.

We'd been out and laid this wire – we'd left the truck and walked it. I'd got a blue pennant to denote it was a signaller's truck. Having completed the job we boarded the truck to make our way home. We were jumped on by an Australian patrol. They man-handled us, roughed us up a bit and lined us up against the truck. We told them we were Tommies belonging to the guns. One insisted that we were Germans and that we were using that pennant as a German flag. I says, "No, we're Pommies!" One of them was going to shoot us – he'd got his gun levelled – young Taffy Roberts got down on his knees and prayed. Then they suddenly realized they were making a mistake and let us go but Ooooh! That was a bad nightmare.

Driver Ernie Hurry, **425 Bty**

Of necessity the regiment formed a close relationship with the Australian infantry of the 9th Division.

On more than one occasion we rescued them from difficult situations and they took us to heart and because of our cap badge they called us the 'Acorn Gunners' and that name stuck with us for the rest of the war. They issued all sorts of wild invitations to us at the time – that all we had to do was stand in the middle of Sydney after the war and say you were an 'Acorn Gunner' and you would be made for life so to speak!

Lance Sergeant Harold Harper, **426 Bty**

The Australians were a wild lot from the British perspective, 'They used to wear virtually no clothes. It was a well known thing to see an

Australian with a tin hat on, a pair of boots and nothing in between – not a thing!'[87] It was not only their eccentric appearance but their refreshing irreverence towards figures of authority which endeared them to the South Notts men.

I liked being with the Australians in the front line position, they were friendly and they had a certain casual way about them. For instance the Battery Commander, Major Peter Birkin, had red sandy hair. When he got into the trench a private soldier would refer to him, "Hi-yah, Red! How yah doing?" Which I thought was fantastic whereas we would say, "Good morning, Sir!"

Bombardier Ray Ellis, 425 Bty

This colonial irreverence did not endear them to a regular soldier like Major Daniell, who considered them a liability in a properly run army.

I mistrusted the Australian element in Tobruk – militarily. I thought they might not do what they were told to do and they never did. They never arrived at an arranged hour for a night attack. They usually never arrived at all, or if they did, they arrived several hours later which was very difficult for me who was arranging the barrage from the guns.

Major Robert Daniell, **Regimental Headquarters**

The original Italian front line observation posts, which included 30 foot high poles, were augmented or replaced as the months passed by with a series of OP towers.

It became obvious that the concrete emplacement OPs were not suitable as they were in full view of the Germans. It was decided that we would build OPs in the form of scaffolding towers. The scaffolding would be about six foot square and stand anything between 40 to 60 feet high. It was like a prisoner of war outlook post. We had to scale up this thing, absolutely perpendicular. These were put about a 1,000 yards behind the ridge so that only the top of these towers could see over the ridge into the enemy land. Very exposed indeed, you got the impression you were there on your own and the rest of the world had left you. You felt as though every German in the German Army was looking at you.

Lance Sergeant Harold Harper, 426 Bty

Newly promoted Battery Quartermaster Sergeant Charles Ward was keen to get a look at his enemies from these vantage points.

Hingston said to me one day, "Look here 'Q' would you like to come up as a change to have a look at the Germans?" I said, "Oooh, all right, Sir, not bad!" Beardall heard about this and he went to Hingston and said, "Look here, Sir! I don't mind you going up there and getting your bloody silly head knocked off, but

our senior NCOs are most precious. I'm not going to have my BQMS taken up there just for fun – he'll get his bloody head knocked off! He's not going!"

Battery Quartermaster Sergeant Charles Ward, **426 Bty**

In view of what happened to Hingston later in the siege Battery Sergeant Major Charles Beardall had shown exemplary foresight. The sheer height of the newly constructed towers was a problem for some of the men and Albert Swinton showed that vertigo can strike the toughest of men – even boxers!

Captain Barber went up and he phoned down and said would I take his compass or binoculars up. I said, "Yes, OK!" Well, I got on this ladder thing and I seemed to be going for hours. I looked up and, "Oh dear!" I looked down and nearly fell off. I was scared to death I was. I eventually got up to the top and I thought, "Now how do I get in?" There was a double row of sandbags with an opening about 18 inches to get through. I got my elbow in to lever in and these sandbags moved and I nearly fell off! I was scared to death! I eventually got in and gave Captain Barber his binoculars and he says, "Righto, Bombardier, off you go!" I says, "Well, it's all right, Sir, I'll stop up here, you go down and have a break." Only 'cos I daren't go down! I sat up there for hours, and hours and hours – because I daren't come down! It never got any better.

Bombardier Albert Swinton, **426 Bty**

The Afrika Korps sought to add physical injury to this vertiginous torment.

They did shoot at us, you could see the guns flash when you were on top of this big pole and you'd say a couple of prayers. Sometimes they'd only fire a few rounds but sometimes they meant it. If you found they did, you watched the guns flash and as soon as the shells burst you were over the side. You could just get to the bottom and in the slit trench before the next lot fell. Flash, Bang, Down – and no messing!

Lance Bombardier Ted Whittaker, **425 Bty**

The observation officer and his specialist OP assistant would climb up the tower before dawn and stay up there all day.

About mid-day we sent down a situation report – sit-rep they called it – and we sent another at night. The usual thing was if you could see movement on the escarpment a few thousand yards in front. Up to the Italian positions the ground sloped slightly upwards. Then it dropped and there was dead ground, that you couldn't see into. Then it rose again steeply to this escarpment, which must have been several hundred feet high, on top of which was the El Adem aerodrome. We could just see the tops of the hangar from the little pole and we could see about half the hangar from the big pole. They built a road that by-passed Tobruk and you could see traffic from the big pole, from the little pole you could see movement but you'd estimate – you'd look through the binoculars – and say maybe 50 vehicles convoy moving east, jot the time down and put it in the sit-rep.

Lance Bombardier Ted Whittaker, 425 **Bty**

Owing to the serious shortages of ammunition at Tobruk they could not open fire on every possible target they could see moving around behind the German lines. 'There were times when we were limited to about five rounds per gun per day, when things got really tight. There was ammunition there for if anything really drastic happened, but we were rationed very severely.'[88] When a worthy target had been identified the OP would get into contact with the gun positions.

You first of all identified the target. If it was a GF target, gunfire, it meant it was a moving target or one that had got to be engaged very quickly. Say it was some vehicles moving you'd say, "Troop, GF target" and everyone ran to the gun even quicker than normal, because the shells had got to be off quickly. You'd then give very fast fire orders. If it was an ordinary target you would just say, "Troop target" and that meant there was no great emergency. Then you gave the type of ammunition that was to be fired. If it was HE 119 that meant it was more of a penetration ammunition; 117 was immediate impact if you wanted to kill troops on the surface; 119 cap on meant that you were firing at something heavy and you wanted a delayed explosion. So, "Troop Target, HE 117". Then you gave the gun which was going to range, right ranging or left ranging, because only one gun would fire. That was more or less a whim! Left ranging meant the gun that was firing was in the middle of the troop, right ranging meant the Number 1 gun would fire. Then you would give your line from the zero line; left or right of the zero line. If there was any angle of sight you would give that. Then the estimated range and the word, "Fire". All that would be passed to the guns. Then all four guns would move together but only one would fire. When it was put on the guns they would say, "Ready, Fire!" You would receive from the gun position the words, "Number 1 shot!" The shell would come over your head and land and you'd make the necessary corrections.

Bombardier Ray Ellis, 425 **Bty**

Theoretically this was a fairly simple procedure, although quite difficult in practice.

You always try to bracket the target either on line or on range. If you had a shell which is on line, but way over the target, you

134

would drop 800 and that would land a round in front of the target. Then you would add 400 and hope that that dropped your round behind. Then drop 200 and then add a hundred until you'd got a hundred yard bracket on the target and then go to fire at the fifty yard split.

Sergeant George Pearson, **425 Bty**

Back at the guns the specialist assistants had surveyed in the guns so that they could place the guns, OPs and target on the 'map'.

That is to get the correct grid reference in eastings, northings and height of the gun position. To use the director which is rather like a simple theodolite to lay the guns out on the correct bearing. Thereafter to plot the gun position on an artillery board which is in fact a gridded square. From that you can mark the eastings and northings rather as the normal ordnance survey map is marked. You plot on the gun position then any targets that you engage; you

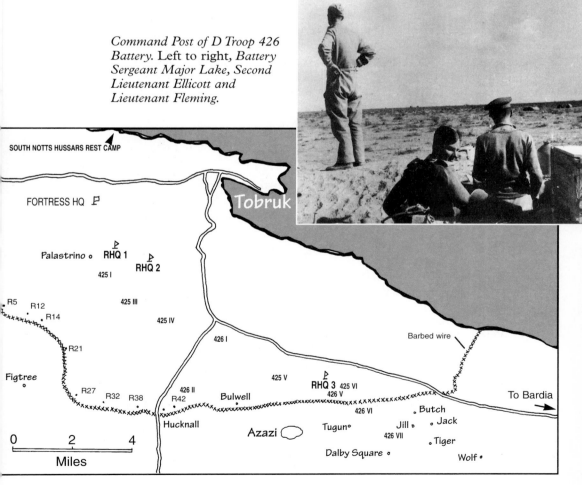

Command Post of D Troop 426 Battery. Left to right, *Battery Sergeant Major Lake, Second Lieutenant Ellicott and Lieutenant Fleming.*

SOUTH NOTTS HUSSARS REST CAMP

FORTRESS HQ

Tobruk

Palastrino ○ **RHQ 1**
RHQ 2
425 I

R5   R12   425 III
.R14   425 IV

R21   426 I   Barbed wire

Figtree   425 V
○   R27   R32 R38   426 II   **RHQ 3** 425 VI   To Bardia
R42   Bulwell   426 V
Hucknall   426 VI   . Butch
Azazi ⬭   Tugun○   Jill ○   . Jack
426 VII
Dalby Square ○   . Tiger
Wolf ●

0   2   4
Miles

also plot in the grid reference of them. Then you have an arm – a metal rule – which is marked out in thousands and hundreds of yards which swings on a pivot which you put over the gun position. Then there is an arc which measures degrees and you lay the arm out on what was known as the zero line. You set your arc up with the zero in the centre, with the arm on the zero and then any reading right or left of the zero line is measured in degrees and can be passed to the guns because they have been laid out on that same zero line. Any predicted targets you would plot in their grid reference on your artillery board and you were able to read off the bearing and range to those targets. Another thing was to work out from meteor telegrams provided by the RAF meteorological service the differences that temperature, wind and barometric pressure made to gunnery from range tables. It was terribly important, because if you got a head wind blowing against a shell, it reduces its range; if you get a freezing cold temperature when you fire a shell the cordite doesn't expand so quickly as it does when its hot and therefore the shell doesn't get as much punch behind it; and of course if you get a cross wind the shell can be blown off to the left or right. All these things had to be corrected.

Sergeant George Pearson, 425 **Bty**

The mathematical skills required from these specialists were either simple or devilishly complicated depending on their own personal numeracy.

One had done logs at school and they were merely something you had to learn. When you came down to gunnery you were actually using logs to calculate. If you had the grid reference of the gun position and the grid reference of the target. You have your grid references eastings and then northings to fix your gun position and then eastings and northings to fix your target. Between the two you can get a right angle triangle. Suddenly logs that you learnt at school became useful and it was in fact very interesting.

Sergeant George Pearson, 425 **Bty**

Captain Charles Laborde had more of a problem!

I wished often that we had calculators – it would have made life so much easier. My family has a failing for mathematics, we cannot do maths, my father was hopeless at it, I'm hopeless at it. Working out the angles, range and lines of sight you have an army form to do it on and I always had to use the army form and the log tables to work these things out. We had all these hostile batteries with their co-ordinates and every so often, six or seven times a day, the meteor telegram would come in and you would have to work out the line and range to them all over again. Ivor

Birkin was marvellous, he'd do the whole thing in his head and he never got it wrong!

Captain Charles Laborde, 426 Bty

Herbert Bonnello had a mnemonic to remind him of the trigometrical formula required to work out the angles and ranges.

Some people have curly black hair to push back – that was it. Sine equals perpendicular over hypotenuse – Some people have! Curly black hair – cosine equals base over hypotenuse. To push back – tangent equals perpendicular over base! That's how we used to know it – some people have curly black hair to push back!

Bombardier Herbert Bonnello, 426 Bty

The gun position officers usually took a relaxed view of the calculations. 'The officer would do a rough check to make sure that we were in the right area. It gradually got to the situation where the officer would say, "Right, fair enough" and wouldn't bother to check.'[89] The gun officer would then pass the order to the guns, 'You get the order, "Take Post". We had tannoys but we'd discarded them because you got a distortion of sound, "Blowchh, Blogh, Blurrk!" We went back to the hand held megaphone.'[90] The orders were received by the sergeant of each gun team.

He was in charge of everything to do with the gun and to see it was effective in every respect: supervise the work of the layer, see that the ammunition was there, organize the gun tower and the driver, all the gun numbers. He was responsible, if anything went wrong he was to blame. Physically on the gun he had to put his shoulder to everything else that was happening. If the gun wanted moving round from one line to another he helped as much as he could, but basically he was there to see that everybody else did their job. And he gave the order to fire.

Lance Sergeant John Walker, 425 Bty

The next most important member of the gun team was the gun layer. 'The layer was the key position as far as putting into effect all the instructions. The layer put the line on the gun, the lateral angle and the vertical angle.[91] The rest of the gun team then swung into action.

You put in the shell which is rammed, then you put in the cartridge which is really bags of cordite. You close the breech and pull the firing lever. A pin strikes the percussion cap which explodes the cordite. The cordite burns with great rapidity causing gases, which expand, to project the shell. If you're putting bags of cordite into a gun that is red hot you don't need to pull the firing lever it explodes itself. If you're not quick and you don't get the breech closed in time then it will blow the breech back and the gun blows up. So you musn't jam the breech by getting the cartridge in at a wrong angle. You have to have people who work as a team very well. In goes the shell rammed in, the man loading the cartridge has got to be very adept at loading cartridge and the man closing the breech has got to follow his hand so that it closes quickly. Very often before the layer had time to pull the firing lever it would fire itself!

Bombardier Ray Ellis, 425 Bty

And so the shell would be fired. As the 25 pounders only had a range of 14-15,000 yards and many of the choice targets were beyond that mark, risks had to be taken in order to move the guns forward.

> We carried out shoots when we brought our guns right up to the wire amongst the infantry lines. We were guided on to our targets by the 4th Field Survey Regiment who had sound ranging and flash spotting equipment. They devised a very, very effective system whereby they had already plotted in exactly where the enemy artillery were. They ranged our guns by spotting through their sound ranging equipment where our shells fell and then they would move our fall of shot on to the gun pit. As soon as we had done our shoot we upped sticks and pushed off as quick as we possibly could and left the infantry to collect the return gun fire!

Bombardier Charles Westlake, 425 Bty

At other times these forward shoots were less scientific as was discovered by Sergeant Ian Sinclair, who had been placed in command of an extra troop which had been formed and armed with 4.5″ howitzers. The troop had been given a nickname appropriate to his rather dazzling good looks.

> I was sent up with our 'Glamour Troop' to a forward position. We had some spare guns, 4.5 gun howitzers and only skeleton gun crews – three or four per gun. We went up well forward, within a 1000 metres of the wire, took up position and fired regularly for no good reason. We were only in touch with the command post and we were told to fire on a certain line because they thought there was a target there but nobody was observing for us. There was no urgency about it – it was a nuisance value. The whole idea was to make the enemy think that we had a damn sight more guns than we had.

Sergeant Ian Sinclair, 425 Bty

Another means of achieving this was through the use of captured Italian guns. 'They were all over the place. The old Eytie, when they decide to bale out they bale out – they left everything! We'd got thousands of rounds of ammunition for these guns.'[92] One abandoned battery of guns was situated close to the 426 Bty gun positions.

> They must have been 150 millimetres, real first war veterans. They had huge slatted wheels, wooden flaps round the outside of

the wheel. Just behind them they had a movable ramp and you had to put this into position. They had no dial sights of course, but we used to point them roughly in the right direction of the El Adem aerodrome and then try and fire a shell up on to the escarpment. They were very large shells, much larger than anything we had – they must have weighed over a hundred pounds. When you'd lined the gun up you put the ramps behind it in the right position and took hold of the lanyard – nobody pulled the trigger of course, a lanyard was tied on to it and you retired. You pulled the trigger with this very long lanyard made of signal wire. There was a colossal bang, off goes the shell and the gun would run straight back, there was no re-cuperator, up the ramp at the back and then run forward again. Marvellous sight – it was simply fascinating! You could see the shell going away, then you'd wait for quite a long time and there would be this lovely WHHUUMPHH in the distance, a great cloud, a huge shell burst.

Captain Charles Laborde, 426 Bty

The gun crews were exposed to a considerable risk as no-one really knew what they were doing.

I pulled the lanyard for that many a time standing at a distance of about 30 yards from the gun, we never used to stand close to it because we never trusted it. The first round we ever fired with that we put so much cordite in the barrel we never observed the shot

Making good use of captured ordnance – an Italian 75mm artillery piece is being readied for action, but note the long lanyard to ensure safety for the SNH men.

139

falling – we think its still going!

Lance Sergeant Harold Harper, **426 Bty**

The ever eager Australian infantry became keen amateur gunners in their spare time.

These Aussies said, "Well how do you get these things in action?" So we showed them how to do it and they said, "Right, lets have a go!" One evening they started firing a bit tentatively saying, "Right, fire one round, let's see where it goes and then we'll adjust it." Eventually we got onto target and we said, "Fire, two rounds gunfire!" "Two rounds! We're not firing two rounds – its 25 or nothing!" They just let rip until Jerry got a bit fed up and fired back and they were off like an alarm clock – into their trucks and away!

Bombardier Albert Swinton, **426 Bty**

Gradually the Australians' efforts were harnessed.

They started merely banging away haphazardly in the direction of the enemy. The British artillery units showed these Australians how to use the 'bush artillery' effectively. Each gun would be laid on a bearing individually with a prismatic compass – chaps standing behind with a prismatic compass to lay the gun on a particular bearing. On many of them the sighting equipment had been damaged or destroyed by the Italians when they left them, so the range was done by a wooden stave which was marked every six inches or foot. That was put in front of the muzzle and you learned the sort of range that you'd got so that the order for the ranging would be, "Twenty eight notches!" and the chap would cock his muzzle up until he'd reached the twenty eighth notch and it would be fired. The Australians did have a rather nasty habit from our point of view. The Italian guns were the type where charges were put into a cartridge case and put in behind the rammed shell. If they weren't getting sufficient range from the three or four charge bags that were in the cartridge case they'd cram in an extra bag! "That'll make the bastard go!" Of course they blew a few guns to pieces that way! Luckily they didn't lose any men by it because when they'd done that they used to fire the gun with a lanyard. But it was not a habit to be recommended. You wouldn't have seen my rear end for dust!

Sergeant George Pearson, **425 Bty**

The *ad hoc* gun teams, whether British or Australian, were inevitably known by all as the 'bush artillery'. They received a unique kind of firing orders from the OPs.

We'd got these guns lined up and we used to have a stick at the side of them with notches in it, beside of the barrel; along this escarpment were all these telegraph poles that the Eyties had stuck up. The OP would look out and see something, perhaps a truck zooming about somewhere in the desert and thought, "Well, it's not costing us anything let's have a go!" The fire orders would be something like, "Up two notches, along three telegraph poles, fire!" They were just used for bloody nuisance value really, just to keep them on their toes on the other side.

Bombardier Albert Swinton, 426 Bty

The risks were enormous but it was at least a way of hitting back at the enemy, 'We kept firing it until when we opened the breech there were flames shooting out. The 'tiffy' examined it after and he said that if we had fired it another half hour it would have blown up in our faces.'[93]The artificer discovered that, 'The barrel had cracked and that was the end of that with the Italian 'Biff Bertha'!'[94] Sometimes the warning signs were not noticed in time.

I remember I was up there with old Barker and they wanted a bit more range so they decided to put a bit more charge in. They fired this gun and we all started running because this gun disintegrated. Old Barker got a lump of the barrel, fortunately flat on, BANG, this big lump of cast iron hit him smack on his backside! He was bruised and couldn't sit down for days. That put paid to that nonsense!

Bombardier Albert Swinton, 426 Bty

As the siege of Tobruk dragged on the barrels of the 25 pdrs began to wear out. Sergeant Bob Foulds with D Gun, B Troop, 425 Battery.

The 25 pounders of the SNH were also suffering from over-use and required constant maintenance if they were not to become inefficient or dangerous, 'You had to pull through the barrel the same as you did a rifle and you had to see that all the parts were polished, clean and lightly oiled.'[95] There were other sources of concern.

> The buffer and recoil systems depend upon pressurized air and oil sections, with a piston which separates the oil and the air in the re-cuperator system. These are maintenance problems that the Number One will be keeping an eye on. He's got an oil level indicator and also if the gun becomes sluggish in the recoil he's probably lost air pressure in his buffer and re-cuperator system. Then he would get his 'tiffy', the battery artificer, to check it out. He might say, "The piston needs re-packing we shall have to pull this gun out of action for a day". It would be pulled out and the Number One would act as labourer to the tiffy to put a new packing in.
>
> *Sergeant George Pearson,* **425 Bty**

As the siege wore on the gun barrels began to wear out from the sheer number of shells that they had been required to fire, 'You can always tell when a barrel is wearing because instead of a shell going off, "WWWhhhhhhhh" into the distance it goes off, "Whhh..Whhh..Whh.. Whh". If a barrel wears you can take it off down to the Royal Army Ordnance forward section and they will change the barrel.'[96]

★ ★ ★ ★

It was not only the guns which were worn out at Tobruk. The men endured a miserable existence with an enervating combination of danger and boredom. 'Time in Tobruk was endless. One day was very much like another, and another, and another, and another....'[97] There was no end to their torture in sight.

> We were on duty 24 hours a day, seven days a week, week after week after week for nine months. No newspaper, no radio, no cinema, no beer, no time off, no recreation, no sport – just sat there for nine months. You couldn't wash or bath: at one time you couldn't even shave. The food was monotonous, dreary and not enough of it. The water was brackish so that you were continually thirsty. That itself was a terrific strain – forgetting all the dive bombing and fighting! Just sitting in a gun pit for nine months.
>
> *Bombardier Ray Ellis,* **425 Bty**

Although Tobruk itself was a sizeable town, most of the defensive perimeter was out in the Western Desert, with all the discomforts that this entailed.

The lot of the embattled defenders of Tobruk: daily hardships and boredom punctuated by deadly danger from enemy barrages and air attacks. The strain is beginning to show among Sergeant Ian Sinclair's gun team from A Troop. On the left is Tommy Foley, fourth from left is Ian Sinclair, with Ray Ellis on the right.

You couldn't get away from the dust – the grime round your eyes, your mouth, your nose. The khamsin, the hot blast of wind, means you're sweating like fury. The dust, the filth in the atmosphere sticking to your sweat. You can't move your eyelids, you try to breathe, you can't blow your nose – it's a nasty sensation.

Signal Sergeant Fred Langford, **425 Bty**

When the wind got up to a certain point a sandstorm would ensue.

You saw the sandstorm coming along. It just looked like one red mass in the air blotting out the sun and everything. The sand would hit you so hard that on occasions it would even make your skin bleed. We used to dress ourselves up and looked like these cowboys with scarfs over our faces and all you could see was a little bit of eyes. Of course your ears all got bunged up and goodness knows what else! The only consolation was that there was never any firing done in a sandstorm.

Lance Sergeant Harold Harper, **426 Bty**

You could easily get lost in such a storm.

We were at the observation post, right on the perimeter of Tobruk and it was in the form of a concrete emplacement obviously put there by the Italians. We were down there one evening and there was a sand storm raging outside. There was about four or five of us there and we were playing cards by the light of a hurricane lamp. Lo and behold, the flap of the tarpaulin came back and a pair of legs descended. We thought, "Well who the dickens can this be at this time of night?" The next thing was a dixie full of stew and then this German lad came down, a very young boy, 17 or 18 at the very most. He was in the cook-house and he'd strayed in this sandstorm, lost his way, seen a chink of light we'd left uncovered, thought it was his own crowd and appeared in our dug-out. Then we committed what might have been described in Whitehall as a crime. All we did was eat the lad's stew and then I took him up to the top, pointed him in the direction of the German lines and told him where to go!

Lance Sergeant Harold Harper, **426 Bty**

Other peculiarities of the desert were the mirages and related visual disruptions.

By the middle of the morning, as the heat of the day became more intense, you could walk about without compunction. They could see you but in a distorted way. They did the same thing and we would see them walking about but you'd see a man walking upside down fifteen foot in the air – distorted visions – you couldn't aim at it, because you didn't know where he was really. Sometimes by a trick of the light, or fate, it would all revert back to normal again in a second and they had a complete view of the front again, maybe for quarter of an hour, and then it would go again. You'd be looking out and everything would be distorted; then it would all be clear and everyone dived for cover as the war started again.

Bombardier Ray Ellis, **425 Bty**

The fauna of the desert were varied but almost uniformly unfriendly. The troops suffered from lice or fleas and some developed a spectacularly dangerous method of delousing which it would not be in anyone's interest to emulate at home.

Your clothes do get lice in them and we used to get a half petrol tin, put petrol in it and soak your overalls or shirt in petrol. You'd then put that over a low petrol fire so that the petrol heated up and that seemed to get rid of these lice. Then you let your shirt dry out and washed it in such water as you could get! It sounds so ridiculous now!

Sergeant George Pearson, **425 Bty**

As you might expect, the widespread cheerful use of highly inflammable fuels did lead to accidents.

We used to put a lot of petrol on the floor – scattered on the floor – to kill these sand fleas. Somebody lit a cigarette and threw the match on the floor. All of a sudden there was a BANG! It didn't set fire, it exploded! I wasn't the first out through the door but I was second. When Penny (Penlington) came out he'd got no eyebrows. He looked ever so funny! He said, "What silly bugger struck a match!"

Driver Ernie Hurry, 425 Bty

The desert was, above all, the domain of the fly, although the men could not understand how they came to be there.

You could drive into totally empty desert, miles from any civilization at all, and stop. While the truck was moving there was no sign of life, but the moment you stopped, the flies would settle on you. Where they came from, what they lived on and how they existed I've no idea but they were an absolute menace.

Sergeant Bob Foulds, 425 Bty

The flies made the men's lives a misery as they swarmed around greedy for any kind of moisture – be it sweat or tea.

If you got your mug of tea, before you can get it to your lips, there would be fifty flies in the top of it – they'd pounce! To get rid of them we developed a skill where you gave a circular little flick and it took the top quarter of an inch off and all the flies off with it. Then you could get a drink – it was a race between you and the flies as to who got the most and of course you couldn't spare to waste your tea. It became an art.

Gunner Reg McNish, 425 Bty

Despite all this effort some flies usually prevailed, 'You were lucky to be able to drink a mug of tea without at least ten flies drowning themselves in it as you drank! There were millions of flies. It was a common saying, "You've got the whole bloody Mediterranean to drown yourself in and you pick my tea!"'[98] Nowhere could a man be alone with his thoughts – the flies accompanied them literally everywhere! 'Where there was a toilet there was thousands of flies. If you sat on a toilet the flies would be in there and tickling your arse!'[99] In such circumstances, the flies were not only incorrigible, but a serious threat to health.

This was something we learned in the early stages – flies cause dysentery. There was nothing you could do about them. To eat a slice of bread and jam was a nightmare. You'd swat the flies off and in the split second between swatting them off and getting the jam in your mouth, you'd have another couple of flies in your mouth.

Lance Sergeant Harold Harper, 426 Bty

More overtly threatening than the flies were the scorpions. Many of the troops started off their career as desert warriors in mortal fear of scorpions but that soon faded, 'A scorpion couldn't do much through a

145

boot. It's just if one had got in your bed roll. We checked them when we first went to Palestine but when you've checked your bed roll every night for a month and nothing there, you stop doing it!'[100] Other insects were in fact much more dangerous to health and fitness. 'The worst things in Tobruk were what they called camel ticks. They were a sort of beetle which got under the skin and the only way that you could get them out was to get a hot match and put it on the head of this thing and it would get itself out.'[101] Other gunners hated the centipedes which could cause serious discomfort and had no proper respect for the sanctity of a man's underwear.

There were some centipedes about four inches long – revolting looking things – and Ernie Hurry had one crawl up his leg. You've got to brush them off but if you brush him the wrong way his legs come off and stick into you. Ernie got rid of it quick and one of these legs went into one of his balls. It swelled up just like a rugger ball – ever so big – and Ernie Hurry was very worried! It was night time and he went to see the Medical Officer Finnegan who I think had been having a bit to drink and gone to bed. He wasn't very pleased and told him to, "Bugger off and come and see him in the morning!" We all thought Finnegan was a bastard then because

Managing a cheerful grin for the camera, close friends Bill Hutton and Ken Tew during the nine months' siege.

Ernie's balls were really swollen. But next morning, when it was time for him to go to the MO, it had gone down again.

Driver Bill Hutton, **425 Bty**

As at Mersa Matruh the men wore the bare minimum of a uniform, 'You used to wear a pair of shorts, no shirt, no socks. Socks got sweaty and hard with sand, no water to wash them, so we just had to throw them away.'[102] Many did not even wear their tin helmets, 'Generally they were a nuisance and there was an attitude as well about wearing tin helmets. I think it was considered slightly cissy to wear a tin helmet and not many people did, until things got really warmed up.'[103]

Overall, conditions of service were undoubtedly tough. On many previous occasions the food had been limited, but Tobruk was a real trial to the normal stomach, 'Bully beef, bully beef, bully beef. biscuits, biscuits, biscuits. It was a problem!'[104] The regimental cooks tried to vary the menu but to little avail. Cook Sergeant Ted Hayward had set up his equipment in a cave.

We were on very simple rations – six days a week corn beef and one day a week tinned M & V, meat and vegetable ration. Never such a thing as menu planning, you went off the cuff – what was there. If we had curry powder, we used to make a curry stew of bully beef with a bowl of rice, not too hot because most of the chaps wouldn't like it. Then you would mix some of your meat and vegetable ration with your bully beef to get a certain amount of vegetables inside a stew. We did meat pies on tin plates. You put your bully beef and vegetables on the plate, put a bit of pastry on the top and push it in the oven. The cave was reasonably cool and we were able, to a degree, to cut the bully beef so therefore we were able to make bully beef fritters, which were very popular. Make a flour and water batter, cut a slice of bully beef, drop it in the batter, fry it in a pan on the Number 1 burner for two or three minutes.

Cook Sergeant Ted Hayward, **425 Bty**

Despite his efforts some of the SNH have never touched bully beef since. The biscuits, essential accompaniments to bully beef, were not delicate wafers but had more in common with dog biscuits, 'The biscuits were really hard, about four inches square and an inch thick. You had to really bite – in fact you could only gnaw at them'.[105] Tobruk recipes were by no means sophisticated, 'You got a few biscuits, soaked them overnight. Then in the morning, some sugar, cook it and it became like a porridge called Biscuit Burgoo.'[106] There was a field bakery but it was cursed, 'Jerry was very, very clever – he always bombed the field bakery and it would be a week or two before they got it mended again. As soon as they mended it Jerry used to bomb it again! A slice of bread was a luxury!'[107] When they did get the bread it was slightly unusual.

> A peculiar thing about this bread was that it was like a seed cake – a flour mixture with tiny seeds. When we were relieved and we went down to Cairo, we happened to bump into some people from the bakery at Tobruk. We asked what the seeds were that were in the bread? He started to laugh and he said, "They weren't seeds, they were fleas in the flour and we couldn't afford to waste it – we'd got to cook it!"
>
> ***Driver Ernie Hurry,*** **425 Bty**

Although other types of food were occasionally available, the basic diet was unrelenting and dietary diseases were a real threat in the absence of fruit. 'We took ascorbic acid tablets every day. A bitterish sort of taste, you just swallowed them and they gave the body vitamin C and prevented scurvy.'[108]A further trial for the garrison was the constant shortage of water.

> We had half a gallon of water a day and a good portion of that

Ted Holmes, wearing the cap, was the water tanker driver and a battery cook. He is seen here with two unidentified SNH men

Making the most of every precious drop – Bill Adams attempts a 'bath' in previously used water.

went to the cook-house. We used to have our water bottle, which holds about a pint and a half, filled every other day. It was very bad, our lips were all swollen up, split and bleeding. Like you see with these pictures of anyone what's got lost in the desert. We used to dream about putting your head under the tap at home.

Gunner Ted Holmes, 425 Bty

The men tortured themselves with visions of all the water that had literally gone down the drain in England.

It was thirst, thirst, thirst – you were talking about how when you got home you wouldn't waste a drop of water. We used to suck a button or a small pebble – it brings the saliva up – I did that right through.

Gunner Victor Harrold, 426 Bty

The most rigid self discipline was necessary if what little water they had was not to be 'gorged' in one orgy of transient satisfaction.

I used to have half a mouthful first thing in the morning, before the sun came up, have a gargle, and then spit it out. That was it until you had your tea. Then when the sun went down you drink the rest of it and think, "Thank God for that!

Bombardier Albert Swinton, 426 Bty

The manifold functions of water soon became apparent once its supply was restricted and the same water would be used many times over.

It was a matter of real economy of priorities really and truly. Drink first of all. Any water that was left over that would be a matter of washing your shirt. Maybe, before it got too thick, you'd have a shave and when it was really no good at all – that was the time to wash your socks!

Signal Sergeant Fred Langford, 425 Bty

What water they had to drink tasted a little unusual, 'It was well and truly chlorinated. We got so used to the taste of chlorinated tea that when eventually we tasted the real stuff it tasted queer.'[109] Some of the old regulars found an illicit supply which they exploited without a second thought.

Me and this Liverpool bloke were coming on our way back from Tobruk and we went on a round-about way. We saw this water seeping through in the rocks. We scratted about a bit and we found a break in the water pipe, not a big break, but just enough to fill a dixie and pour it into a barrel. It took ages and ages. We used to take a 44 gallon drum down to the doctors and one to the gun position. We didn't let on because we wanted to keep that to ourselves. You daren't spread it around or, crikey, you'd soon be in trouble!

Driver Harold Thompson, 425 Bty

149

At one point in the siege the men were promised blessed relief from brackish water – beer!

They announced, rather rashly, that somebody had paid for a whole consignment of beer. There would be one bottle of beer per man for the whole garrison. And they said when it was coming. The day the ship arrived, in daylight, the Stukas let it come all the way up and they came over as it got into the harbour. All we ever saw was this big plume of smoke. I drew this cartoon with two chaps talking and a big column of smoke in the background just saying, "Oooh I see the beer ship's come!"

Lance Bombardier Ted Whittaker, 425 **Bty**

Even when beer was available it was in minute quantities for a regiment of thirsty men in the desert.

Occasionally there'd be a ration of beer which was usually so small that it wasn't worth having. The Aussies had the right idea with the beer – they used to cast lots for who should have the beer. One chap would get gloriously drunk and that was that! What was half a can of beer – it wasn't worth drinking really!

Captain Charles Laborde, 426 **Bty**

There were of course no water closets at Tobruk and the latrine arrangements were primitive.

You usually waited until dark, took a shovel and walked away until you found an empty area. You did whatever you had to do and covered it over again. The men knew that they had to cover their excreta because of the flies. You lived with the flies all around your mouth and up your nose. The very thought that those flies might have been in somebody's excreta made them really keen.

Sergeant Ian Sinclair, 425 **Bty**

Thunder-boxes were installed, but even there, privacy could not be guaranteed from the random shell burst.

We had a Welshman with us who was a member of the Communist Party, a local councillor, a miner of course. He was sat on the thunder-box, which was a good 200 yards away from our command post. Out of the blue came half a dozen shells, two or three of which landed not ever so far from his thunder box. I'll swear that Taffy covered the 200 yards in two bounds with his trousers waving. When he got in he said, "Boy, they knew I was an anti-fascist!"

Lance Bombardier Ted Whittaker, 425 **Bty**

The inadequate diet and insanitary conditions formed two thirds of a vicious circle which was completed by dysentery, 'I can recall one very strong sergeant major one morning crawling from his dugout on his hands and knees, trying to get to the troop latrine and leaving a trail behind him all the way. He was taken away and we never saw him again for six months.'[110] Under these conditions jaundice was also prevalent.

THE BEER SHIPS HERE AGAIN

I started to feel ill and every time I ate anything I just threw it up and this sort of very bitter, biley, colourless stuff came into my mouth. It was terrible. I had a camp bed and I was lying out in the open. If there was an air raid I just used to roll off the bed and just lie there – then I hadn't got the strength to get up and get back on to the bed. Finnegan had a tough time because a lot of people were pretending to be ill to get out. He came to see me and didn't reckon there was a deal wrong with me and left me. A couple of days later Max Miller came and looked at me and I'd gone yellow, like a banana and my eyes were yellow so he went back and fetched the doctor. As soon as he saw me he had me taken straight down into Tobruk – jaundice! All I was having up to then was tea, with condensed milk and sugar in it, and bully beef. Well you just spew it up straight away. But if you're on the right sort of food, like chicken broth, you don't spew. As soon as they changed my diet I didn't feel so terrible.

Driver Bill Hutton, 425 Bty

Boredom was almost as much an enemy to the men as the Germans and the desert. For many, cigarettes were a crutch to lean on, 'We got 50 a week and that wasn't enough for me. I smoked as many as I could get. I've seen the time when I smoked my ration straight off! Then I would go without or a friend who didn't smoke might be generous towards you.'[111] The cigarettes they got were for the most part of low quality, 'We used to get cigarettes called "Cape to Cairo" and that's probably where they ought to have been sent. I was a smoker in those days but I could easily give them up and "Cape to Cairo" were the best reason for giving it up. They were rank.'[112] Early in the siege men could afford to be fussy but the situation soon worsened.

We'd been issued with some Egyptian cigarettes that were ostensibly a present from King Farouk. Most people threw them out or buried them because they'd got this 'Turkish' aroma to them – they weren't Virginian tobacco – not what we were normally used to. Then when British cigarettes dried up we were looking for those we had slung!

Signaller Frank Knowles, 425 Bty

It was a case of any port in a storm but King Farouk's gesture still remained unappreciated, 'Then we'd dig them out and try them again, but they were horrible. I don't know where he got the tobacco from – I'm sure it was cattle dung!'[113] Men grew increasingly desperate, 'People missed their cigarettes more than anything. They were making cigarettes out of tea leaves and army form blank. Break a cigarette open, mix it with tea leaves and roll it back up again.'[114] Pipe smokers had an advantage, 'With having a pipe you got your tobacco rations and you could also go looking around for dog ends. You used to get a pipe full out of that now and again – it smoked hot but it was a smoke!'[115] Harold Harper could have made his fortune, 'I didn't smoke at Tobruk. For my 50 cigarettes I used to have a raffle every week. Just bits of toilet paper, anything. The blokes would go mad for cigarettes, everybody would go in for this raffle. I did enormously well with it but I used to give the money to the Red Cross.'[116] The men were paid but there was very little opportunity to spend it and the Tobruk economy bore some resemblance to the mercantilist systems introduced by various Seventeenth Century European monarchs.

I used to make up the pay when we drew some money. I went out on Thursday to each gun position and I remember walking across the desert carrying five or six hundred pounds thinking, "What happened if I got bombed here there'd be all these notes floating about the desert!" The men would be lined up, the officer would supervise and I would give them all their pay in Egyptian piastres. The following day I went round with the NAAFI truck. The regimental clerk went to fetch it from the big NAAFI and I went to regiment to collect it from him. I went round with the battery canteen truck and they bought their tins of fruit, cream, toothpaste. You couldn't have more than two bottles of beer or one tin of fruit – I sold out. Very often the money I collected in was equivalent to the money I'd taken out. They were making direct payments home – if they'd got a wife it was stopped from their pay – and all they were getting was spending money. It balanced to within thirty to fifty pounds and that was all I had to make up. The money just stayed in Tobruk going round in circles!

Battery Clerk Ted Coup, **425 Bty**

The men very occasionally received parcels from home but they could bring bitter disappointment.

I was 21 and I got a parcel that my stepfather had done up. He'd really gone to town on it, put it in sacking and sewn it up. When I got it the cake was missing, somebody had swiped my birthday cake. Other bits and bobs were in there, but somebody down at the base had pinched me cake. There was me sticking me neck out up the desert and then there's people down in Cairo pinching all our stuff.

Bombardier Albert Swinton, **426 Bty**

Some of the officers were in a more privileged position and were able to arrange for parcels of 'luxuries' to be brought in by the navy. Major Robert Daniell, the regular who had commanded the Composite

Battery in December 1940, before being actually posted to the SNH in April 1941, relied on his wife who was living in Egypt.

Betty, from Alexandria, with great ingenuity filled a kerosene oil tin with whisky, tinned fruit, underclothes, socks and shoes, chocolate, cigarettes... sealed it, describing its contents as nails. She then charmed one of the two officers of the two very gallant Australian destroyers to deliver it to me on the next run, until they were both torpedoed.[117]

Major Robert Daniell, **Regimental Headquarters**

On occasions a rum ration was issued to the men.

One evening Sergeant Bill Barker said, "Hey, go across the command post, Bert, there's a rum ration!" The Battery Command Post was two or three hundred yards away and I went up there and said, "I've come for the rum ration". They said, "Righto, there it is", and they gave me a rum jar three parts full of rum. "That's your ration for the troop". I set back across the desert and had got halfway back when old Jerry started shelling us something rotten. I thought to myself, "Do I be British and walk through this lot, or do I hit the deck and break this bottle of rum!" I thought, "If I lose this rum, I'll get killed anyway!" I was between the Devil and the deep blue sea! I eventually got through to the troop – the first rum ration it was!

Bombardier Albert Swinton, **426 Bty**

The rum ration was officially considered medicinal rather than recreational.

The Number One would go to the Command Post with a mug or mess tin and be issued with the ration for his sub section which was eight measured tots. Everybody didn't have it because they didn't like it, so they used to trade it for bacon or whatever. I had a gin bottle and that was constantly full of rum to drink whenever you wanted – you weren't supposed to, you were supposed to have it when it was issued and knock it straight back. It was the only drink you could get hold of. It was just to have as, and when, you wanted it. There was no question of a binge on it.

Sergeant Ian Sinclair, **425 Bty**

Sergeant Sinclair was wrong!

We had been issued with rum – about three tablespoons. Some of the lads, five or six of us, had decided to save this in a corked bottle. We were also issued with limes which we squeezed to make a passable lime juice. As soon as this corked bottle was full we decided to have this terrific binge. We mixed the lime and the rum together and all five of us got really drunk. I can remember walking into my dugout and I hit the cross bream at the entrance – that was the last thing I remember! The next morning we were all on a charge. From then on you lined up with your mug for your rum ration and there was another man to make sure you drank it!

Battery Clerk Ted Coup, **425 Bty Headquarters**

The most basic form of entertainment was plain ordinary conversation, 'You did a lot of talking about your own life. What you had done, your way of life at home. I don't think you showed off about whether you were better or worse than the next bloke because you were so much one of a party.'[118] The officers slowly began to unbend and talked to their men.

Women, usually the number one subject with a soldier, what was happening in the war in the rest of the world. They were always wanting to know what would happen if Hitler won – you always answered that by saying, "He won't!"

Captain William Pringle, **425 Bty**

The men could write home but real communication with their families and loved ones was difficult as a result of the restrictions imposed by the censors. 'That was one of the most difficult things. You certainly couldn't write about the war because you weren't allowed to. So to find a subject to write home about was almost impossible.'[119] Many of the officers hated censoring letters, 'Censorship of letters was one of the jobs I did not like, I was reasonably conscientious but I didn't like reading other people's letters. It seemed to be prying into mens' private affairs.'[120] In desperation, the men often employed simple codes to let their family know where they were. These were hardly sophisticated but usually eluded the censoring officer.

We used to write home but obviously we weren't allowed to put where we were – but we would put on a type of a code. I would put on the bottom of mine, 'Give my regards to Tom and Olive' – 'T' 'O' – then the next time, 'Give my regards to Bob and Reg', which eventually would spell out Tobruk.

Gunner Dennis Mayoh, **426 Bty**

Letters from home were welcome but, given the state of the war in the Mediterranean, were often delayed, or never arrived at all. One source of news came via the signallers who could illicitly turn off the regimental network at quiet times to listen to the German broadcasts for a little biased news which was sometimes directly aimed at them.

We'd listen to the wireless at night and pass the news round to the troops. For instance the BBC announced one night, "A Midlands town has been heavily bombed, some casualties." We switched to Lord Haw Haw and he said, "Good evening South Notts Hussars, as you've heard Nottingham has been obliterated tonight."

Lance Bombardier Ted Whittaker, **425 Bty**

The propaganda was fairly crude and most of the men seem to have rather enjoyed William Joyce's propaganda broadcasts in his guise as 'Lord Haw Haw'.

We used to listen to Lord Haw Haw, we used to have a good laugh about him! In one particular case he was on about a big battle taking place out in the Mediterranean. His aircraft had sunk our ships and shot down our planes and he played a record, 'How deep is the ocean, How high is the sky!' He used to call us the 'Rats of Tobruk'. He would say, 'Good morning, Rats of Tobruk' Have you said, 'Good Morning', to your airforce? Oh, I beg your pardon, don't worry, ours will be over to visit you soon!' We used to think it was very humorous! We didn't believe him – I can honestly say that when things got really tough, I can put my hand on heart and say that we never, ever thought we would lose. Never!

Gunner Dennis Mayoh, **426 Bty**

Sometimes, however, the propaganda would be very personal indeed, directed as it was straight at the real or imagined fears of men long separated from their wives.

The only effect I can ever remember of German propaganda getting through to certain members of the battery was the lady who originally sang 'Lilli Marlene'. She used to call us the "self contained prisoners of Tobruk" and this seductive voice would say, "Of course while you are here and slaving away your girlfriends and your wives are enjoying life back in England." Occasionally you would get a bloke who would say, "I haven't heard from my wife for six months" and it would get through to him that way. Of course I was single so it didn't bother me!

Lance Sergeant Harold Harper, **426 Bty**

Leaflets dropped over the British positions were another German propaganda weapon, 'Then Jerry dropped the surrender pamphlets, "Lay down your arms, slaves of the Western Desert!"'[121] These had little or no effect other than provoking a marvellous 'raspberry' from Gunner Victor Harrold when asked of his reaction fifty years later![122]

In desert conditions gramophones were rare, but the selection of music, although limited, seems to have helped maintain at least Gunner Mayoh's morale.

We had a gramophone it used to come round to the gun positions to each gun crew. We had 'The White Cliffs of Dover' and 'When the Lights go on Again'. It was an unforgivable sin for anyone to lose it or drop it. Whatever happened one bloke was detailed to look after the gramophone and record – irrespective of what was happening. It was passed round all the time. Nobody will ever really know what good Vera Lynn did for us. She was really terrific, she really kept our spirits up and people will never, ever, realize the value of her.

Gunner Dennis Mayoh, 426 Bty

Playing cards was a popular distraction, although gambling was difficult without much disposable money or access to credit. Naturally some managed it.

We had a vicious game – 'Shoot!' Probably six people would take part and you would take turns to be a banker. You would have three rounds of the six people as a banker. You would deal each person three cards and then you would turn over the next card whatever it may be it might be, shall we say, the ten of clubs. A chap musn't look at his hand but the banker would put 50 Egyptian piastres in the middle to start the bank off. The chap would look at the ten of clubs and would say, "Now, have I got anything to beat the ten of clubs!" If he said, "Yes!" he would double the kitty, he would turn over his three cards and if he'd got anything in his hand to beat the ten of clubs he'd take the kitty. On the other hand he would just dump it! This could go round doubling up the whole time! You could imagine the amount of money there could be at the end of it! Inevitably you get winners and losers. We had no money coming into the regiment, so the losers' money disappeared and therefore they couldn't take part in the gambling school. You got an élite number who were the winners gambling among each other until in the end you came down to a very small group of people with money in the unit. I wasn't one of them unfortunately!

Cook Sergeant Ted Hayward, 425 Bty

Some of the more cerebral began to learn the arcane arts of contract bridge.

Sergeant Pat Bland taught us bridge, his family were county bridge players. Bridge proved to be a magnificent mental therapy. We would play for hours but Pat insisted that we were learning the game, he was a very, very, strong minded young man. He would tell us off horribly if we made silly mistakes. Once he had told us we were supposed to remember. It drilled it in.

Lance Sergeant John Walker, 425 Bty

Another intellectual pursuit attracted some devotees, 'We'd have spelling bees. They came out just before the war on the radio, they were very popular. Somebody would quote a word from the dictionary and you had to spell it. We had different teams, each troop was against each other and battery headquarters had a team.'[123] Reading was an obvious distraction with one NCO appointing himself an unofficial regimental librarian.

> I'd always been a great reader and it occurred to me that we didn't have any books. I borrowed a 15cwt truck and went all around the regiment scrounging books. In the end I got quite a collection and I made a library in my dugout on the gun position. I'd got two or three hundred books and made shelves in the dugout and put them up. I used to have library periods during the day when men could come and change their library books. I went to a lot of trouble documenting the books, got mens' names and filled in the library system and they'd come and change their books. I was just passing the time really, trying to occupy my mind with something different. It was a good thing for the blokes, but it illustrates how I personally was desperate to occupy my mind.
>
> **Bombardier Ray Ellis,** 425 **Bty**

On a more physical plane the boxer Tommy Foley helped maintain his own and other mens' fitness with some gentle sparring.

> Tommy used to take one after the other of us on and lightly touch us for a round at a time to keep himself fit. As many as 12 or 15 people would put up their fists against him for one round and he would never stop. You had to try and hit him but he never really hit you. The only way you could ever get Tommy down was to tickle him, he used to laugh like mad, he couldn't stand being tickled!
>
> **Lance Sergeant John Walker,** 425 **Bty**

Some gunners adopted faintly surrealistic amusements, 'Billy Bloggs used to go fishing! He'd sit on an empty 40 gallon drum of petrol and he'd be casting his lines, reeling it in – all the motions!'[124] A successful 'craze' would be taken up throughout the troop or battery and could

A knocked out Italian tank could provide items of distraction for bored SNH gunners.

even reach exalted heights.

In front of the positions there was a knocked out Italian tank. One day we went forward to it and levered off the turret and there was two or three hundred inch ball bearings. So we confiscated these and set up a marbles league! In the charge cases there was a cardboard cup about two inches in diameter and about an inch-and-a-half deep. We used to set these out into the desert and scrape a board along so that all the sand was level. We'd flick these ball bearings into these various cups. One day the Colonel came along and there was all his troop on their hands and knees flicking these ball bearings about! He said, "Most intriguing! What's happening?" So we told him, he said, "Can I have a go?" And there was the Colonel on his hands and knees playing marbles with us!

Bombardier Albert Swinton, **426 Bty**

The grinding day-in day-out boredom encouraged activities which were frankly all too redolent of a second childhood, but which served their purpose by providing harmless amusement whilst releasing stress.

We actually sometimes played cowboys and Indians, schoolboy games around the gunpits! Once we were doing this and I was an Indian with a stick which was supposed to be a tomahawk charging across. This is ridiculous – this is men in action! Jim Hardy, the Sergeant Major, was a cowboy he came charging up and, in the excitement of the thing, he forgot, drew his revolver and fired and nearly put a bullet through me! That sobered us down a bit!

Bombardier Ray Ellis, **425 Bty**

Other pastimes were equally farcical for grown men facing a situation of life or death in the desert.

We would call a lodge of the 'Noble Antediluvian and Most Noble Order of Jerboas'. This was a take off of the Buffaloes but we were Jerboas – the desert rat. We would all sit round and, "The Lodge is now in session!" When in session we were not allowed to laugh, you had to keep your face absolutely straight. You had to sing the Lodge anthem. It was a song from the Boer War and the words went like this, "The Boers have got my Dad they have, My soldier Daddy". We changed it to:

"The whores have got my Dad they have
My Soldier daddy
I don't like to see my Mummy sigh
I don't like to see my Mummy cry

The SNH lads as they sing their hearts out to the accompaniment of a ukelele banjo.

> I'm going across the ocean on a big ship
> I'm going to fight the whores I am
> And bring my Daddy safely home!"

You had to sing this without laughing! Then we had to sing:

> "See them on the platform
> Early in the morning
> Standing on the station all in a row
> Daddy's on the engine
> Pulls a little lever
> Chuff, chuff, whoof, whoof off we go!"

It was so bloody ridiculous. A lot of hairy arsed gunners sitting round in a circle singing these stupid little childish songs! If you laughed you had to pay a forfeit and these were pretty terrible. They varied, you might have to piss in your boot, or take out your penis and allow one member

The rest camp wadi at Tobruk. This gave the defenders the chance to swim and 'fish' in the Mediterranean.

of the team to lash it three times with a bootlace! Horrific things! While this was taking place everybody could laugh, but when the punishment had taken place, Jim Hardy, who was usually in charge, would say, "Calling the Lodge to order!" and you'd have to somehow take any smile off your face. Of course you couldn't and so it went on!

Bombardier Ray Ellis, **425 Bty**

Very occasionally the men could get away from the gun positions.

> The best recreation was the rest camp down on the beach on a little inlet which was quite secluded. You can imagine what the weather was like, this was summer, you didn't need tents you just had a sleeping bag. You could get a pass for a couple of days and lie on the rocks or dive into the most gorgeous clear sea water that was possible. It was quite tepid for the top three foot but as you dived further down it got cooler and cooler until it got quite cold. It was just like eating a lovely ice cream in a way, it was delicious.

Lance Sergeant John Walker, **425 Bty**

The Mediterranean also offered the tempting prospect of a variation in diet, but fishing Tobruk style was not a relaxing occupation!

> We used to fish there – it was very primitive done with the aid of a Mills bomb. We'd all try to win a Mills bomb from the Australians before we were going down. Then you pulled the pin out, we really had no idea, you have to be very careful with them. Then we lay down on the flat rock and tossed this Mills bomb into the water. There was duly a 'WHAM' underneath, a great column of water, you waited two or three minutes and then the dead fish

160

started to come up to the surface. We then all popped into the water and picked out the best of the fish – so that we got a change of diet from the bully beef, which was very pleasant as you can imagine.

Captain Charles Laborde, **426 Bty**

However the Luftwaffe were capable of bringing trouble even to this simple paradise.

There was about a dozen of us swimming in this bay. It was lovely, no ladies about so we were swimming in the nude. A Messerschmitt came, flying low. Naturally we got onto the sand and raced back towards the wadi and caves. This pilot, just for a bit of devilment, he machine gunned just at the back of us. We were all running along in the nude, just imagine it, picture it in your mind! Machine-gun bullets just tickling the sand up at the back of you. We could imagine him laughing, "That'll warm their bottoms!"

Gunner Ted Holmes, **425 Bty**

★ ★ ★ ★

There was no real escape from danger because every part of the Tobruk area was continually under the threat of fire of one sort or another. As the long hot summer wore on, the unending stress told on the men in a manner which evoked comparisons with their predecessors' experiences in the trenches at Gallipoli in the First World War. The presence of the Australians made the analogy even more striking.

A man could walk up, one shot could be fired and he would be killed. We thought about this a lot actually. You looked for all sorts of omens – I can remember looking for omens in the sky – shapes of clouds which would suggest good things. Your mind was involved in this sort of thing. What were the omens or the chances? But I never thought of being killed – it was always the other man who was going to die. You had this feeling that, yes, you would survive! Really at the back of your mind you realized you were kidding yourself.

Bombardier Ray Ellis, **425 Bty**

In these circumstances the idea of a supreme being who could perhaps intercede for an individual and protect him from harm had an obvious comforting attraction.

You can talk to who you like but there's no atheist on the battlefield, I can say that in all sincerity. I've known blokes say, "No, I've got no time for religion." You put them in a battle and they're all there praying mate, there are no atheists on a battlefield!

Bombardier Albert Swinton, **426 Bty**

Such ephemeral religious beliefs were usually, in essence, a kind of wish fulfilment. Signaller Bill Adams had a close escape which started him thinking, 'One of these shells went into the slit trench where my stuff was, so I thought, "I think I'd better turn religious!"' The initially flippant urge persisted and, after special classes with Padre Parry, Adams was actually baptised in Tobruk, 'It took some of the fear out of it when you knew that somebody was looking after you. You didn't worry so much.' For some the front line of defence against battle fatigue was a sense of humour which asserted itself in stories both real and apocryphal, 'Padre Parry was driving around when there was an air raid and he said to his driver, "It's all right my boy, God will protect you!" The driver said, "Aye, God will protect me just as much, if not better, with great respect, Sir, in that slit trench!"'[125] Herbert Bonnello was in charge of the pay for 426 Bty and he conceived an amusing ploy, 'Whenever there was an air raid I used to get this tin box out of our little dugout and put it out in the open. One of the officers one day said, "What's in the tin box?" I said, "The pay records and if it gets a direct hit, we're made!" It never did!' But for many the strain never became such a joking matter.

> I had one gunner in my sub-section he'd only got to hear the drone of an aeroplane and he would get fidgety. If it became obvious that you were going to be bombed, he would just rush madly around. We just used to knock his feet from under him and a couple of us would lie on him. It was just sheer panic that it set off in him. You might say, "Oh he's not a very good chap to have in a gun crew!" But when we were being fired on by shellfire it didn't bother him a bit!
>
> *Sergeant George Pearson, 425 Bty*

The men were generally tolerant of such temporary failings.

> If a man broke for a few moments you sort of forgot it – you didn't notice it because you knew he'd been all right till then and he'd be all right again. Anyone who was really cowardly he was out, he no longer belonged to the club, we had no pity for people who couldn't sustain their courage. The man in the line doesn't have pity for the man who runs away. It's a fine drawn line.
>
> *Bombardier Ray Ellis, 425 Bty*

As the garrison battled against the fluctuating threats posed by the Afrika Korps, desert conditions and boredom there was the real potential for a disastrous collapse in unit morale as a whole. Officers occasionally had to exert more tact than would have been their former practice.

> There was a definite low point when the push that was supposed to get to us didn't. They were unco-operative. You might

say, "Come on, So and So, you haven't shaved today!" and he would say, "So what!" I realized there was no point in trying to tell the chap off, because it would only make it worse. I would tell him that life wasn't as bad as that; he was still alive – there were plenty far worse off than him buried in the desert!

Captain William Pringle, **425 Bty**

As at Mersa Matruh a few men broke under the strain and tried to get away by means of trickery – as Ray Ellis and his gun team noticed with one NCO.

His act was that he was becoming mentally unsound and he was doing all sorts of peculiar things; but we noticed that he always did it when there was an officer present. He would put his head in front of the barrel of the gun and say, "Fire!" We were very tempted to do so! He referred to himself as 'Bubbles' all this sort of silly nonsense. It could be that he was becoming mentally unstable under the pressure, but we honestly thought at the time that he was working his ticket.

Bombardier Ray Ellis, **425 Bty**

Such conduct does seem to have been the exception and most of the officers and NCOs held up well under the pressure.

As an NCO you have a great advantage because everyone is looking to see how you behave and that bolsters you up. I think the chap who is really brave is the poor soldier who is a gunner who nobody is looking to for any support and he's the chap who really has to hold himself in check. You looked to the officers to see how they were behaving and if they're not behaving particularly well you think, "Silly so and so!" or "Windy Devil!"

Sergeant George Pearson, **425 Bty**

The officer was expected to lead by example, but many of the men were curious as to what the officers actually felt in tense situations.

They were at the advanced position waiting for the word go and one of the chaps asked, "Are you scared sir?" Captain Slinn said, "I'm as scared as you are, but, being an officer, I have to hide my feelings. I wouldn't like to go out on a job with a fellow who wasn't scared, because a scared man takes every precaution, looks twice before he does anything. A man who's not scared – he gets careless."

Driver Ernie Hurry, **425 Bty**

The only respectable way of leaving the unit in action was the 'Blighty' wound, 'Everyone dreamed of the marvellous painless wound – the impossible! The painless wound that didn't inflict any permanent injury but got you home!'[126] Until then they just endured it as best they could, 'Generally speaking, it was a matter of doing your duty. I don't believe in the slightest that there's any such thing as a hero. I think the average bloke just did his duty.'[127]

Overall the Hussars seem to have drawn strength from their shared ordeals and the officers, NCO's and men of the SNH emerged as a battle hardened unit. In such circumstances an individual's strengths and weaknesses could be accurately assessed. Above them all was the Colonel who, although still a remote figure, was to be seen at times of crisis.

> Colonel Seely always gave me the impression that he was a very efficient chap. Always there in the thick of the action. It was always good to see the Colonel come round. He visited us on a number of occasions in Tobruk and that always instilled a lot of confidence into the men. Bill Seely was quite popular.

Lance Sergeant Harold Harper, **426 Bty**

Harry Day saw a different side to the Colonel – literally!

> Colonel Seely had a bad back and Doctor Finnegan said, "Now take this bottle of rubbing oils, give the Colonel a good massage and no doubt you'll get your third stripe!" Full of glee, off I went across the desert, gave him a massage and said, "How do you feel, Sir?" "Oooh, much better, that's great, thank you very much!" The next morning Finnegan said, "For God's sake, what have you done to the Colonel, Harry, he can't get out of bed!" Sometimes, if you overdo it with massage, you get the reverse effect!

Medical Orderly Harry Day, **Regimental Headquarters**

The officers were still considered by their men to have more than their fair share of physical and mental idiosyncrasies, but they now valued their proven skills. 'Graham Slinn, everybody liked him. He was one of these chaps you'd have followed anywhere. Great tall chap, well over six foot, thin. I always used to draw him as the old fashioned gas lamp, the first one with this gunner saluting this lamp, obviously drunk and saying, 'Goodnight, Captain Schlinn!'[128] They were now accorded respect based on their military achievements, as well as their rank. 'Slinn was very, very, very good at his job, but I don't think he liked it. I wouldn't be surprised if at night he didn't worry about all the people he killed because, by God, he did kill some! I should think he hated war.'[129] Such officers had little trouble with the men. 'A man like Graham Slinn in B Troop could maintain his authority and when necessary call you by your Christian name, or all the bloody fools under the sun, and you'd take no offence.'[130] As they gained in experience and got to know their men many of the officers also showed a real caring side to their natures which had perhaps been lacking in the early days of the war.

Captain Graham Sl.
a lamp post of a m

Gerry Birkin was possibly the most efficient officer. Very

human, he was there when the padre told me my mother had died. Gerry Birkin, that particular evening outside Tobruk, I think he was really marvellous. I made a mistake on the director and he just patted me on the back and said, 'Its the first mistake I've ever seen you make'. He was a very human character.

Lance Sergeant Harold Harper, **426 Bty**

Nevertheless there were differences of opinion about the overall worth of the officers. Major Robert Daniell, the second in command, remained aloof from the regiment and held strong views which he did not hold back from expressing.

There were two or three officers I liked, but the officers did not as a whole like me, as their second in command. I was a regular officer, I had been brought up in a Horse Artillery Regiment and I was accustomed to carrying out anything I was told to do immediately to the best of my ability. I did not find that the majority of these officers copied me in any way whatsoever. They found difficulty in obeying orders in carrying out any operation that they themselves did not care for. I found that the warrant officers, NCOs, and men were of a very high standard. Their discipline was excellent, they themselves were strong and intelligent, and they took advantage of every order that was given them.

Major Robert Daniell, Regimental Headquarters

In turn some of the senior NCOs and officers harboured strong feelings about Major Daniell himself.

Major Daniell had a great deal of experience and went about his job with a great deal of aplomb. He treated our officers with contempt because, "All you lot are bloody amateurs!" He would talk to them in a tone of voice that was contemptuous. His attitude and the way he acted was wrong. He should have appreciated, like Freddie Porter did, that he was coming into a territorial unit which had a great deal to offer – we were all volunteers – a great deal of good will and courage. But you don't get the best out of people like that by treating them as semi-illiterate idiots. That's where he made his mistake. In a territorial unit there is a certain *esprit de corps.* You realize you're not like the regular army, you don't want to be like the regular army. You have discipline but you have a certain kind of camaraderie being a local regiment.

***Quartermaster Sergeant Charles Ward,* 426 Bty**

The warrant officers and senior NCOs had a crucial role in the regiment.

I would think that the sergeant majors were more responsible for running the battery than anybody. The two troop sergeant majors and the battery sergeant major. They maintained what little bit of discipline was necessary. But they were always very friendly with the troops, they knew that the troops would respond as and when necessary.

Lance Sergeant Harold Harper, **426 Bty**

One of the most fondly remembered was the leader of Ray Ellis's informal 'Lodge' – Sergeant Major Jim Hardy.

Hardy was a nice man – they used to call him 'Nellie' Hardy because he was a bit of an old woman in the nicest way. A little bit older than the others and he kept a fatherly or motherly eye on us that saw we came to no great harm. He was heart and soul the South Notts Hussars.

Sergeant Bob Foulds, **425 Bty**

He had another even less reverential nickname amongst the men, 'Sergeant Major Hardy, now then his nickname was 'gnat scratchers'! For the simple reason he used to be scratching there all the time. Everybody called him 'gnat scratchers'![131]

Below the warrant officers, the gun sergeants welded the disparate elements that made up the gun teams into efficient units. Their methods varied according to their personalities, 'Sergeant Barker was a right laugh. Very efficient, but he took things very, very lightly. He used to mess about something rotten but when it came down to doing the job he was a 100% efficient.'[132] Such men often showed enormous potential which was not always recognized in time, 'Sergeant Cliff Smedley was one of the finest men I have ever met – a great man. Very, very clever, physically big, a born leader he should have been at least a Captain with his ability, knowledge, bearing and powers of leadership.'[133] In the context of a World War, where every trained competent officer with battle experience was invaluable, such men were wasted in charge of the six men of a gun team.

There were men in our troop who were far more intelligent and with a better standard of education than some of the officers. They were definitely officer material. I don't think we were ever so much aware of the fact they should have been sent to Officers Cadet Training Unit, because we were not really *au fait* with what it all entailed. We just accepted the fact that if you weren't an officer at the beginning of the war that was hard luck! Looking back in retrospect, it was disgusting that some of the men were still sergeants and bombardiers at the end of Tobruk who should have been captains at least.

Bombardier Ray Ellis, **425 Bty**

Some of the prospective high fliers were aware that not all was well.

If ever there was any resentment it was because we reckoned we ought to have been sent to be officers because of the way that we had done our work and knowing that they must be needing them. Several of us felt that we had been passed over because we had spent all that time in Mersa Matruh and Tobruk and nobody knew anything at all about us. We found out that we were being kept in the regiment because of the feeling by the Colonel and the officers that they didn't want to lose anybody – wanted it kept as a family. They kept sending nil reports in for people for OCTU. We kept hearing of other people going but nobody from South Notts ever went. Eventually they were detailed at RHQ that they should send somebody – "This regiment of yours, that is supposed to be so bloody wonderful, how is it that you have no officer material?" Well of course we had, we'd got lots and lots of officer material and Bill Seely didn't want to lose us!

Sergeant Ian Sinclair, **425 Bty**

Some of the officers were aware of the potential of their men and tried to encourage them. Captain Hingston felt that his Troop Sergeant Major Claude Earnshaw, was an ideal candidate for a commission.

I was sitting talking to Earnshaw and he was worried, "I don't think I ought to go there, Sir, I don't think I'm up to it". I said, "Damn it all, Earnshaw, you can do the job of a Second Lieutenant on your head!" "Aye", he said, "but I don't talk like an officer". I said, "I don't think that matters now, I quite agree it would have a few years back, but now I don't think that will matter at all. He said, "I hope you're right, Sir!"

Captain Bob Hingston, **426 Bty**

Towards the end of the siege Colonel Seely gave in and the process of selecting men suitable to be officers began in earnest. Nevertheless only a few ever left Tobruk to attend the Middle East Officers Cadet Training Unit. Claude Earnshaw was amongst them but, to Hingston's fury, he was rejected in the middle of the course and returned to the unit. Despite his qualities as a soldier, a man with his accent and background remained unacceptable to the more hidebound element in the British Army hierarchy. It was largely the grammar school educated, the 'cut glass boys' who succeeded in getting commissions.

★ ★ ★ ★

As the summer of 1941 dragged on both sides launched occasional frontal attacks whilst nightly patrols scoured No Man's Land. An attempt to relieve the garrison was thwarted in June and it became obvious, that for the moment at least, the Germans could not break in and the Garrison could not break out. Both sides were forced to accept the *status quo*. Rommel moved his armour away and the investing troops

The Poles arrived in Tobruk to take the place of the Australians. Here Lieutenant Weller Polley visits the Polish positions.

were reduced to three Italian divisions and only one German division. The artillery dispositions were revised so that the SNH were now separated out and assigned the left of the southern sector, whilst the 1st RHA took the right. However, continuing shortages of ammunition meant that they were restricted to only ten rounds per gun per day, with a discretionary allowance of a further ten rounds for exceptional targets. Air attacks diminished and the Royal Navy was able to change over much of the hard pressed garrison.

This situation endured until late October when the 9th Australian Division was gradually replaced by the 1st Polish Carpathian Brigade and the British 70th Division. The Midlanders of the SNH found some of the exotic new accents of these recent arrivals rather intimidating!

> If wire had been broken up during the day by shelling, or whatever, we would go out at night and repair it. We were repairing this wire and these blokes came over the cliff and we could hear them talking and I thought, "Christ!" I couldn't understand them hardly and it turned out they were Durham Light Infantry. You know how they talk and I thought they were bloody Germans! It frightened the life out of me! "Wye aye, lad!" and all that!
>
> ***Signal Sergeant Jack Sykes,*** **426 Bty**

As the garrison was strengthened the German armour began to return to the Tobruk area and the whole scale of operations began to increase. Stuka attacks were vigorously renewed and there was a great deal more German shell-fire for the men to contend with. They were also becoming more successful in targeting the scaffolding observation post towers.

168

I went up to the OP and an officer called out to me, "Can I come up there, whenever I appear on top of the ridge in front of me I get shelled off it?" I said, "Yes, come along up – a bit of company would be very nice." Lieutenant Weaver turned out to be a very nice chap. An ardent politician – he was a Conservative – he was talking about his political career in a rather more pleasant way than most politicians talk. He was really telling comic stories about it which were really very funny. We were having quite a good time when, for some reason or other, they decided they didn't like us up there and a battery opened up on us. That gunner, I hand it to him, he knew his job. He landed a shell short of us and another over us. I remember remarking in a rather tight voice with a rather dry mouth, "Damn, they've bracketed us!" Then he landed two shells right at the base of the tower. Weaver looked at me and he said, "Should we get down?" I said, "I don't think so, I think it's very unlikely he'll ever hit us up here and these things can stand an awful lot of battering around. He might see you getting down and then promptly land one on the ground just as you get there!" I'm sorry I made that decision. Just as I did so they got a direct hit. There was a roar, it wasn't a bang, it was more of a roar in my ear. And something hit my right leg like a stone. The silly things one does – I remember shouting out to the world at large, "That's buggered me!" Then I looked to Weaver and there he was sitting beside me with the top of his head blown off... I was splattered with blood and everything.

Captain Bob Hingston, 426 Bty

With a great deal of difficulty Hingston was got down and sent to Tobruk Hospital for treatment. Throughout the siege the regiment was lucky in that casualties came in as a trickle rather than in a rush. Any wounded were got away for treatment as quickly as possible.

If they had any casualties the orderly at the battery would just administer first aid and then he would whip them down by truck to the Regimental Aid Post. They would be seen by the surgeon, he would decide which were the more seriously wounded men and treat them accordingly. I would take the dressings off and display the wound for his inspection and diagnosis. It would be looked at properly, re-dressed and splinted. They would be given anti-tetanus serum and morphia where it was necessary and they would be down to the hospital at Tobruk. It was always marked on the forehead with skin pencil – what time they had been given anti-tetanus serum or morphia and how much they had been given. If there was any injury to the head then it was marked somewhere where it was easily seen.

Medical Orderly Harry Day, Regimental Headquarters

The seriously wounded would then be evacuated from the harbour by the Royal Navy.

In the evening we were all carried out, fifty or so I should think and laid on a sort of raft tied alongside some aged paddle steamer. We lay there for a bit it, was deadly quiet and rather nerve racking lying there quite helpless. At intervals you would see gun flashes from around the perimeter and hope, "Oh my God, I hope that's not coming this way. One's ear was cocked for bombers! Nothing happened. A voice said, "Won't be long, we're just going to start the engine". The most appalling crashes and bangs occurred and a frightfully noisy engine started. We were manoeuvred out, I glanced to my left and there was a destroyer. The whole thing was beautifully organized, there were lashings of men heaving up the stretchers. There were two burly matelots on the deck and as each stretcher was pushed up towards them, they seized it and passed it on to a chain of men who carted it off. Incredibly quickly we were moved up into the destroyer HMS *Kandahar*. On the other side of the ship they'd heaved off all the ammunition and supplies they'd brought up then they were out again. The orders were they were not to stay in Tobruk longer than absolutely necessary because it was bombed so much.

Captain Bob Hingston, 426 Bty

★ ★ ★ ★

Reinforcements had flooded into the Middle East where there had been a major re-organization of the Middle East Command. At the top a new Commander in Chief, Lieutenant-General Sir Clive Auchinleck, took over from Wavell on 5 July 1941. The growth in the scale of the forces on both sides meant that the Corps not the Division was now the basic unit. As a result Eighth Army was created out of the XXX Corps, which consisted of 7th Armoured Division, 4th Armoured Brigade Group, 1st South African Division and 22nd Guards Brigade; and XIII Corps, made up of New Zealand Division, 4th Indian Division and 1st Army Tank Brigade. By October, Auchinleck felt confident enough to plan the launch of an offensive on 17 November designed to drive the Axis Forces back from within striking distance of the vital Suez Canal and of course to relieve Tobruk. The plan, known as 'Operation Crusader', was for XXX Corps to deal with Rommel's armoured units before occupying the Sidi Rezegh ridge. The Tobruk garrison was then to break out, once the threat from the German armour had been contained, and capture the El Duda ridge to the south east of Tobruk. Meanwhile XIII Corps was to pin down the rest of Rommel's forces, before striking northwards to cut him off from any possible retreat to the west.

As the plans were finalized there was an officers' briefing conference at the Tobruk garrison headquarters.

> Birkin said to me, "Have you got a plain shirt", I said, "Yes, Sir!" So he said, "Put your jerkin on" and I went down to a conference where they were all officers at the Garrison HQ where the General explained what was going to happen. All dead secret and I was just introduced as, "Oh this is Whittaker, my assistant." I should think I was the lowest but I shut my mouth! They had a sand table and we were shown the strongpoints – all given a name, 'Jill', 'Jack', 'Butch', 'Tiger'.
>
> *Lance Bombardier Ted Whittaker,* 425 **Bty**

The SNH were to cover the attack launched south eastwards from the perimeter, striking out some 12, 000 yards to El Duda ridge, where it was hoped they would meet the tanks of XXX Corps.

> We were going to fire a fixed barrage on these strong points and we were supporting the Black Watch. Peter Birkin was going to be the liaison officer with the Colonel of the Black Watch. Tanks were going to go first, and we were going to go out with them in the Bren Carrier. We had one or two practice runs, they'd measured the exact distance, "Stop two minutes while you attack 'Jill'." Just a couple of minutes to overwhelm a strongpoint! They used to put a great stress on this, how fast they could do it, 'Tiger' was our ultimate objective.
>
> *Lance Bombardier Ted Whittaker,* 425 **Bty**

The regiment settled down to play its part in the offensive. Whilst the specialists worked out the programme for the bombardment, the gunners sweated over the burial of huge numbers of shells around the new gun positions, ready for immediate use as required.

> You were given a programme which gave the line, range, angle of sight and the times that they were to be fired. This was printed on a piece of paper which was given to the Number One on the gun. When the zero hour arrived you fired the first salvo and then you followed the programme, according to the times as they were laid down for you.
>
> *Bombardier Ray Ellis,* 425 **Bty**

The start of the operations was awaited with the usual mixed feelings.

They told us there would be two code words, if it was "Tug" we stayed where we were, when it was "Pop" that was it – we were off! For days at six o clock at night we stood to and listened round the command post officer's telephone and we'd hear him say, "Tug". It was November 20th and "Pop". We rushed over to the carrier – new batteries on the radio, fastened everything down, fastening your kit on, making sure the water was on, and off we went to the rendezvous point. It was well to the east of our position and was already marked out when we got up there. The Royal Engineers had put white tapes down. We had to post guard, I did the first shift, always show willing! Next morning we woke up and a tremendous noise – tanks going past. We'd got a lorry next to us with Bombardier Stan Keaton. It was Peter Birkin's brainwave, a 15cwt truck sandbagged to the hilt, so that it could just move and lay wire following the attack – as well as the wireless we would have a telephone line as quick as possible. We brewed up. Peter said, "Now you all know what you've got to do", poured a rather large rum ration into all our drinks and off we went. We were going to meet the Colonel of the Black Watch through the wire.

Lance Bombardier Ted Whittaker, 425 **Bty**

Frank Penlington was the driver in Stan Keaton's sand-bagged truck and he could see that the Black Watch were also enjoying a special rum ration before going into action.

The Sergeant Major of the Black Watch said, "Where's your mugs, lads?" I thought we were having tea, but all the lads of the Black Watch had their white mugs and he filled them up with rum up to the blue rim. He came to mine and filled it up – I didn't drink. They drank it up and I sipped mine just to wet my lips. Then, "Anybody want this?" A soldier of the Black Watch said, "I'll have it!" So I gave it to him and he had the whole lot – half a pint!"

Driver Frank Penlington, 425 **Bty**

In the front line Captain Charles Laborde was acting as a fixed OP officer, ready to observe the effects of the prepared barrage, timed to open as the infantry and tanks were launched into the attack.

Suddenly, in the still of the morning, the wail of the bagpipes as the piper started up. There was about half a minute, a minute, no more than that and then everything opened up and of course you couldn't hear anything more at all. As soon as the guns started to fire, the clouds of smoke and dust – it was just like a thick fog – you couldn't see anything at all.

Captain Charles Laborde, 426 **Bty**

The mobile OP teams moved off with the infantry and Signaller Erik

Infantry attacking out of the perimeter at Tobruk. The SNH gunners were relieved that they could provide covering fire and not have to face the German machine guns.

Morley had good reason to be grateful for the thin steel which gave him a veneer of protection.

The Scots just walked and fell. They were striding forward not turning a hair at all. They were doing their job and doing it bloody well! I was sitting there watching them, they were only a few yards away, and I must say my concentration was on those poor buggers in front of me. Just falling down and the blokes that didn't fall stepped over their comrades. There was no turning back, you didn't stop for anyone, even your own people. Going on relentlessly. I was very glad for that bit of metal that was around me.

Signaller Erik Morley, 425 Bty

So they crossed the bullet torn maelstrom that was No Man's Land.

There was the most incredible noise, I have never in my life, before or since, heard anything like it. It was impossible. There was our barrage, people firing back, tanks, trucks... In the middle of all this a Black Watch piper, standing there, we couldn't hear a thing but he was stood there with these pipes! Shortly after that we met Colonel Rusk and again I was absolutely flabbergasted. There stands this Colonel, stood there with his greatcoat, steel helmet and ash walking stick with a knob on top, "Morning, Peter!" My mind flashed back – I'd read stories about these young infantrymen going over the top with walking sticks and blowing

173

SNH Bren Gun Carrier with driver Bill Hutton. This one belongs to 425 Battery and is the Observation Post for B Troop.

whistles – but I thought a piper and a chap with a walking stick – and me here! We set off constantly checking we were on right lines. The first thing that happened the tanks ran onto a minefield, so that was the tanks gone, but this was horrifying – we were going to follow them. There were shells, machine guns; German machine guns sounded just like a piece of calico tearing, they seemed to fire ten times as fast as ours; occasional bits of stuff hitting the side of the Bren Carrier. Eventually we arrived at this so-called strongpoint. The most miserable little selection of holes and things you've ever seen – that was 'Tiger'! I got a message just after we got there. A voice told me it was Brigade HQ and said, "Report your position". I very proudly said, "'Tiger' repeat 'Tiger'!"

Lance Bombardier Ted Whittaker, **425 Bty**

The assault infantry had suffered heavily in the attack.

The Colonel came and said, "Tell them I've lost 60% of my chaps and I want reinforcements as soon as possible." We had a code book and reserves were 'pigeons'. We had codes for figures and the message said something like, "Sixty per cent casualties, need urgent pigeons". Within an incredibly short space of time, this regiment who had been held in reserve, came over the hill. The Colonel said, "How the bloody hell did they get here?" I said, "Brigade are listening to us." Of course it made all the difference because it kept him up to strength.

Lance Bombardier Ted Whittaker, **425 Bty**

174

German resistance to the attack was unexpectedly strong because Rommel had been preparing his own forces for a final assault on the Tobruk fortress on 23 November, which was why his armoured units had been recalled to the area. The counter-attack was not long in coming, 'In the afternoon there was a counter-attack came in from a strongpoint to the east, 'Wolf'. You could see quite clearly with the naked eye, Italian tanks, not Germans, and we had a real good shoot on them. They soon turned tail and hopped it.'[134] This was the first of several such attacks and Major Peter Birkin showed considerable courage in organizing the artillery response, 'We'd got news of this attack but where we were we couldn't see it. In order to see the Major actually stood right on top of the turret of this tank as bold as brass and shouted fire orders down to us.'[135] Back at the guns they responded to every call that was made on them over the next few days of intense fighting.

The Germans put in a heavy attack and the OP, who thought he was going to be overrun, just gave the quite unconventional order, "And fire like bloody hell!" The wireless set went dead and we lost communication and 'we went to town' – we got rid of the whole 240 rounds behind the gun. My gun was just beginning to glow red round the jacket, the thicker part that goes round the barrel. It was just beginning to glow red. That was very dangerous. You put a shell into the open breech a chap rams the shell up so the driving band engages and then he puts a cartridge behind. They were moving ammunition so quickly that they were waiting for a cartridge case to be opened, these steel square cases where a

A 25 pdr gun crew in action. The firing was so furious during the breakout attempt and German counter attack that the gun barrels heated up and prematurely exploded the shells.

hasp came over with a split pin through which held them shut for normal travel purposes. The chap had to pull the split pins out and lift a cartridge out. On two of the guns they rammed the shell and the loader put his hand behind to take a cartridge which should have been there and the fellow just couldn't get these ruddy split pins out... The shell heated in the barrel and exploded. We had two guns go like that in a matter of seconds.

Sergeant George Pearson, **425 Bty**

It was no wonder that there were problems, for the guns were working right on the maximum limits of both men and machinery, 'The normal rate for a 25 pounder is three rounds a minute, slow is two rounds a minute and intense is five rounds a minute. On that occasion I clocked my gun firing off between 12 and 13 rounds a minute.'[136] This triumph of gunnery efficiency had not been anticipated by the specialists in working out the gun programme!

They had a hue and cry from the gun positions, "We're running out of ammunition!" I said, "Don't be bloody silly! You can't...!" I thought, "Crikey! What have I done?" I quickly did some critical calculations through the gun programme. I had thought the rapid rate of fire of 25 pounders was about seven a minute and I'd based all my calculations on that – which was the right thing to do. But the gunners thought otherwise. "What rate are you firing at?" They didn't know – they were just putting them up – they were that enthusiastic! I reckoned they must have been firing at about ten or twelve a minute. The guns were red hot you could have fried an egg on them!

Bombardier David Tickle, **425 Bty**

The gun teams could not leave their guns even when under fire themselves.

With gunners there are occasions when you can't take cover. If it was a normal day and you weren't firing, or you were firing on a relatively unimportant target, and you got shot at by counter-battery fire, then you would cease firing and take cover. As soon as it had finished you would go on firing. When you are in support of infantry then you don't leave the guns – you must keep firing in support of your own infantry, you can't just pack that up because you are being shelled or dive bombed. That was part of Royal Artillery training.

Sergeant George Pearson, **425 Bty**

The hard back breaking work did not even stop during the occasional lulls.

You'd go into a lull while the OP was re-organizing itself and the infantry were getting themselves in a new position. You would start getting rid of your shell cases because you can imagine 200 odd shell cases just lying behind the gun position. You've got to get rid of those because next day, with sun on them, they provide a nice helio to mark your position. They get shoved into the boxes they came in and then loaded up and taken away in the ammunition waggons. [516]

Sergeant George Pearson, 425 Bty

The situation in the desert ahead of them was by now breathtakingly bewildering and to quote the official historian, 'Over the twenty or so miles of country from the front of the Tobruk sortie to the open desert south east of Sidi Rezegh the forces of both sides were sandwiched like the layers of a Neapolitan ice... A complicated situation indeed, which, if suggested as the setting for a training exercise, must have been rejected for the reason that in real life these things simply could not happen.'[137] Whilst the rival armoured formations continued to manoeuvre across the desert nothing could be certain. Eventually news came through that the relieving forces had reached El Duda, only for it to be almost immediately re-captured by the Germans. It was into this chaotic situation that 426 Bty was ordered forward, supported by tanks, into the corridor which reached out in a south eastern direction towards El Duda.

We found ourselves on the receiving end of terrific barrages, so much so that we had to move out very, very quickly in the middle of the afternoon. We were in full observation from the enemy, that was why we were getting well and truly hammered. We moved to this position about 500 to 600 yards to the right rear. It wasn't until we reached there that I found that I'd left the director stand behind. My officer Captain Birkin was not pleased, although he and I were the best of friends! He said, "You'll go and get it as soon as its dusk!" Dusk arrived about two hours later and I walked across this No Man's Land. I'd just got there when the Germans let fly. I got these all to myself and I dived for the very first trench I could find. That first trench was the latrine and I finished up ankle deep in it! Nobody wanted to speak to me for two or three days after that!

Lance Sergeant Harold Harper, 426 Bty

One man showed impressive calmness as the shells rained down all around.

Suddenly we got very heavily shelled by Italians, they were 75 millimetre shells. We were all lying down of course, shells landing all over the position, and this wonderful Padre Parry was standing up there going on with the burial service with bits of splinter going through his robes – a brave man!

Captain Charles Laborde, 426 Bty

Padre Parry's coolness under fire attracted comment from the gunners.

We'd got Germans on three sides and got hammered something rotten, we were being shelled and all sorts – it was a right dodgy place. The Padre came round and he was a big fat man – Parry. He'd got a little tiny tin hat on the top of his head and he was walking about in amongst all this lot saying, "Have faith, my boys!" We used to say to him, "Why don't you 'F' off you silly old sod!" Anybody with any sense would have been down under the ground but he was walking about amongst it, "Have faith..." The gun position was absolutely pitted with shell holes, you could step from one to another. They were just raining down on us.

Bombardier Albert Swinton, **426 Bty**

On arrival at El Duda, 426 Bty met up with the infantry and played a crucial role in supporting British attacks and repelling the German counter-attacks which were launched intermittently over the next few days.

I crawled forward slowly up the slope with a piece of wire so that I could talk to the truck. I found, to my certain amount of consternation, about 60 or 70 yards away a German 50 millimetre anti-tank gun with its crew. Just on the top of the slope, away to west of me, there was some English infantry. I tried to fire on to this anti-tank gun, concentrated the guns and unfortunately one of the guns got the elevation wrong and shells started falling in the infantry, which was always rather embarrassing, so I had to cry, "Halt", very quickly. Then the anti-tank gun must have tagged onto me. I had a German periscope by that time and I think it must have been waving about above the sangar. This anti-tank gun ominously swung round pointing directly at my sangar so I thought, "Chum, this is where you disappear!" So I backed out very quickly on my stomach...

Captain Charles Laborde, **426 Bty**

Not only did the battery help break up direct assaults by tanks, but they were also able to prevent the Germans from concentrating in strength through the judicious direction of their fire, especially by Major William Barber, whose work at the OP was crucial.

After hard fighting the end was in sight, but still victory could not be taken for granted.

The siege was on the verge of being lifted. We woke up one morning to see a line of trucks which said, 'Eighth Army', they were coming in and it was the New Zealanders. Somebody said to the leading officer or NCO, "Thank goodness you've come and Tobruk's relieved!" They said, "Relieved nothing! We've been chased in by the Germans!"

Sergeant Bob Foulds, **425 Bty**

For some time after the veterans of the Tobruk garrison retained their own perspective of the 'Relief of Tobruk'!

Tobruk put out a corridor into the desert which linked up to the Eighth Army. The first vehicles that came into that corridor and into Tobruk were vehicles from Eighth Army who were after ammunition, provisions and petrol. So we always maintain we relieved the Eighth Army who were stranded in the desert!

Sergeant George Pearson, 425 Bty

At last the Afrika Korps broke under the extreme pressure and began retreating in earnest. This provided the SNH with a plethora of targets as the retreating columns passed within range of the guns in the Tobruk area. The Germans left behind a number of strongpoints in their old lines facing Tobruk and the SNH were pulled back into their former gun positions to provide artillery support for the infantry as they winkled out these pockets of resistance on 8 December. The siege had at last been lifted and the Tobruk garrison were free.

With the relief of Tobruk the SNH gunners could relax for a while. Here Sergeant Flint's team polish up a captured Spandau machine-gun.

179

There was a great feeling of relief that it was over because until that moment we didn't know that Tobruk was going to be relieved, we didn't know that we were going to win any battle. There was always a constant fear that we would be overcome and taken.

Bombardier Ray Ellis, **425 Bty**

The battle then moved beyond Tobruk and there followed a period of order and counter-order in its wake. The SNH moved up as far as Tmini before they were 'forgotten' and left far behind in the main advance across Cyrenaica. In a camp outside Tmini they celebrated their 'freedom' in the traditional male fashion when caches of Italian wine and brandy were found.

Somebody discovered a barrel of Chianti which had been abandoned by retreating Italians. The officers had left the position so the guns were there with the NCOs and the men. The men started to drink it and so did I out of enamel mugs. Everyone was getting quite merry. It occurred to me what was happening so I went and got Sergeant Frank Burkinshaw and said, "Stop drinking, everyone's going to get paralytic – we'd better stay sober!" It was no use telling everyone to stay sober – the men were not in the mood to be told!

Bombardier Ray Ellis, **425 Bty**

The drink in itself was not an attractive beverage but it offered a certain relief from reality for a few hours. 'Horrible purple looking Italian stuff in 44 gallon drums – a truck full of the stuff. The sort of wallop where the first mouthful tasted disgusting, like permanganate of potash or something, but after a couple it tasted all right.'[138] The drinking soon got out of hand, 'We got settled into this Chianti and we were all well and truly plastered! I remember my friend the Troop Sergeant Major sitting astride this barrel of Chianti ladling it out by the mug full to people.'[139] Things became quite lively, 'We'd got some Italian rockets – I think they were like coast guard flares – and we let a lot of these off.'[140] Meanwhile the band played on!

We had a bloke who played the piano accordion – he played all night and gradually his playing got wilder and wilder as he got drunker and drunker until eventually it came home in a great WRRRRRHHH, a last chord and he collapsed!

Sergeant Bob Foulds, **425 Bty**

Fuelled by the raw alcohol, the men went through an accelerated version of a typical night's drunkenness in Nottingham.

It was amazing because every man went through the same changes as they got drunk. They were happy for a start. Everyone was laughing and happy – it relieved all the tensions – we were out

180

of Tobruk. Backslapping, weak jokes were laughed at – all the normal things of men getting drunk. Gradually it changed and they stopped laughing and became maudlin. It was mothers, sweethearts and wives – tears rolling down! Then eventually they just collapsed unconscious down on to the ground. Then Frank and I went round all the gun towers collecting blankets and covering them because it was bitterly cold and they could have died of exposure.

Bombardier Ray Ellis, 425 Bty

Some of the gunners were less tender in ministering to the fallen. I got gloriously drunk and I went outside. I don't know whether you've had a lot of wine to drink but if you get out in the fresh air it makes you keel over! Jack Billngton said to the others, "Parker's outside I think he's dead – I kicked him twice and he never moved!" Next morning when I got up all my ribs were bruised. I felt rough, really rough!

Lance Bombardier Albert Parker, 425 Bty

He was not alone as come the dawn – come the hangover! 'Some people were in a hell of a bad state and putting their heads out of the windows as we were driving along the road and being ill!'[141] Even respectable sergeants like George Pearson suffered the consequences, 'We travelled next day in the gun towers with blinding thick heads over a bumpy desert – we paid dearly for our night before believe me!'[142]

Left to right: *Lieutenant Weller Polley, Gunner Murray, Lance Bombardier Checkland, Bombardier Harris and Driver Cooper. Neither the desert roads nor the vehicle were suitable for travelling when suffering from a hangover.*

CHAPTER SEVEN

Calm Before the Storm

The regiment moved back on 30 December into the Nile Delta as far as Tahag Camp, from where the men were sent back to Cairo on leave. They had been marooned amongst all male company for eight months or more and some slight signs of strain were appearing. 'We hadn't seen a woman for about nine months. We went down on the train and somebody shouted, "There's a bint!" Bint is Arabic for woman. Of course all us were at the window of the train with eyes popping out. She was a real old ragged looking Arabic woman but she was female!'[143]Cairo was another world after the privations of Tobruk, 'Eating, drinking; enjoying things like table cloths, butter and bread. Beautiful meals a lovely polished knife and fork. A hot bath; to be clean to be shaven; to have clean boots and creased trousers. Things we normally take for granted. It wasn't just a matter of getting blind drunk!'[144] Back at Tahag there was a belated Christmas party.

> We had one of our memorable parties at Tahag. Colonel Seely had arranged this, this was our delayed Christmas, and the Colonel and the Ladies Committee paid for the lot. We took over the NAAFI all the drinks were free – I must say that was a fatal mistake in those days – turkey, mince pies, plum puddings. It was all lads together and it was a riot! Peter Birkin who was a rugby player led everybody who could still stand in all the old filthy rugby songs. It was a party and a half and I don't think half of us ever got back to our tents that night, it was lay down and sleep wherever. Anyone who was sober ought to have been court martialled. Can't remember the next day or two!
>
> ***Signal Lance Sergeant Ted Whittaker,* 425 Bty**

By now many of the gunners were hardened drinkers, in contrast to their pre-war selves, as they sought through the medium of drink and good companionship to relieve the strains of war.

> There was a bar with plenty of beer and whisky. We used to go up every night at about seven o' clock, a whole gang of us, to 'write letters'. No one ever wrote a word of course – we would start drinking and drink steadily through until about two or three in the morning. When you got there you ordered a crate of beer and you put it at the side of you. You didn't go buying rounds like you do in the pub, everybody had a crate and you drank your own. Talking and drinking, laughing and joking. The officers used to come in

Xmas day breakfast in the desert. Left to right: *Lance Bombardier Checkland, unknown, Gunner Freeman, Captain Colin Barber, Gunner Shaw, Sergeant Wootton, Gunners Robinson and Peachment.*

UBI PIONEERS QUE

SOUTH NOTTS HUSSARS

107th (S.N.H.) REGT. R.H.A.

WITH · BEST · WISHES · FOR · XMAS · AND · THE · NEW YEAR ·

From .... Ted.

they always stood at the door for a second and someone would say, "Ah! Hello Sir, do come in!" One night we were there at about one o' clock in the morning when Peter Birkin fell off his chair into the sand! We picked hm up and carried him to his tent and put him to bed. About twenty minutes later he crawled in under the tent and said, "Whhosh had the audacsshitty to put me to bed?"

Sergeant Ray Ellis, **425 Bty**

There were signs that the SNH now had little to learn from the regulars or indeed anyone else about 'old soldiering'.

I remember Captain Slinn coming to me one day and saying, "Sergeant, we're short of an EP/IP tent by the way!" There was another regiment camped in Tahag and he said, "They've got some very nice EP/IP tents – need I say any more?" "No, Sir! That's all right!" I went and got my gun team and gun tower, went round the desert to the back of this camp, crawled up over the sand hills, looked over, they were all doing various things on parades. We crept down, took down this huge EP/IP, packed it all up, dragged it off, put it in our truck and went back. I said, "I've got an EP/IP for you, Sir!" "Jolly good, very good, Sergeant! Have it put up over there!"

Sergeant Ray Ellis, **425 Bty**

The regiment moved on 21 February to Sidi Bishr near Alexandria. While they were there a boxing match was arranged for Tommy Foley.

We went into this cabaret and the chap that owned it had something to do with this Egyptian boxing champion. A fight was fixed up between Tommy Foley and this champion. We went back to Sidi Bishr and started sparring with him, like, me and another chap, Nobby Clarke. Of course we weren't much good to him because we'd been out of it so long, but we did our best for him. We got permission, like, to do it. It was an honour for the South Notts to be represented in something like that. It was held in Cairo at their sporting arena over eight rounds. There was a big crowd, Egyptians, British and what have you. I was in his corner. It was a hard fight. Foley eventually won – only just through lack of training. He'd only had a couple of weeks or so to prepare and he was gradually running out of steam. But he'd built up such a big lead in the first four rounds that pulled him through really. We went back to the cabaret place and had a slap up meal!

Driver Harold Thompson, **425 Bty**

On 24 March they moved to Beni Yusef, where the regiment was expanded by the formation of the newly designated 520 Battery. To avoid establishing a completely inexperienced unit, the two original batteries were divided up with Captain Shakespear's B Troop of 425 Bty and Captain Ivor Birkin's D Troop of 426 Bty being used to form the

The South Notts Hussars after the addition of a third battery

425 BATTERY

A Troop

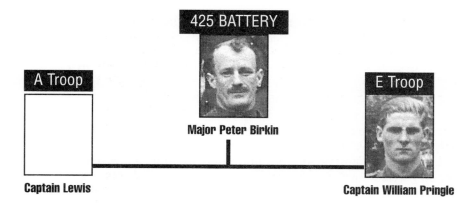

Major Peter Birkin

E Troop

Captain Lewis

Captain William Pringle

426 BATTERY

C Troop

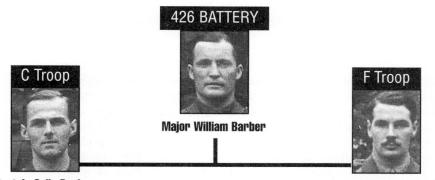

Major William Barber

F Troop

Captain Colin Barber

Captain Tony Chadburn

520 BATTERY

B Troop

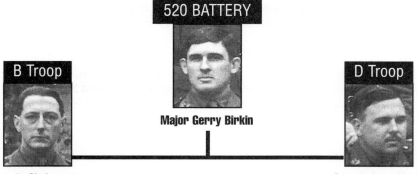

Major Gerry Birkin

D Troop

Captain Shakespear

Captain Ivor Birkin

basis of 520 Battery. Reinforcements were then split up between all three batteries and the line up became: 425 Bty under Major Peter Birkin, consisting of A Troop under Captain C A J Lewis and E Troop under Captain William Pringle; 426 Bty under Major William Barber with C Troop under Captain Colin Barber and F Troop under Captain Tony Chadburn; and 520 Battery under Major Gerry Birkin with B and D troops. An anti-tank battery – B Battery of the Northumberland Hussars was also attached to the regiment.

Despite their Royal Horse Artillery status, the SNH had spent most of the last two years in static defensive positions. During their period in Egypt, they were substantially re-equipped and began re-training for a more traditional RHA mobile role in the Western Desert where the situation remained finely balanced. In December 1941, Auchinleck's 'Crusader' offensive had succeeded in re-capturing the whole of Cyrenaica, but it had been a pyrrhic victory, for his forces had suffered heavy losses and were left exhausted. Their advance ground to a halt in front of the German positions at Mersa Brega. Here the two sides remained in loose contact until Rommel received reinforcements and promptly attacked on 21 January 1942. Once again, as in April 1941, the British fell back across Cyrenaica, but this time stopped some 30 miles west of Tobruk. Here Auchinleck developed a fixed defensive line behind which his armoured units could re-organize in preparation for yet another offensive. This line consisted of a series of self-contained all round defensive positions, or 'boxes', linked by minefields which stretched from Gazala, on the Mediterranean coast, to Bir Hacheim.

In this grand scheme of things the SNH had been designated part of the 22nd Armoured Brigade whom they joined at Fort Capuzzo on 25 April. Each battery was then assigned to work with a tank regiment. Thus 425 Bty was attached to 3rd County of London Yeomanry; 426 Bty to 4th County of London Yeomanry; and 520 Battery to the Royal Gloucestershire Hussars. The OP officers were equipped with Marmon Harrington Armoured Cars or light Honey tanks so that they could keep up with the forward units.

It was solid steel, made in South Africa and with that weight behind it wasn't the easiest of vehicles to manoeuvre because your vision wasn't all that good. Next to me was Gerry Birkin; directly behind me was a wireless operator and behind Gerry there would be two wireless operators. One into regiment, the other into brigade and one direct back to our own battery.

Driver Bobby Feakins, **520 Bty**

The unit was accorded the honour of a Royal inspection before going back into action, this included an examination of the vehicles. Major

His Royal Highness The Duke of Gloucester, seen here inspecting a Grant tank, was soon to be brought down to earth by a SNH radio operator during an inspection of one of their vehicles.

Gerry Birkin took the Duke of Gloucester round his armoured car.

He got in at the back and I think I was sat at a radio set. Gerry got up through to the turret and stood on the turret. The Duke of Gloucester went up through and he broke wind quite badly pulling himself up through the turret. One of the operators who had his phones on, not hearing too much of what was going on, turned round and said, "Jesus Christ, who the bloody hell has shit?" – the Duke must have heard it. I gave him a great smack across the head and he suddenly realized what he had said and to whom he had referred!

Driver Bobby Feakins, 520 Bty

★ ★ ★ ★

As the brigade moved slowly up into the desert they trained in the new concepts of armoured mobility.

We were training to move about in box formation. The soft vehicles were in the middle. The guns were on the outside with the armoured units coming up in the rear in their own box formation. These huge dispositions moved about the desert like ships at sea – like a flotilla of naval vessels sailing. It was rather like that in effect, because as the vehicles moved along through the sand, they left a trail of dust behind them just as ships leave the wake in the water.

Sergeant Ray Ellis, 425 Bty

At first their inexperience of mobile warfare showed, 'We got into a terrible mess on one of these night exercises. There's no doubt about it. Vehicles were going in the wrong direction, we were getting mixed up with people we shouldn't get mixed up with. It was a little bit disheartening because we just hadn't had long enough. There were conferences galore.'[145] A controversial role was assigned to the regiment for they were to act as decoys on the edge of the armoured box. This caused considerable doubts amongst both officers and men.

The idea was that we should be in this vulnerable position tempting the tanks to attack us. When the German tanks came out our armoured units would come in and destroy them. It was a stupid theory. The amount of time it would have taken for German tanks to come onto our position and wipe us out didn't allow enough time for our tanks to come from wherever they were in hiding to protect us. The time limits were too fine. We didn't like it at all, we were all well aware that the 25 pounder was not an anti-tank gun and it was being pressed into service because the British Army hadn't really developed an anti-tank gun at that time. It was not manoeuvrable enough – it would only traverse a certain distance with the traverse wheel and if you wanted to move the gun you had to move the whole bloody gun round by moving the trail; it was too high with a shield that gave you no protection except from blast. Very often HE wasn't very effective against tanks. If you were firing and hit the armoured part of the tank, the projectile would fail to pierce the armour and the tank would continue virtually unchecked. Armour piercing shells were more effective but we carried very few. The main hope of destroying a tank was to knock off its tracks, set it on fire, or catch it somewhere at the back.

Sergeant Ray Ellis, **425 Bty**

Nevertheless, despite these misgivings, the men were proud of the progress they had made.

On May 26 I remember our officer turning to me and saying, "I do not know what else we can do to make this troop more efficient". By that time we'd reached the situation where we could be driving along and suddenly get the order and within 35 seconds we would have a round up the spout and in the air.

Sergeant Harold Harper, **520 Bty**

With their training completed the whole of the 22nd Armoured Brigade was rushed forward into a position close to the junction of two desert tracks that was known as 'Knightsbridge', lying behind the defensive minefields of the Gazala lines. The South Notts Hussars who had endured their rites of passage at Tobruk were about to face their destiny.

Major P. L. Birkin.
425 Battery.
(Middle East Model!)
(The longer the service - the)
(longer the moustache!)

CHAPTER EIGHT

Knightsbridge: The Death of The Regiment

The Battle of Gazala, which was about to commence, was a confusing series of engagements which resulted from the almost simultaneous attempts of the British and Axis forces to launch offensives in the Gazala sector in late May 1942. Unfortunately, the British left flank south of Bir Hacheim remained exposed, presenting Rommel with an ideal opportunity for manoeuvre and he was the first to strike. In order to pin down the British reserves in the north, he feigned a major attack in the coastal area throughout 26th May, while that same night a highly mobile force consisting of the Italian XXth Corps, the 90th Light Division, the 21st and 15th Panzer Divisions, swept round the south of the Bir Hacheim minefield to fall on the vulnerable British southern flank early the following day.

On the night of 26th May the SNH were ignorant of any approaching danger. At dusk 425 and 426 Batteries were in positions near Knightsbridge, while 520 Battery was well to the south in front of a gap which existed in the minefield at Bir el Harmat. Driver Bill Hutton, for one, was completely at ease with the situation. 'The Colonel came round and I heard him telling everybody, "We're having a very early move in the morning so nobody need dig in..." Well that suited me – I wasn't very fond of digging. I was very pleased.' Of course, although the guns and vehicles were not being dug in, any desert veterans worth their salt would always dig slit trenches for their own protection before they settled down for the night. Second Lieutenant Herbert Bonnello, who had recently returned to the regiment after his officer training at the Middle East OCTU, was equally unaware of the danger posed by the approach of Rommel's right hook round the British defences.

> The guns were pointing westwards over the minefield. All the supporting trucks were in line, dispersed at the back. I noticed, as I was getting ready to get down in the old sleeping bag, there was a tremendous amount of activity by flares on the other side of the minefield. No-one realized the import of these flares. Nobody had the slightest idea of what was coming. I can remember we kicked a football about that particular night.
>
> *Second Lieutenant Herbert Bonnello, 520 Bty*

For Sergeant Harper it seemed to be just another night in the desert with no particular cause for alarm.

190

Sergeant Major Earnshaw, the Battery Sergeant Major, and myself went across to one of the B Troop positions and sat in the back of a 15cwt truck where under the direction of Sergeant Bland we were taught the elements of contract bridge by the help of a hurricane lamp. When we left just after midnight and wound our way across the moonlit desert you could have heard a pin drop.

Sergeant Harold Harper, **520 Bty**

On awakening the situation still seemed normal and when, after breakfast, Harper and his comrades spotted a dust cloud on the horizon, they paid no attention, presuming it to be some of their troops on manoeuvres.

The first sign that trouble was brewing came in a telephone call from Regimental Headquarters, announcing that the Germans were very

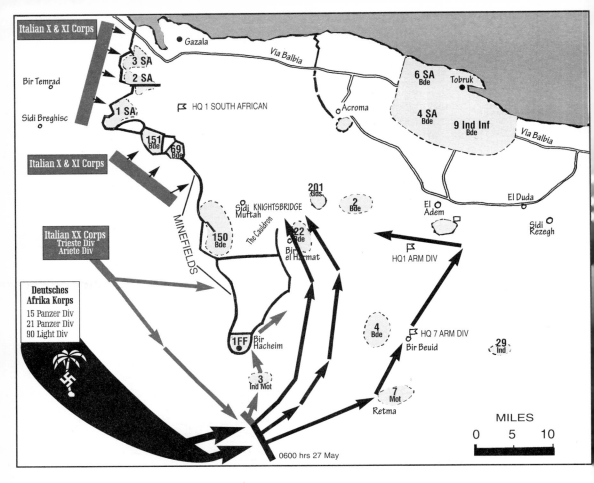

Gazala

Via Balbia

3 SA

2 SA

Bir Temrad

1 SA

Sidi Breghisc

151
Bde

69
Bde

⚑ HQ 1 SOUTH AFRICAN

6 SA
Bde

Tobruk

Acroma

4 SA
Bde

9 Ind Inf
Bde

Via Balbia

El Duda

Italian X & XI Corps

MINEFIELDS

Italian XX Corps
Trieste Div
Ariete Div

Sidi
Muftah

KNIGHTSBRIDGE

The Cauldron

150
Bde

201
Gds

2
Bde

El
Adem

Sidi
Rezegh

22
Bde

Bir
el Harmat

⚑
HQ1 ARM DIV

Deutsches
Afrika Korps
15 Panzer Div
21 Panzer Div
90 Light Div

1FF

Bir
Hacheim

4
Bde

⚑ HQ 7 ARM DIV

Bir Beuid

29
Ind

3
Ind Mot

7
Mot

Retma

MILES

0   5   10

0600 hrs 27 May

close and seemingly moving down from the south. The 520 Battery Commander, Major Gerry Birkin, and his brother, Captain Ivor Birkin, in command of D Troop, went out to investigate in two of the armoured cars used as mobile observation posts. They were *en route* to the Royal Gloucestershire Hussars' regimental headquarters when they ran right into the German tanks sweeping round the Bir Hacheim minefield. Major Gerry Birkin seems to have seen them first.

He'd sighted a lot of dust and we were getting firing lines. He was up through the turret and he came down and said, "Bombardier would you just check this?" I went up and a shell landed a bit behind us. He said, "Whoops!" Then I said, "Oh Sir! Quick!" I thought I'd seen a vehicle moving in direct line towards us. I came down and sat in my seat and he went up. I had a map on my lap facing the front of the vehicle, he was up through the turret, looking out of the back of the turret facing the Germans. The next round came straight inside the armoured car. I didn't

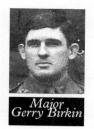
Major Gerry Birkin

realize it had hit us and I turned and there was two radio operators without heads – absolutely nothing from the shoulders. I had blood and muck all over me. Gerry slumped into my arms and he was actually dead at that point, hit right in the tummy – the abdomen. I was wounded in the legs. On the inter-battery radio I said, "We've been hit, we've been hit!"

Driver Bobby Feakins, **520 Bty**

Sergeant Harold Harper was in Captain Ivor Birkin's armoured car where he was acting as his observation post assistant.

We had only gone about six or seven hundred yards when we heard a gabbling on the battery commander's radio which immediately told us something was wrong. Captain Birkin jumped out and dashed across, fifty to sixty yards. I followed him.

Sergeant Harold Harper, **520 Bty**

The badly wounded Feakins was in a desperate state as he tried to get the armoured car away from the immediate area of danger.

One of the radio operators, Gunner Wright, was unhurt. I thought, "Well I'm no good operating as a two man band". I was bleeding profusely all round my legs, so I decided to make back to the battery to get out of a sitting duck position. I said to the chap – I didn't even look round, "Hang on!" I slammed it into gear, tried to put my foot on the accelerator because I was losing the strength in my legs and I hit a slit trench. It just went 'Whuumph' – right in – and I can assure you it was a very nasty smack – everything came forward and the seat hit me in the back... I turned round and there was nobody there and I wondered what had happened.

Driver Bobby Feakins, **520 Bty**

Unfortunately, in the chaos of the moment, Wright had jumped out of the armoured car and taken shelter in that same slit trench. There the wheels unluckily ran straight over him and he suffered a broken leg, which meant that he too was out of action, although Feakins was not immediately aware of what had happened.

I crawled out as best I could, pulling myself out and I was hanging on the back of the vehicle when Sergeant Harper came racing across. I have to admit that I was in a bit of shock – headless bodies – the inside of my armoured car was just nothing but blood and flesh, bits of body all over the place.

Driver Bobby Feakins, **520 Bty**

Harper was horrified at the sight before him.

When we reached the truck – I've never seen anything like it in my life. Major Birkin lay flat on the floor, obviously dead. I went to the back and opened up the two doors at the back of the armoured car. Apparently the armour-piercing shell had gone clear through the middle of the battery commander as he was standing up and chopped off the heads of the two radio operators. All you could see was these two lads, their hands still holding their mouthpieces, although their heads were lying on the floor. The third radio operator was the one who was gabbling the message. He jumped out of the truck. My biggest problem was to persuade Birkin to leave his brother. There was a little bit more than just a couple of officers involved here. I said, "Come along you must come back". He said, "No, you get back I'll see what I can do" and he ordered me back to our original armoured car.

Sergeant Harold Harper, **520 Bty**

Although he obeyed the direct order, Harper decided he must try to pick up Ivor Birkin. The armoured car started to manoeuvre round.

Just out of a cloud of sand came a Royal Gloucester Hussars' Grant tank. We hit it head on and we literally bounced back, five or six yards. The next thing we saw the engine was on fire so we all had to jump out and dashed across and told Captain Birkin what had happened. There we were, stranded.

Sergeant Harold Harper, **520 Bty**

The German tanks were still in the offing and their situation appeared truly dire when they were lucky enough to sight and board the only remaining functioning British tank in the immediate locality.

A tank came past and we all jumped on it – saying that I jumped is an over statement – it was Ivor Birkin's driver who lifted me on and hung on to me because from my waist down I couldn't feel a thing. I don't think they had any idea we were on the tank. I was on the back, Ivor Birkin's driver, Harold Harper, Ivor Birkin and Wright the signaller with the broken leg. There was stuff flying around we were under shell fire. Ivor Birkin's driver was hanging on to me like grim death.

Driver Bobby Feakins, **520 Bty**

Their situation had thus improved, but was still not exactly comfortable, as the tank was actually in action with the German tanks.

We all jumped on the back of a tank of the County of London Yeomanry and lay flat. The tank commander had no idea we were there and kept firing. We had to keep dodging as best we could when the turret and barrel kept swinging round. One of our fellows fell off and we thought he'd been crushed to death. Most of us received wounds of some description from the German shelling, although at the time we weren't aware of their extent – there was too much happening. *Sergeant Harold Harper,* **520 Bty**

It was the wounded Feakins who had fallen off when Ivor Birkin's driver, who was the only thing keeping him on the slewing tank, was wounded himself.

We hadn't gone very far when he was hit right across the bottom and when you get hit like that on the cheeks of your arse the immediate thing is to grab them. In doing this of course he let me go and I fell off the tank. It continued on its way and I was left out in the open miles from anywhere in No Man's Land. Where tanks turn their tracks throws up a ridge and that looked like a haven to me and I was hiding behind tank tracks. The pain had started to come in and I just couldn't use my legs. I had a great gaping hole in my right leg and my left leg and knee was full of shrapnel. I must have still been in shock, but I was *compos mentis*, I knew what was going on around me and my one issue was to keep safe. After a while another tank came by, saw me out in the open and came over. They said, "What the hell are you doing here?" I said, "Having an afternoon cup of tea, you silly bugger!" He said, "Well, I'm sorry old chap, I'm going into action now, but on my way back I'll pick you up and take you back". Away he went. An hour and a half to two hours. Hell on earth watching shells drop all around me, but none too close. Just wondering about the things you've done and the things you'd like to do! An element of fear of course because you didn't know what was going to happen. But he did come back and I felt heaven had opened up. One of the crew got out, lifted me on and made me safe and they drove me back.

Driver Bobby Feakins, 520 Bty

Back on Harper's tank, the survivors' desperate shouts were eventually heard and they were taken back to the 520 Battery waggon lines for medical treatment. The wounded, including Harper who had crushed ribs and shrapnel in his knee, were then taken to a field dressing station. He was still there when it was over-run by the advancing German troops. As a prisoner Harper's conduct was exemplary, 'One had been trained to do this. I noticed for instance that the German tanks used purple smoke every time their planes came over to indicate who they were. I took note of how many tanks there were and the signs on the sides of the tanks and goodness knows what else.'[146] Armed with this useful information he decided to try and escape.

A Welsh sergeant and I noticed that the Germans had been pushed back. So, after about four nights, we decided to make a break for it. My theory was that if we went due south-east we would be edging out into the desert where there was less likelihood of anybody being around because nearly all the fighting was in the coastal zone. All I had was a pair of shorts, full stop! We waited until after dusk. We passed one tank full of Germans so I started speaking in German, just to make sure that if we were spotted they would think that we were part of them. At first light we laid up. We found one or two derelict British vehicles, put our hands under the radiator and swilled our mouths out with the radiator water. We had the sense not to appear in the daytime. When the sun was belting down, we just got under a vehicle. We never slept to any great extent, kept awake all the time because you daren't sleep. Then unfortunately the next night, when we were walking, this laddie trod on a land mine and that was the end of him. So I was left on my own. Eventually I had to drink my own urine, you started by swilling your mouth out with it and hoping for the best. We'd got used in the desert to reading the stars, so I knew which direction I was going in pretty well and I could tell from the firing where the battle was and the right way to approach. My only fear was when I got near to our lines – I walked in with my hands up and started shouting as much in English as I possibly could. I was in a bit of a bedraggled state when I got to the Guards Brigade Headquarters.

Sergeant Harold Harper, 520 Bty

Harper finally succeeded in getting back to the British lines on 6 June and was able to pass on the intelligence he had gathered.

Back on 27 May, however, before Harper had even been captured, neither of the OP armoured cars had been able to get off a warning radio message to the SNH. As a result back at 520 Battery they were totally surprised as the German tanks swirled up out of the desert. Bill Hutton was attending to one of life's necessities in the vicinity of the waggon lines.

I'd made myself a permanent lavatory seat out of a petrol tin – all cut with a pear-shaped hole. I took that and a spade, dug myself a little hole, put this seat on top of it and I sat on it reading some magazine. I was sitting there and in the sand round me there were bits of stuff flying up all round me. "What the bloody hell's that?" I couldn't hear any bangs or whistles, but it was like somebody was bloody well shooting at me. I could see a tank way back on the horizon – I presumed it was one of ours practising, trying his gun out, and not seen me. I smartly pulled my trousers up and, all of a sudden, one of the new officers came rushing up and said we need every spare man to help dig the guns in.

Driver Bill Hutton, 520 Bty

The Quad gun towers were next to the guns totally unprepared for action.

I had a load of NAAFI stuff dropped to my truck and I had to give it out to the men. Cigarettes, tins of fruit, anything. I'd left my vehicle and walked across to another one. They hadn't been dispersed at all, they were still in column of route, one behind another. All of a sudden I heard the schmozzle the other side of the hill. Gunfire, machine-gun fire. I said to a chap, "Somebody's having it pretty rough over the other side!" I didn't know how far or near it was because sound travels in the desert. We were sat there talking and then I saw this German tank pull over the hill.

Driver Ernie Hurry, 520 **Bty**

At the guns chaos reigned.

We were trying to find what was going on with the radio, standing by the side of the pick-up truck. As far as B Troop were concerned, it seemed to happen so quickly, that we were more flabbergasted than panicked. B Troop had to turn round and face the other direction. D Troop were able to go, they were on the other side of all this line of vehicles, that shielded them and they managed to get their gun towers, limber up and push off. We were in the middle in a slit trench under fire. I should have gone. Clearly the attack was coming from the south and it was too late to go back towards Cairo, you had to go north. We should have gone much sooner. When do you scarper, when do you go into action? That was the biggest worry, that's the nightmare.

Second Lieutenant Herbert Bonnello, 520 **Bty**

The confusion was total and in not knowing what to do many of the men did nothing.

I said to one or two of the drivers who were congregated round this vehicle, "We shouldn't be here at all – the guns have got to fire up the column of vehicles, we ought to get at the back of the guns." They said, "We've had no orders to move – we've got to stay put!" I said, "You don't want to stay put in a situation like this, you've got to use your common sense – its common sense now! Anybody coming?" They said, "No, we're not moving!" I said, "I'm moving!" While we were making our mind up more tanks appeared over the hill, six or seven.

Driver Ernie Hurry, 520 **Bty**

Hurry ran back to his truck and drove it round to take up position to the rear of the guns out of the line of fire.

The guns opened up as I waited there, firing down the column of vehicles. The Germans were very close – let's face it they were close on the back of our vehicles when they came over the hill – about half a mile. Then Captain Bennett, he stood up in his vehicle with a blue flag, which meant everybody was to withdraw. I went back on the gun position and picked up three or four signallers – Bruce Meakin was one of them – I'd got them on the running boards. I was fired at and chased by one of the tanks, I could see

the bullets spurting in the ground in front of me. I put speed on
and kept going.

Driver Ernie Hurry, 520 **Bty**

Hurry was one of the lucky ones as the guns had little chance of escape.
As the tanks closed in, Lieutenant Bonnello saw an act of outstanding
heroism.

> I had a close picture of Sergeant Taylor's gun action. It was an
> amazing thing. He did an open sight action all on his own. I think
> most of his chaps had been killed. He hit this tank at fifty yards
> and it was just like a knife going through butter. The turret came
> straight off and bounced at the back.

Second Lieutenant Herbert Bonnello, 520 **Bty**

*Lieutenant
Bonnello*

Sergeant Taylor later got the DCM. But Bill Hutton heard a slightly
different version of the story from Taylor himself!

> MacNamara was Taylor's gun layer and this tank was coming
> straight for the gun. MacNamara looked through his telescopic
> sight and the thing was so near that he didn't see anything, just a
> grey mass. Fred Taylor was telling him to fire and he turned round
> to Fred, off his gun seat and said, "I can't see a f****** thing!"
> Taylor said, "Pull the bloody trigger man!" So he pulled the trigger
> just as the tank was going to climb over the gun. It blew the turret
> right off and killed everybody in the tank and it carried on and
> climbed over the gun.

Driver Bill Hutton, 520 **Bty**

Sergeant Taylor

Bonnello had been forced to take cover in a slit trench and the situation
was by then utterly hopeless. 'If tank crew see enemy in a slit trench they
can crush you – that was a big worry. I saw this big tank coming and it
just missed us.' The tanks swept in and Hutton, ensconced in the
waggon lines, was forced to take cover.

> There I was, all by myself. I could hear this squeaking, creaking
> noise that tanks make. I bobbed my head up and soon put it down
> again – they'd got dirty big black crosses on! Three German tanks
> all within spitting distance. Our guns are shooting at these tanks
> and they're shooting at our guns. All bloody hell was let loose.
> There's a hell of difference from being in action with one of your
> pals so that you can make silly jokes about it, but when you're on
> your own it's a different cup of tea altogether. I sat in there and I
> thought that if I was Errol Flynn and I'd got some sticky bombs
> I'd got a perfect chance to put those tanks out of action. "Well," I
> thought to myself, "thank God, I haven't got any sticky bombs!"

Driver Bill Hutton, 520 **Bty**

After two of the tanks had moved forward to overrun the gun position,
the supporting German infantry appeared and Hutton was captured. 'I

saw chaps walking about with their hands up so I came out with my hands up. It wasn't long before your arms begin to ache!'[147] Major Daniell saw the Padre evacuating some wounded, 'Beside me, out of the corner of my eye, I saw Padre Parry, hauling a couple of wounded into the back of his truck. I shouted to him, "GO! GO!" Just in time he disappeared, six wounded in the truck and four bullets in Padre Parry. Exhorting his driver to go faster, yet faster, they eventually reached safety.'[148] Although D Troop escaped this debacle with few casualties, B Troop had ceased to exist as a fighting unit.

To the North, 425 Battery started the day facing out on to one of the minefields, some two miles to the south west of Knightsbridge. Gun Sergeant John Walker, in charge of Number 1 gun in E Troop, had his first inkling of the attack on 520 Battery from under his feet. 'We felt the ground shaking which we knew by experience was either artillery or dive bombers. We immediately went to our guns and we could then see smoke on the horizon and knew that there was a battle.' Lance Sergeant Ted Whittaker was the signaller in the armoured car of Major Peter Birkin, commander of 425 Bty, and the cousin of Gerry and Ivor Birkin.

Major Birkin got all the information he could and said, "We'd better go to see what's happened to 520", as we were about the nearest. We were very apprehensive: this was the complete unknown, this was mobile warfare. We simply went towards the noise. Before we got far we met Captain Shakespear in his truck, coming back in a tearing hurry. We stopped and he shouted across, he was absolutely hopping mad.

Signal Lance Sergeant Ted Whittaker, 425 Bty

Shakespear explained what had happened and said, "'The bastards have killed Gerry". Peter said, "Oh My God, are you sure?" he said, "Absolutely..."' While the OP teams were investigating the situation 425 Bty, 426 Bty and the remnants of 520 Battery moved back to the north east, taking up independent positions immediately alongside the Knightsbridge 'box', which was occupied by the Guards Brigade and the 2nd Royal Horse Artillery. Soon after this, German tanks made a concerted effort to break from the south. For Walker and his gun team it was a tense period.

Willie Pringle, our Captain, walked along and said, "Under no circumstances must you fire until you're given an order." The heat haze slowly dissolved into physical things. On the horizon you saw a vehicle which looked like a shadow and the heat haze made it jump up and down and it slowly became a vehicle or tank. Our Sergeant Major, George Attewell, walked round and asked if we were all right. We just lay there until they started to shoot at us. We were under a hail of machine-gun bullets and lost fairly quickly the layer on the next gun to me and one of my team got a bullet through his leg.

Sergeant John Walker, **425 Bty**

Not everyone in the gun teams appreciated the tactic of holding fire until the enemy were so close.

> We'd got a round up the spout ready. We'd been told to load but not fire until they came in close – until we could see the whites of their eyes. Daft! We had to just sit there. I remember this Irish gunlayer said, "I wish they'd let us fire, I've got two in me sights". We were firing from open sights when we started. If you hit him it's all right – but meantime he's firing at you with his gun, machine-gunning you at the same time, twisting and turning, zig-zagging towards you. We got one or two shots off when this one hit us. It dropped just underneath the gun shield as far as I know. I was on the left hand side of the gun, where you load up with your right hand, crouched down, me head right under the gun layer's seat with this 25-pounder round ready to load up again. It was just like someone gave me a big bang on the shoulder. Me arm went all dead, it was just like an old rope, just hanging all sort of any road. You could see the bones through me flesh.

Gunner Ted Holmes, **425 Bty**

He was taken back to the Regimental Aid Post, 'I met Ted Holmes after he'd been wounded. You couldn't stick a pin into anywhere that hadn't got shrapnel in it! He was absolutely spattered in shrapnel.'[149] Back at the gun positions, Walker had also opened fire on the tanks.

> We didn't shoot until they were well within range, you could identify them and train your gun on a particular tank. We all opened fire at the same moment at little more than two thousand yards. We were firing cap on HE – it hit and exploded a fraction later – the idea being that it would blow up inside the tank rather than outside. The first one that we hit – the whole tank went red – my layer, Frank Bush, threw his hat in the air. Willie Pringle said in his Scotch accent, "Never mind that, get another one!"

Sergeant John Walker, **425 Bty**

Pringle felt that his tactics were justified by the results.

> The German tanks wouldn't face concentrated 25 pounder fire, when they got within close range we put down a barrage of shells, a nice little line of shells in amongst them and I noticed they stopped every time. You had to be sure to get more accuracy. Armour-piercing is no good over distances because it must have a flat trajectory.

Captain William Pringle, **425 Bty**

Anti-tank actions were fought at a frenetic pace.

You take scant notice of the tank you've just fired at because you're looking at the next. You're very excited, not afraid, its before and after that you're afraid. In the actual battle you're not so much afraid as excited and trying to get things done quickly. If a high explosive 25 pounder shell hits the track of a tank it is going to blow the track off and the tank will slew and stop. That means you can put another one into it, bang one into the back and he'll explode and brew up. By this time you can see something coming over from the left getting close to you, so you whip the gun round to have a go at him. Sometimes the shell will hit the tank, explode and the tank would keep coming. It's probably given everyone in the tank a headache, but it didn't stop the tank, or kill them all. But you're not just firing at one tank you've got tanks all over the place. You think, "I'd better have a go at him – he's getting a bit close!" and so it goes on. To be absolutely honest all you're looking at are the few tanks that are coming near your gun. All you're thinking about is not saving the British Empire but protecting your gun and yourself – knocking out any tanks that look dangerous to you!

Sergeant Ray Ellis, 425 Bty

Major Peter Birkin and his crew spent the day liaising with the tanks of 3rd County of London Yeomanry, organizing support fire for them from the battery.

This Colonel operating his tanks like a fleet of ships at sea. It was more than a bit exciting because you could see through the binoculars these big grey monsters with umpteen times more range. The General Grants had gone in a flash because they picked them out. We were bringing fire down. It was absolute chaos – a scrap, then fall back – because our tanks were no match for these Germans. The infantry, I didn't know where they were.

Signal Lance Sergeant Ted Whittaker, 425 Bty

Whittaker found himself right in the epicentre of the tank battle with shrapnel and bullets flying all around him. Then, right in the middle of this action, there came a memorably dramatic incident noted in the regimental history. 'One of the tyres on the exposed side of Major Birkin's armoured car had been punctured by a machine-gun bullet. Though the car drew intense enemy fire Gunner Worley coolly changed the wheel under a hail of small arms fire.'[150] Whittaker remembered his own – rather more colourful – account of the incident.

All of a sudden the car started to lurch. David Worley said something gentle like, "What the f****** hell's happened to us?" We hopped out and we'd got a puncture – front wheel. You can imagine! The tanks were at fairly long range, but by this time they'd come over the hill and there was quite a bunch of them. Machine-gun bullets were landing round us. We couldn't get the spare wheel off. I don't know whether it was because we were terrified or whether the nuts were tight. Talk about fingers and thumbs! We finally got the spare wheel off. Then jacking up an armoured car – it's heavy – we were frantic. We got this ruddy wheel off. We put two wheel bolts on and Dave said, "What do you reckon?" I said, "In the bloody car!" We hopped in, the Major said, "OK?" and off we went.

Signal Lance Sergeant Ted Whittaker, 425 Bty

They found that night that they'd cross-threaded both nuts! 'That's what they called "Coolly changed the wheel under fire!"'[151]

As the British forces overcame their initial surprise they were able to compensate for the inferiority of their Crusader tanks by digging in 'hull down', so that only the turrets were visible to the German Panzer Mark IIIs, who were consequently much easier targets as they advanced across the open desert. As the artillery support became better organized they took an increasing toll until eventually, after hard fighting, the advance of the German tanks was stemmed and they fell back to regroup in the 'Cauldron' area between Knightsbridge Box and 150 Brigade Box. The stiff resistance offered by the SNH and their fellow units in the Knightsbridge area meant that Rommel's plan had not been as successful as he would have wished. Although he had penetrated deep behind the British position, as a result of his sweep round the Bir Hacheim minefield, it was at the cost of a third of his tanks and others were immobilized due to shortages of fuel. At this stage all such supplies had to travel right round the British minefields in order to reach the advanced German forces. Rommel persisted with his attempts to break through to the north behind the British lines until 29 May, but by then his communication and supply situation was so critical that he resolved to turn back to the west and smash through those British minefields that were guarded by the 150 Infantry Brigade Box. If this could be achieved it would serve the dual purpose of providing a greatly shortened supply route and of course a means of escape back to his own lines should such a course of action become necessary.

His gambit succeeded and after severe fighting 150 Brigade Box was overrun on 1 June and Rommel thus secured a direct route through to his forces which were then concentrated in the Cauldron. In the wider confusion of the battle the British generals remained unaware of this development and it seemed to them that Rommel had been beaten back.

We could see the big minefield and we were shooting at vehicles

202

which were coming through from west to east. Instantly we reported this because the only known path at that time was further towards Bir Hacheim where it was fairly narrow. Back came someone from Brigade on our frequency and said, "Regards your sit-rep. Suggest you mean east to west, enemy retreating." We were incensed at this and Birkin got on the mike himself and said, "Troop movements, west to east, through minefield." Blow me they came back again and said, "Other reports definitely indicate east to west, enemy retreating." This was one of the fatal mistakes of that action. They'd opened a huge gap through the broadest part of the minefield and they were pouring supplies through.

Signal Lance Sergeant Ted Whittaker, 425 **Bty**

Although, if fully appreciated, such reports could have provided adequate warning that the Germans were building up their strength in the Cauldron, the belief that they were mistaken persisted and consequently a small general advance was ordered into the Cauldron on 5 June in order to capitalize on a non-existent success. The plan was for 10th Indian Brigade, which was part of 5th Indian Division, to move westwards, after a heavy preliminary artillery bombardment and drive a wedge through the German anti-tank screen. Once this had been achieved the 7th Armoured Division would then follow up through the gap to destroy the German forces in the Cauldron.

Since 1 June the SNH had been in position north east of the Knightsbridge junction in company with the 7th Armoured Brigade and the 11th Regiment RHA. Many of the men shared the optimism of their generals. 'The impression we got was that we had almost won it and that we were going to go forward, that we were chasing them.'[152] Throughout 4 June the specialists were kept busy preparing a fire programme to support the advance of the 10th Indian Infantry Brigade. Once this had been carried out the unit was to return to the control of the 22nd Armoured Brigade. After making rendezvous with their tank regiments near Bir Harmat at 06.00 they were to advance west into the Cauldron, where it was expected they would only be facing a weak German rear guard. The artillery barrage started at 03.30 in the morning.

The worst part of a battle is before the battle – waiting for it to open – that is when you have the fear. I was tired, physically tired; and tired of battles, fighting, deserts and killing – sick of the whole thing. My gun crew were new and this was there first experience of warfare. I felt sorry for them because they were all obviously frightened, I don't say this in any way to belittle them – everybody's frightened – but by this time I'd got past that stage. I was only 22, but as far as warfare went, I was an old man. They were also homesick. It was only a matter of months since they'd been at home in England with their wives and sweethearts. Again we'd passed that – by this time it was two or three years since we'd been home so that had also gone. So I felt sorry for these men who were homesick, frightened and cold. I knew what it would be like when the barrage started, the first 'FLASH' and 'CRASH'. All the noise and the screaming of shells. Then you knew the enemy would reply and back into the old carnage. I wished that no gun would ever fire again. I was war weary. Then you got the "Take Post!" You get on the gun just tensing yourself. Everything is very still and quiet then the shout through the megaphone, "Zero, Minus Five... Four... Three... Two... One... FIRE!" A screaming 'CRASH' as every gun along the front opens up and the battle is started. There is no longer then time to think about being wounded, or killed, or lonely, or tired – you're involved, the gun is firing and leaping about and you're firing the programme.

Sergeant Ray Ellis, 425 Bty

Captain William Pringle was acting as forward observation officer in his Honey tank with the 3rd County of London Yeomanry, when they ran into a battery of German 88mm guns. Led by their Colonel the tanks just charged straight at the guns without any tactical sophistication whatsoever.

He spun round and waved his flag, "Yoiks, tally ho to it, tally ho, tally ho!" A bit childish, we were there to win a war as far as I was concerned. When I eventually got him on the radio, because he wouldn't answer to start with, he told me that he knew where he was going, what he intended to do and that it was my job to do as I was told! We went straight at them. The barrels were facing that way. The first gun was on him in seconds and BWHUUFF – he'd gone and the whole lot came to a screaming halt, there was total chaos everywhere. The tank I was in had a burst petrol tank so they'd tied 100 gallons in 5 gallon tins on the back with string! I tried to bring some gunfire down on the positions, but there was that much smoke and dust around you couldn't see it! I thought, "Well, there's only one place for Pringle and that's out of here!" The British government spent a lot of time training me – I was an expensive asset! I said to the driver, "Turn round and get on back!" "I can't!" I said, "Why not?" "Can't get it into gear the clutch has gone!" I said, "Stop your engine and start it", "I've tried that, Sir, it doesn't work!" I told him to, "Rev it up, full revs, put the gear in a reverse position, then let me get my feet in it and I'll see if I can push it in with my legs!" . The Honey gear lever went down into the entrails of the tank. The first time it didn't go in. There was a right old battle going on outside of the tank, but I was more interested in getting this bloody engine started. There was no getting out on foot because you'd have been shot to bits. I said,

204

"Keep the revs on whatever you do and if we go don't you stop!!"
I straightened my legs, the tank gave one hell of a bunny jump and
kept going backwards. We reversed seven miles! I told the chap,
"Don't you stop, I'll murder you if you stop!"

Captain William Pringle, **425 Bty**

The guns moved forward as planned, but they were soon aware of the
mistake the British generals had made in deciding that Rommel was
retreating.

> After the barrage was fired it was, "Cease Firing! Rear limber
> up!" We closed down, clamped the gun, hooked it onto the limber,
> the gun towers came up and we moved into the advance as the
> whole front moved forwards. It was just before dawn when we
> came up to this crest and everything opened up around us. He was
> waiting for us – he must have had it all ranged and ready – because
> the very first shells landed right among us. It was appalling. The
> sky ahead was a sea of flames as all their guns opened up. It was
> carnage but we just kept going because what the hell else could we
> do?

Sergeant Ray Ellis, **425 Bty**

The SNH had run into a trap.

> I have never seen anything like it. In the distance there was this
> big arc of little tongues of fire. I realized to my horror that this was
> practically the whole of the Afrika Corps waiting for us. Soon after
> the first flashes, everything fell on us. The fire was absolutely
> murder. We were on this down slope and they were sitting on the
> edge of this shallow bowl. Absolute chaos, that really was the
> beginning of the end.

Signal Lance Sergeant Ted Whittaker, **425 Bty**

In the face of this fire the guns dropped into action in a hollow. The
seriousness of the situation was obvious as the gun positions were,
'intended for the support of infantry and not defence'.[153] It was in every
way a bad place to have been caught.

> It was a little bit like a saucer, sloping upwards from the centre.
> We were put in position on a very exposed piece of ground with
> the enemy in front of us where they could see us better than we
> could see them. They had the opportunity of coming round both
> of our flanks underneath the lips of the saucer. From the moment
> we dug ourselves in as best we could, it never felt like a happy
> place to be.

Sergeant John Walker, **425 Bty**

As Harold Thompson found any differences between the ranks tended
to evaporate in such moments. 'I can remember when we were moving
into our last stand, my officer was stood up with his head poking out.

He said to me, "Are you frightened?", I says, "I am!" because there were shells bursting all over the place. He says, "Yes, and so am I!"

To the left of 425 Bty were the survivors of D Troop of 520 Battery; whilst 426 Bty was to the right and slightly in front. In all they had 21 guns. The battle began in earnest.

> On 5 June we had a major attack on us which culminated in the evening in them taking up positions almost on our doorstep. Although they didn't overrun us, they were able to stay where they were instead of withdrawing, finding protected positions for their tanks. I remember shooting with a rifle at Germans digging in. It was a very unpleasant sensation having a rest on the evening of the 5th knowing that they were going to start an attack. Most of us actually went to sleep and, this might sound very far fetched, but I put my pyjamas on! But I don't think anybody had more than an hour or so's sleep. It wouldn't be until about eleven when things were quiet and we were ready at our posts by three in the morning.

Sergeant John Walker, **425 Bty**

The situation was truly dire. The guns were in a basin with only a few British tanks between them and the best part of two German Panzer divisions, who were gradually working round the open flanks to surround the whole position. Throughout the night the officers conferred amongst each other with mounting alarm.

> The tanks kept creeping closer and more of them seemed to be around. We couldn't see our tanks anywhere until that night we saw them behind us trailing away up to the north which was the last place they should have gone. The British High Command said that all the German tanks were up north and the ones that were opposite us were wooden ones! Well I nearly exploded because we'd been in the desert three years, we'd seen every German tank that ever came into the bloody desert and if we didn't flipping well know then I didn't know who the devil did! I went and saw Peter Birkin and played hell and said if we don't get out of here tonight we've had it. He agreed with me and we both went to the Colonel.  He said, he'd put it to the Divisional Command. I said we'd got to have more ammunition and a lot of it! He said, "Don't worry, Bill, don't worry, there's plenty of ammunition on the way!" I said, "Well, I hope it gets here before daylight!" He said, "Why?" I said, "The German tanks are round behind and they'll shoot it up!" "How do you know?" "I can hear them!" You can't move tanks around without making a horrible squawking of tracks and God knows what! I was annoyed, probably wrongly, with his lack of ability to convince Higher Command that they'd got it wrong.

Captain William Pringle, **425 Bty**

206

Panzerkampfwagen MkIII advancing against British positions. With the German break-through around the southern flank of the Gazala Line the SNH were ordered to stand and fight to the last round.

The SNH had been given orders by Major-General Herbert Lumsden commanding the 1st Armoured Division, that they were to 'stand and fight to the last man and the last round'.[154] Nevertheless, in view of the situation, the senior officers asked for permission to withdraw.

> Just before dawn, I got through to our Brigadier, Brigadier Carr. I told him the situation was untenable, but I thought with the help of all my smoke shells, I could get the wounded out, most of the guns and what few men remained.[155]

Major Robert Daniell, **Regimental Headquarters**

Daniell's intention was to take advantage of the known reluctance of German tanks to advance into areas masked by smoke shells, to withdraw the SNH back towards the Knightsbridge escarpment. He met with short shrift from Brigadier Carr.

> He said, "Bob, you are to stand and fight in the position where you are now, you are not to move! Do you understand me? You are not to move at all!" I told him that if I obeyed I would lose every single man I had. He replied, "You are a Horse Artillery officer, you have been properly brought up and you know that in battle you will obey orders, or take the consequences".

Major Robert Daniell, **Regimental Headquarters**

It seemed that, rightly or wrongly, the SNH were considered expendable in the overall scheme of things.

> It was dark and cold and I was standing by the gun when two figures approached, Captain Slinn and Lieutenant Timms. They stopped for a chat and I asked, "What's the situation, Sir?" Captain Slinn said, "We're being left to fight a rearguard, Sergeant. We're going to stop and its one of these fight to the last man and last round jobs! Its going to be a bloody awful day. I think there will be very few of us left alive at the end of this day."

Sergeant Ray Ellis, **425 Bty**

As the infantry of 10th Indian Brigade had been driven back, the SNH were almost totally exposed to attack from both German tanks and infantry when dawn broke on 6 June. They were also almost completely cut off and, as Pringle had suspected, the supply column carrying ammunition, petrol and food was faced with a difficult, if not impossible, task.

We got there more or less at first light and it was quite obvious that the Germans had practically surrounded them. This Lieutenant came to me and he said, "Quartermaster, I'm going to take the petrol and ammunition in. Its up to you to take back all the other soft vehicles with the food and everything". I rounded the others up and told them and suddenly he came dashing up and said, "I'm taking the lot through!" I think really he was after a medal, I can't think of any other reason, because what he did was stupid. As we went in we were actually machine-gunned. I'd got a driver who'd just come out from England – not very good, certainly not very brave. As we were machine-gunned he almost went to pieces and said, "What do I do? What do I do?" I said, "Drive on, and put your so and so foot down!" He did and we got in just as the Germans closed the ring. The first thing I saw was all the petrol trucks we brought in going up in flames.

Quartermaster Sergeant Charles Ward, **426 Bty**

The ring was now closed and there were clear signs of impending disaster. 'The Stukas came over and I looked out and there was purple smoke all round us. That was the identification system for the Jerries. It showed them where their positions were and we were completely surrounded.'[156] Their British tank support, which had withdrawn overnight, had not returned.

During the night they told us not to be alarmed: the British tanks were going out to re-fuel and re-arm. On 6th June we stood to from before first light. As it got light we looked up the ridge and there were the tanks in position – we could just see the tops of them silhouetted. As it got a bit lighter we knew we were for it – they were German tanks hull down.

Signal Lance Sergeant Ted Whittaker, **425 Bty**

The young gunners realized that it really would be a fight to the death.

Then you knew that was it! I felt shattered. How does a young man feel when he thinks his life's going to finish there and then... You'd made a picture in your mind of the Germans and he was about nine feet tall, big, strong and swarthy – invincible.

Bombardier Albert Parker, **425 Bty**

The fighting re-commenced early on 6 June.

The infantry laid low and we carried on shooting where

appropriate, but the tanks didn't come forward so fast on the immediate front. But there was the roar of the tank engines coming up the sides. It was a much more confused battle than the 27th. It was very confused, fast, we were shooting like mad. I remember shooting at both lorried infantry and tanks. We still never got hit ourselves, not even by a machine-gun bullet, yet they were spurting along near us all the time.

Sergeant John Walker, **425 Bty**

The gun layers had a difficult task in keeping their guns trained on the ducking, weaving tanks as they approached the SNH position. Even a direct hit would not necessarily cripple a tank unless it hit in a vulnerable part.

If the tank was going sideways from right to left, or left to right, we had to hit him in the tracks. If the tank was coming for you, as it moved up and down, we had to try and aim for the belly. If not the belly then the top of the gun, which should have knocked his turret off. That was how we were trained to hit them. Although I say it myself we were good! Sergeant Faulkner was at the trail giving orders and at the same time looking for any danger to the left or right. I was laying the gun. On the telescope you've got a cross and you would wait for the tank to come across there and as he got there you would say, "On! On! On! Fire!" You would fire just as the tank's nose reached the cross allowing for the distance.

Gunner Dennis Mayoh, **426 Bty**

The first attack was beaten off and the Germans withdrew.

They wheeled off and went back. Once they were out of effective range, we stopped firing, because we were concerned with ammunition. I doubt if we had more than twenty rounds per gun of armour-piercing, so I always tried to keep a few in reserve, so that if something did get through and was looking really dangerous, at least I'd got an armour-piercing to pop up the chute as a reserve. Then you cleared all the shell cases from the back of the gun, made sure the ammunition is to hand, generally tidy up the position to make it as efficient as possible. See if you can find a few more stones to pile up in front of the gun or scrape a bit more depth to the slit trench you are in.

Sergeant Ray Ellis, **425 Bty**

Captain Pringle even believed that they could have held out with more ammunition.

You were saying to the chaps as they fired a shot, "For Christ's sake go easy we won't have any left!" I was quite happy we could cope with the situation – we could have done if we'd had enough ammunition. We wanted lorry loads of the damn stuff.

Captain William Pringle, **425 Bty**

Battery Sergeant Major Beardall tried to take up a convoy of ammunition trucks from B Echelon to the guns but, after his tank escort and 12 of the 15 lorries were destroyed by enemy fire, he was forced to turn back. Gradually the German pressure began to grow.

> They brought in their artillery and we heard it open up. You think, "Oh, bloody hell!" Then that started to fall among us. Then we took cover, that's when you get in your slit trench and you hide behind any little rock you can find. If you press flat you could probably get your body under the ground, but the hams of my bottom were probably just sticking above the surface! They called in their airforce as well and it was absolutely devastating. The noise, the bombs crashing down, shells at the same time, all onto the area round the guns.
>
> **Sergeant Ray Ellis, 425 Bty**

Again the German tanks rumbled forward and by then the SNH had suffered severe casualties, with most of the gun teams sorely depleted.

> In the middle of the morning they came again with their tanks and they got very close. Their artillery were still firing, the Stuka raids were coming over regularly and when the tanks attacked you had got to get out of your slit trench and go and sit on the gun amidst all the shell fire, machine-gun fire and cannon fire from the tanks. The air was just alive with red hot steel. I hit a Mark IV tank and it slewed round and burst into flames. The next thing I remember I was in the air as if someone had picked me up and thrown me in the air – spinning in the air! We'd had a direct hit on the gun. I dropped, 'WHHOOMPH', on to the ground. I lay there a second or two dazed and then, before I picked myself up, I went up spinning in the air again and dropped again. This time I think I was unconscious for a short time. An 88 millimetre had dropped two shells straight on the gun position. When I came round I was dazed and I can remember kneeling and hearing the battle going on in a dazed sort of way. I stayed like that for quite a long time. Then it went quiet again and I realized the tanks had been fought off. I looked round and my gun was upside down and the crew were draped on the floor all round. I thought I must be wounded but I couldn't feel anything. My shirt and body was all black my clothes were all blood stained and I was in a hell of a state. The whole crew had been killed and my next thought was for self preservation – a very strong instinct – "Get your head down Ray!" I found a little hole, lay in it and started to try and build rocks around it. Then the shelling started again and they changed it to air-burst spraying down all their red hot shell splinters.
>
> **Sergeant Ray Ellis, 425 Bty**

The shells burst all around the position – nowhere was safe, 'It was terrifying, like thunder but worse than thunder. They were bursting in the air. Pieces of metal about an inch square coming from right above you.'[157] In such a chaotic situation many of the more specialized members of the batteries found that they had little to do. Thus Signal Sergeant Fred Langford found that, 'There were very few people to communicate with so I was nearly redundant. I just tried to help wherever help was necessary. If people were trying to move a gun, lugging ammunition about.' Similarly Ted Whittaker found himself almost useless as the regiment struggled to survive.

> What use is a forward observation expert when the enemy is on your position – its like the proverbial spare at the wedding. I've never felt so helpless. I had a word with my mates, told them what the Colonel had said – "We've only got to hang on twelve hours" – and the reply to that was, "A fat lot of f******* use that's going to be...!"
>
> *Signal Lance Sergeant Ted Whittaker,* **425 Bty**

Two of 426 Bty headquarters staff had the rare experience of playing children's games under heavy fire.

> During the last hour or more I was with this chap Sergeant Buckley and we were pinned down completely. He was an amazing bloke, he got out a piece of paper, drew on it and said, "Let's have a game of Battleships!" There we were in this slit trench playing 'Battleships' with all this hell let loose.
>
> *Quartermaster Sergeant Charles Ward,* **426 Bty**

Charles Ward

One person who was kept busy was the new Regimental Medical Officer, Captain A McFarlane, and his Medical Orderly Harry Day. 'We set up a regimental aid post in and around a three tonner truck with canvas covering in a shallow depression. Inside the truck were four stretchers. In the space of half an hour we had thirty casualties or more and as the morning went on the casualties grew.'[158] Bombardier Albert Parker used his truck to bring in the wounded, 'People were scattered all over the place. One bloke was like a rag doll – no arms, no legs, smoking – it frightened me to death.' In these circumstances the medical staff were severely over-stretched.

> I had great difficulty in restraining men suffering from shock and in a comatose condition from walking away from the comparative shelter of the shallow basin around the truck and walking towards the enemy guns. One had to be very careful, they were very badly wounded and they had to be slowly shepherded back. They didn't know where they were going, they wanted to go away.
>
> *Medical Orderly Harry Day,* **Regimental Headquarters**

All this had to be carried out under shell-fire.

One of the wounded in the truck had a compound fracture of the humerus. The doctor was replacing the splint and the man's head was resting on my thigh as I was kneeling on the floor of the truck. An armour-piercing shell came straight through the truck and took the man's head completely off. I rolled over with the near miss and my shorts were covered with his blood.

Medical Orderly Harry Day, **Regimental Headquarters**

Shells constantly burst all around the SNH position and it seemed only a matter of time before everyone received a wound of some description.

I saw, looking out the rear of my truck, a shell air-burst felled Captain Slinn and Lieutenant Timms. They had severe head wounds. It was within 12 foot of the rear of my vehicle and I got out to see if I could do anything, but Pete Birkin told me to get back in and leave it to the MO and his orderly.

Lance Bombardier Signaller Frank Knowles, **425 Bty**

Frank Knowles

The over-stretched medical team tried to respond to the calls for help.

A runner came across from 425 Bty Headquarters where we had seen airbursts and one such had mortally wounded Captain Slinn and Lieutenant Timms. The Doctor went across and a few minutes later the runner came back again and asked me to go across with another medical pannier. He went and I saw him within a few yards blown to bits. I put the medical pannier on my back and I ran zig zag across to 425 Headquarters. The Doctor had received an injury in the knee and Captain Slinn and Lieutenant Timms were both taken by stretcher back to the RAP. I put my arm around the Doctor to assist him back and he told me to walk in front, at first I couldn't understand this order, but obviously one of us had to be left alive. Had a shell burst when we were both together, it would have killed us both and nobody of any consequence would have been left to look after the wounded. Eventually we arrived back at the RAP. The men's wounds were … I can't elaborate, they were beyond talking about. The actual decision about giving these men a lethal dose of morphine rested entirely with the Doctor who was completely justified. That included Captain Slinn and Lieutenant Timms – they would never have been normal human beings again. It was a relief for them and it was my duty to do it by hypodermic syringe under the instructions of the Doctor.

Captain Graham Slinn

MO Orderly Harry Day

Medical Orderly Harry Day, **Regimental Headquarters**

Shortly after this Frank Knowles was hit.

You could see clouds of dust and flashes. I received a leg wound from shrapnel or rock splinters – we were on hard ground. I was lying beside the pick-up. 'Cheddar Turner' rolled me into a slit trench and applied a field dressing.

Lance Bombardier Signaller Frank Knowles, **425 Bty**

As casualties mounted Ted Whittaker realized the grim extent of their losses. 'I began to realise that these were my friends, people I knew...' Nothing could be done to staunch the flow of casualties.

I was sitting there passing messages when all of a sudden there was a bloody great bang. It filled with cordite and smoke. I remember Walter shouting, "Jack! Jack!" I was pretty well half unconscious because the shell had hit underneath my seat and I got the blast of it. I was wounded in my arms, back and knee. I remember he dragged me out and put me at the bottom of the slit trench. After that I took no further part in it.

Signal Sergeant Jack Sykes, 426 Bty

The German tanks came ever closer to the position. 'Three tanks appeared around the escarpment, Dr McFarlane said, "Harry, we're saved. Its the Gloucester Hussars!". I said, "Sir, the Gloucester Hussars don't have white crosses on them!"'[159] Last ditch resistance continued and as gun teams were knocked out scratch teams formed to try and keep the guns firing. Major Daniell struggled to form scratch gun teams to replace the dead gunners.

I heard Major Daniell shouting, "Are there some gunners? I've got a 25 pounder here – somebody man it." I thought, "I can't sit here". I jumped up and said, "Here, Sir!" and there were two other fellows. He said, "There's a few rounds in there you might as well fire them". Then off he drove. There was this German tank a few hundred yards away. I guessed the range. There were three rounds, no armour-piercing. We loaded this HE and fired and it went over the top of this tank. The turret turned and WHHUMP. To my horror I was the only one standing. The machine-gun bullets had gone straight through the gun shield.

Signal Lance Sergeant Ted Whittaker, 425 Bty

Ellis who had recovered from being blown up made his way over to a crewless gun.

A shell burst right over Number One gun and the crew just fell to the ground and nobody moved. It occurred to me that with two guns out of action that was half the strength of the troop gone and the next time they put in an attack this could mean they would get through. With a great deal of reluctance I got out of my hole and went over to Number One gun. The gun was in a parlous state, the shield was all riddled, at least one of the tyres was flat, but it was workable. From somewhere men started to appear – they were signallers or specialists or drivers, but they helped to man the gun. These men were not gunners but you could tell them what to do.

Sergeant Ray Ellis, 425 Bty

The tanks were now very close and the makeshift gun teams were suffering heavy casualties.

As one was mown down then somebody else appeared. It eventually got to the point where they were not just South Notts Hussars, they were strangers. I remember a man from the Royal Corps of Signals coming on to the gun position. This man caught a burst of machine-gun fire right in the bottom part of his body, he jumped in the air then fell to the ground. I looked at this lad and he was frightened – his eyes were terrified. I crouched down to try and console him, all the noise going on round, "You're all right lad, you're all right, don't worry you're not badly wounded we'll soon have you away, I reckon you've got a Blighty!" Trying to ease his fear. I noticed the sand was settling on his eyes, he was dead, he died in my arms.

Sergeant Ray Ellis, 425 **Bty**

It was a brave fight, but stocks of armour-piercing shells were now exhausted and with hindsight many of the survivors now believe that the regiment's resistance continued longer than was strictly necessary for sensible military reasons. It appears that the driving force behind this resistance was Major Daniell. As we have seen Brigadier Carr had invoked his pride as a Regular Royal Horse Artillery officer. Daniel had accepted the challenge and no longer cared for the consequences of prolonged resistance.

Never mind. We were told to stand and fight to the last man and the last round and that's what we did! I was directly given the order and I had no idea of surrender at all. My natural inclination had been to move the whole bloody lot half a day earlier and get them out of trouble. I never would order anybody to surrender and no Horse Artillery gunner officer has ever surrendered.

Major Robert Daniell, **Regimental Headquarters**

The action he took was quite remarkable and had its antecedents in the Napoleonic age of warfare.

I knew that the guns behind me had no ammunition. I knew that Barber's battery had got ammunition if I could get guns to it. If I could get the four guns together I could face four ways. I could therefore stop any tank from running over them. You must remember I'd seen the German tank run right over the British gun. I found these two guns and shouted to them to follow me, I was in my 8cwt truck and I started to drive off towards Barber's position. I never saw them again.

Major Robert Daniell, **Regimental Headquarters**

His last ditch orders were a death sentence to many of the men who struggled to obey.

There was ammunition exploding, gun limbers and ammunition trucks blowing up. Flames, smoke, horrible stink of gun powder. I went up to E Troop, I thought I might as well be with my pals. Major Daniell drove up and shouted, "Form British square, go and form up on 426 Bty". They were over to our right. The gunners went to hook the guns in and I went to get on the limber of the first gun in the troop. There were two or three chaps sitting on the limber. The nearest one, Harrison, was a Derby County footballer. They told me to "F off". The truck was moving and I put one foot in the foot rest, so I was hanging on the side of the door. We went a few yards and there was the most horrible explosion, the most enormous crash – it brought us to a standstill. There was some awful moans and it was a terrible sight: this shell had hit these blokes and this poor Harrison was practically in half... I dropped off the door and threw myself flat. The driver Stevenson, had got half out of the door and the next armour-piercing shell came straight through the driving cab and he was left hanging over the door. I was absolutely horrified at what had happened to these people I had been talking to only minutes before. I felt I could have sat down and cried.

Signal Lance Sergeant Ted Whittaker, **425 Bty**

Gun Sergeant John Walker can only have been a few feet from Whittaker when the shells hit the gun towers from point blank range.

Our Second in Command Major Daniell drove on the position in a staff car and he told us to pull our guns out and form "a hollow British square". He immediately pushed off – he didn't stay there to organize it. I was able to pull my gun out, my driver came up with the vehicle, I hitched in and we started to climb into the vehicle when a shell came right through my driver and the front of the vehicle. The vehicle was wrecked and my driver was killed and we decided that was enough. There was nothing we could do. The German tank was about fifteen yards away, no more. Other guns on the same site had already surrendered and they were just driving through us.

Sergeant John Walker, **425 Bty**

Captain Pringle's E Troop suffered the most by Daniell's intervention.

Captain William Pringle

The first thing I knew was a gun was going across my rear heading north. It was nonsensical it broke up what was a very tenable position. Straight into the tanks. They never got where they were supposed to get to – they couldn't have got to where they were supposed to go – they were shot to bits 20 or 30 yards out of the gun positions. I told the other guns to stay where they were I wasn't going to have them shot up.

Captain William Pringle, **425 Bty**

Major Daniell himself had driven over towards 426 Bty but the truck never made it.

One of the German tanks blew one wheel off my truck. I got out and walked across to where one of the subalterns, Chadburn, was sitting behind a gun in his Honey tank. Behind him were blazing lorries and the place was covered with smoke. It was five o'clock and I knew I had an hour of light to get through before it would be dark. machine-gun fire was very heavy all round. I rolled into the smoke but I found I couldn't breathe in it. So I rolled back again and I was on my way walking across the ground, the machine-gun fire was coming up like hail. I walked as far as Chadburn's gun and I saw a German tank about 120 yards away. He was in his tank and I shouted at him to jump down and help me with the gun and a wounded gunner appeared from somewhere. He and I swung the gun round, loaded it and I pulled the trigger and blew the tank sky high – I couldn't miss it.

Major Robert Daniell, **Regimental Headquarters**

Captain Peal

Colonel Seely had spent the entire day travelling from troop to troop in his Honey tank helping organize the defence wherever needed. Finally the tank was hit and burst into flames. Driver Chadbourne managed to drag out the mortally wounded Adjutant, Captain Peal, but Seely and his wireless officer were trapped and died in the flames. At this stage in the action men could almost choose for themselves whether to live or die, 'Chadburn stood on top of a stationary tank and waved his pistol, shouting and suddenly he was machine-gunned down. You're committing suicide aren't you, there wasn't any point, you couldn't win the battle.'[160] The more pragmatic Captain Pringle decided to surrender but spiked his guns when they had run out of ammunition to prevent them being captured, by a simple but effective method, 'There was no more left to fire – we left the last two rounds to blow the guns up. You put one down one end and one up the other and pull the trigger.' One way or another most of the guns had been destroyed by this time and Ellis believes his was the last in action.

Colonel Seely

Eventually I was left with just one man, a complete stranger, he wasn't a South Notts Hussar, and he was standing on the right of the gun. I was pulling the gun round and aiming at the tank then getting on the seat, aiming and firing. He was opening and closing the breech and I was loading. It was a bit chaotic. I'd just fired a shell and I'd got hold of the trail arm when I heard a machine gun which sounded as if it was a few inches behind me. This man was just splattered as he was flung, spinning against the inside of the gun shield. I looked behind and could see the tank within twenty or thirty yards behind me with the gun still smoking. I tensed myself waiting for this burst of fire which never came. I shall never know whether the gunner had compassion, ran out of ammunition or saw something that distracted him. I like to think he had

Lieutenant Chadburn

compassion realizing that it was the end. Every gun was out of action and as far as I know that was the last shot fired by the regiment.

Sergeant Ray Ellis, **425 Bty**

The fighting was over and the cost of resistance was horribly clear to the few survivors, 'The trenches were full of dead infantrymen. The smell of burning and exploding ammunition – a burning tank, a burning truck, a case of ammunition banging. Fires all over the place.'[161] The fears of those Nottingham parents had been more than justified when they reluctantly waved their children off to war.

I was very, very thirsty and I walked over to Peter Birkin's armoured vehicle. In it were the bodies of the driver and Jim Hardy. He had been cut in two but his water bottle was sort of hanging there. I got my knife, cut his webbing, took the water bottle and drank this lukewarm water from old Jim's bottle. I looked down at his lifeless face and I just burst into tears – reaction I suppose – seeing an old pal from the day I joined the regiment.

Sergeant Ray Ellis, **425 Bty**

Sergeant Ted Whittaker

Captain Pringle was captured and a German officer told him, "We said we'd get you South Notts boys at the finish!" Surrender was almost inevitable as the German tanks rolled over the gun position.

A big clank, clank, clank right on the side of me and a German tank stopped. A German officer, with his cap on and earphone, leaned out and said, "Where are you going?". I looked at him and made the classic remark, "With you!" "Hop up", he said, "For you the war is over!"

Signal Lance Sergeant Ted Whittaker, **425 Bty**

Signal Sergeant Jack Sykes lay wounded in a slit trench: 'the next thing I looked up and there was this German officer looking and they dragged me out. He said, "For you the war is over!"' Some did try to escape in the confusion of the battlefield. John Walker and his gun crew tried to sneak away into the desert.

I told my men to take what they could – greatcoat, water bottle, anything they could grab. The firing had ceased. We lay down and the tank that was closest moved past and probably assumed we were dead. We lay down for no more than a minute, then we slowly edged away, walked backwards almost until we were a hundred yards away. The machine guns on the tanks were hustling men into groups but we moved away east. We started to walk in a proper sense, looking for a vehicle. There were four of us. We got away for an hour-and-a-half and we got out of sight. A German scout car came along, they must have just spotted movement, three men jumped out with guns and said "*Hände Hoch!*" We put our hands up. They took our revolvers off us. One of them said in English, "For you the war is ended!"

Sergeant John Walker, **425 Bty**

*Sergeant
John Walker*

The Germans certainly seem to have shown a grasp of at least one line of their phrase books! Ironically, in view of the devastation his orders had unleashed, Major Daniell escaped.'The awful noise of battle ceased completely. A solitary lark flew up into the sunset sky. I prayed for a miracle and my prayer was answered.'[162] He was absolutely determined not to surrender under any circumstances. As he tried to persuade his driver to accompany him in a last desperate bid for freedom, he encapsulated many of the contrasts lurking behind the facade of the British Army: apparently hidebound regular traditions; territorial courage allied with pragmatism; if and when to surrender; valour in the face of insuperable odds; suicidal actions when nothing of any military value could be achieved.

I walked back to my vehicle, which I saw about 40 yards away, by this time it was half past five. There were Germans collecting wounded and picking up dead here, there and everywhere. The driver said, "I've just changed the wheel", I said, "Thank God for that! You've got one minute to make your mind up! Do you see those six German tanks that are approaching in line towards this position – I'm going to drive straight for them, they will be taken by surprise and unable to swing round their turrets to open up with their machine-guns". He said, "Major, you are asking to be killed, I'm sorry but I'm going to leave you." He went to the back of his truck, took out his bundle and I saw him walk off to join two or three Germans carrying some wounded. I jumped in my truck and did what I said! I drove straight for the tanks. Five of them were unable to get their turrets round. One did and blew off my canopy at the back of the 8cwt. I swung hard left, right round them.

*Major
Robert Daniell*

Major Robert Daniell, **Regimental Headquarters**

After many tribulations and with his usual unbelievable luck he managed to regain the British lines. Behind him the shocked survivors who had looked to him for leadership had learnt something about both themselves and the nature of war.

A German tank rolled up and there was a German with his head poking out the top and he just beckoned me up onto the tank. I jumped up there and I could see he was a sergeant. We looked at one another, we'd been fighting each other all day and we both shrugged our shoulders and looked up to heaven – what a bloody silly thing it was! It was a matter of two enemies who had no enmity.

*Sergeant
Ray Ellis*

Sergeant Ray Ellis, **425 Bty**

218

For most of the SNH originals the war really was over and the unit had temporarily ceased to exist as a fighting force. The captured survivors faced three years as POWs in North Africa, Italy and Germany. The regiment was reformed by new drafts grafted on to the very few who escaped the carnage. As first 107 Battery and then, on reformation in March 1944 as 107 Medium Regiment, they continued to serve with great distinction throughout the war in North Africa, Sicily and North West Europe. But none of the regiment ever forgot the disaster and even now more than fifty years later many of the survivors are re-united every year at the Regimental Association's 'Knightsbridge Dinner' held in Nottingham in remembrance of their less fortunate comrades who died in the Cauldron.

Casualties – South Notts Hussars, 1939-1942
Commonwealth War Graves Commission

Alder, Gunner James William 1097323
Died: 6 June 1942 aged 35 Knightsbridge War Cemetery, Acroma, Libya, Plot 12, Row D, Grave 5
Husband of Ethel Alder of Cheltenham, Gloucestershire.

Bailey, Sergeant William Henry 852471
Died: 1 December 1941 aged 23 Tobruk War Cemetery, Libya, Plot 7, Row J, Grave 4
Husband of Doris Bailey of Aldercar, Derbyshire.

Balls, Gunner Alfred Jones 556094
Died: 5 June 1942 aged 28. Alamein Memorial, Egypt, Col.12
Husband of Mary Balls of Smethwick, Staffordshire.

Barber, Captain Colin Browne 50166
Died: 6 June 1942 aged 29 Benghazi War Cemetery, Plot 8, Row D, Grave 12
Son of Walter and Violet Barber of Hucknall, Notts.

Barker, Lance Sergeant Arthur George 784856
Died: 5 December 1941 aged 31 Alamein Memorial, Egypt Column 11
Husband of V Barker of Westcliff-on-Sea, Essex.

Barnes, Gunner Arthur Edward 850514
Died: 6 June 1942 aged 21 Alamein Memorial, Egypt Col.12
Son of Albert and Gertrude Barnes of Battle, Sussex.

Batt, Major Edgar Cossley 31527
Died: 8 October 1940 aged 35 Alexandria (Chatby) Military and War Memorial Cemetery, Egypt, Row N Grave 19
Son of Lt Col Reginald Batt and Violet Batt of Norwich, Norfolk.

Bennett, Gunner Joseph 938461
Died: 27 May 1942 aged 23 Alamein Memorial, Egypt Col.12
Son of Thomas and Emily Bennett of Hadfield, Derbyshire.

Birkin, Major Philip Gervaise (Known as Gerry) 50165
Died: 27 May 1942 aged 33 Knightsbridge War Cemetery, Acroma, Libya, Plot 4, Row E, Grave 20
Son of Major Philip Birkin and Frances Birkin of Birmingham.

Bland, Sergeant Patrick Selwyn Fraser 896291
Died: 27 May 1942 aged 22 Alamein Memorial, Egypt Col.10
Son of William and Florence Bland of Nottingham.

Bleakley, Gunner James 902237
Died: 14 September 1941 aged 25 Tobruk War Cemetery, Libya, Plot 6, Row H, Grave 2
Son of Mr and Mrs J W Bleakley of Bolton, Lancashire.

Bucknall, Gunner John Geoffrey 896290
Died: 6 June 1942 aged 26 Knightsbridge War Cemetery, Acroma, Libya, Plot 10, Row J, Grave 18
Husband of Margaret Bucknall of Basford, Nottingham.

Carr, Lieutenant Arthur Angus Philip 91535
Died: 27 May 1942 aged 24 Knightsbridge War Cemetery, Acroma, Libya, Plot 4, Row E, Joint Grave 14
Son of Arthur and Ivy Carr of Knightsbridge, London.

Carrigan, Gunner Edward 2753053
Died: 16 June 1942 aged 31 Benghazi War Cemetery, Libya, Plot 8, Row G, Grave 4
Husband of Mary Carrigan of Glasgow.

Chadburn, Captain Alan William 85442
Died: 6 June 1942 aged 25 Knightsbridge War Cemetery, Acroma, Libya, Plot 11, Row B, Grave 18
Son of Claude and Ethel Chadburn of Popplewick, Notts.

Charles, Lance Bombardier Frederick 866384
Died: 7 June 1942 aged 21 Knightsbridge War Cemetery, Acroma, Plot 4, Row H, Grave 13
Son of Percy and Ethel Charles of Carrington, Notts.

Clark, Second Lieutenant Harry Reginald Dixon 85443
Died: 26 August 1940 Cairo War Memorial Cemetery, Egypt, Plot P Grave 252
No next of kin details.

Collihole, Lance Sergeant Philip Hunter 892633
Died: 1 May 1941 aged 28 Tobruk War Cemetery, Libya, Plot 3, Row P, Grave 13
Husband of Isabella Collihole of Belfast.

Collins, Gunner Albert William 938449
Died: 29 April 1941 aged 22 Tobruk War Cemetery, Libya, Plot 3, Row O, Grave 9
Husband of Lois Collins of Small Heath, Birmingham.

Cooke, Gunner Dennis 1115711
Died: 6 June 1942 aged 22 Knightsbridge War Cemetery, Acroma, Libya, Plot 12, Row A, Grave 15
Son of Henry and Annie Cooke of Mansfield, Notts.

Corry, Lance Bombardier Walter 1443468
Died: 6 June 1942 aged 23 Alamein Memorial, Egypt, Col.12
Son of Joseph and Ethel Corry of Osgodby, Yorkshire.

Coyle, Gunner George 1101215
Died: 6 June 1942 aged 33 Alamein Memorial, Egypt, Col.12
Husband of Olive Coyle of Manchester.

Denny, Lance Bombardier Charles Patrick 529281
Died: 11 October 1941 Tobruk War Cemetery, Libya, Plot 6, Row N, Grave 5
Husband of Annie Denny of Twickenham, Middlesex.

Dexter, Gunner Frederick Thomas 852045
Died: 30 November 1941 aged 23 Knightsbridge War Cemetery, Acroma, Libya, Plot 10, Row G, Grave 12
No next of kin details.

Flannery, Gunner William 961627
Died: 12 June 1942 aged 31 Benghazi War Cemetery, Libya, Plot 8, Row D, Grave 8
Husband of Emily Flannery of Stockport, Cheshire.

Fox, Gunner Arthur 871867
Died: 29 November 1941 aged 21 Tobruk War Cemetery, Libya, Plot 8, Row H, Grave 7
Son of John and May Fox of Lenton, Notts.

Freeman, Gunner Herbert Francis 852536
Died: 6 September 1940 aged 34 El Alamein War Cemetery, Plot 29, Row J, Grave 5
Husband of Elizabeth Freeman of Leicester.

Godden, Gunner Charley 937759
Died: 27 May 1942 aged 23 Alamein Memorial, Egypt, Col.13
Son of John and Elizabeth Godden of Rochester, Kent.

Gorman, Gunner Thomas 1085142
Died: 6 June 1942 Alamein Memorial, Egypt, Column 13
No next of kin details.

Granshaw, Gunner Arthur 977861
Died: 13 June 1942 aged 27 Halfaya Sollum War Cemetery, Egypt, Plot 11 Row H, Grave 9
Son of Rebecca Granshaw of Walthamstow, Essex.

Gray, Gunner George Sidney 898062
Died: 6 June 1942 aged 21 Alamein Memorial, Egypt, Col.13
Son of George and Ethel Gray of Gateshead, Co Durham.

Hall, Gunner Ronald Hubert 909137
Died: 4 December 1941 aged 21 Knightsbridge War Cemetery, Acroma, Libya, Plot 12, Row E, Grave 14
Son of Harry and Florence Hall of West Bridgford, Nottingham.

Hanlon, Bombardier Harry 974445
Died: 6 June 1942 aged 26 Alamein Memorial, Egypt, Col.11

Husband of Annie Hanlon of Middleton, Manchester.

Hardy, Battery Sergeant Major James Henry 852477
Died: 6 June 1942 aged 24 Knightsbridge War Cemetery, Acroma, Libya, Plot 11, Row B, Grave 20
Husband of Edna Hardy of Radford, Notts.

Harrison, Lance Bombardier Albert Richard 900997
Died: 6 June 1942 aged 33 Knightsbridge War Cemetery, Acroma, Libya, Plot 12, Row A, Grave 22
No next of kine details.

Hayward, Lance Bombardier Harry George 938915
Died: 6th June 1942 aged 23 Alamein Memorial, Egypt, Col.12
No next of kin details.

Higgins, Gunner James 798692
Died: 8 October 1941 aged 30 Tobruk War Cemetery, Libya, Plot 6, Row M, Grave 8
No next of kin details.

Hill, Lance Bombardier Albert George 904198
Died: 11 October 1941 aged 22 Tobruk War Cemetery, Libya, Plot 6, Row N, Grave 3
Son of William and Kate Hill of Radford, Notts.

Horrobin, Lance Bombardier Herbert 1091958
Died: 6 June 1942 aged 21 Alamein Memorial, Egypt, Col.12
Son of Herbert and Florence Horrobin of Kearsley, Lancashire.

Humphreys, Gunner George Frederick 888231
Died: 6 June 1942 aged 24 Knightsbridge War Cemetery, Acroma, Libya, Plot 2, Row K, Joint Grave 23-24
Son of Ernest and Florence Humphreys of Nottingham.

Humphries, Gunner George Ralph 938380
Died: 29 April 1941 aged 22 Tobruk War Cemetery, Libya, Plot 3, Row O, Grave 8
Son of George and Alice Humphries of Birmingham.

Jones, Gunner Clifford Raymond 986733
Died: 27 May 1942 aged 21 Alamein Memorial, Egypt, Col.13
Son of Daniel and Sarah Jones of New Inn, Carmarthenshire.

Lake, Battery Sergeant Major William Albert 1071589
Died: 6 June 1942 aged 34 Alamein Memorial, Egypt, Col.10
Husband of Janet Lake of Thorpe Lea, Surrey.

Lamb, Lance Sergeant Fred Neville 887234
Died: 27 May 1942 aged 22 Alamein Memorial, Egypt, Col.11
No next of kin details.

Layton, Gunner Harold 1108821
Died: 6 June 1942 aged 29 Alamein Memorial, Egypt, Col.13
Son of John and H Layton of Walworth, London.

Lee, Gunner William 913100
Died: 4 December 1941 aged 35 Knightsbridge War Cemetery, Acroma, Libya, Plot 12, Row E, Grave 15
Husband of Alice Lee of Swinton, Notts.

Lewis, Gunner Thomas 1091180
Died: 6 June 1942 aged 32 Alamein Memorial, Egypt, Col.14
Husband of Glythen Lewis of Pontardawe, Glamorgan.

Lilburn, Bombardier Clifford Herbert 899560
Died: 27 May 1942 aged 24 Knightsbridge War Cemetery, Acroma, Libya, Plot 2, Row D, Grave 8
Son of Herbert and Agnes Lilburn of Leicester.

Lloyd, Gunner William 777891
Died: 27 May 1942 Knightsbridge War Cemetery, Acroma, Libya, Plot 4, Row E, Grave 20
Husband of Isobel Lloyd of Tipton, Staffordshire.

Logan, Gunner Joseph Bill 975828
Died: 8 June 1942 Knightsbridge War Cemetery, Acroma, Libya, Plot 2, Row B, Grave 21
No known next of kin details

Lovesay, Gunner Thomas 1110417
Died: 6 June 1942 aged 32 Knightsbridge War Cemetery,

Acroma, Libya, Plot 12, Row D, Grave 4
No known next of kin details.

Mack, Sergeant Arthur Leonard 865157
Died: 27 November 1941 aged 21 Tobruk War Cemetery, Libya, Plot 7, Row G, Grave 15
Son of Arthur and Alice Mack of Buddington, Notts.

Marsden, Gunner Charles George 978100
Died: 6 June 1942 aged 22 Knightsbridge War Cemetery, Acroma, Libya, Plot 12, Row A, Grave 13
Son of Daniel and Mary Marsden of Wirksworth, Derbyshire.

Martin, Gunner James 892594
Died: 25 November 1941 aged 22 Tobruk War Cemetery, Libya, Plot 7, Row F, Grave 13
Son of Mr and Mrs Joseph Martin of Notts.

Mayes, Sergeant John Charles 1415250
Died: 1 December 1941 aged 39 Knightsridge War Cemetery, Acroma, Libya, Plot 12, Row H, Grave 18
Husband of Annie Mayes of Linby, Notts.

McManus, Gunner Thomas 977463
Died: 6 June 1942 aged 26 Knightsbridge War Cemetery, Acroma, Libya, Plot 11, Row C, Grave 16
No next of kin details.

McMinn, Gunner Lawrence 938922
Died: 6 June 1942 aged 24 Knightsbridge War Cemetery, Acroma, Libya, Plot 4, Row H, Grave 16
Son of Josiah and Elizabeth McMinn of Tunstall, Stoke on Trent.

Mills, Lance Sergeant Ronald 938345
Died: 6 June 1942 aged 23 Alamein Memorial, Egypt, Col.11
Son of Arthur and Louise Mills of Nottingham.

Monsheimer, Gunner William Ernest 807656
Died: 6 June 1942 aged 33 Alamein Memorial, Egypt, Col.14
Husband of Mrs B Monsheimer of New Lenton, Notts.

Morgan, Gunner George Edward 969301
Died: 6 June 1942 aged 25 Alamein Memorial, Egypt, Col.14
Son of Albert and Elisa Morgan of Dinder, Somerset.

Pardon, Gunner Cyril James 983215
Died: 6 June 1942 aged 22 Alamein Memorial, Egypt, Col.14
Son of James and Ellen Pardon of North Lopham, Norfolk

Paulson, Gunner Robert 912360
Died: 16 May 1940 aged 19 Ramleh War Cemetery, Israel, Plot D, Grave 27
No known next of kin details.

Peal, Captain Henry Douglas 113160
Died: 7 June 1942 aged 30 Knightsbridge War Cemetery, Acroma, Libya, Plot 1, Row J, Grave 23
Son of Douglas and Winifred Peal of Ealing, Middlesex

Phillips, Gunner Olaf John 909854
Died: 31 May 1942 aged 21 Knightsbridge War Cemetery, Acroma, Plot 1, Row H, Grave 3
Son of Rowland and Eveline Phillips of Pontrhydyrun, Mon.

Platt, Gunner Arnold 995765
Died: 6 June 1942 aged 25 Knightsbridge War Cemetery, Acroma, Libya, Plot 11, Row B, Grave 23
Son of George and Annie Platt of Stockport, Cheshire.

Powell, Gunner Wilfred 938319
Died: 27 May 1942 aged 23 Knightsbridge War Cemetery, Acroma, Libya, Plot 4, Row E, Grave 8.
No known next of kin details

Reid, Lance Bombardier James William Priest 879345
Died: 6 June 1942 aged 24 Alamein Memorial, Egypt, Col.12
Son of James and Margaret Reid of Farndon, Notts.

Riggall, Gunner Eric George 990160
Died: 27 May 1942 aged 25 Knightsbridge War Cemetery, Acroma, Libya, Plot 4, Row E, Grave 20
Husband of Betty Riggall of Bricket Wood, Hertfordshire.

Robinson, Gunner Herbert 873195
Died: 27 May 1942 aged 25 Knightsbridge War Cemetery, Acroma, Libya, Plot 4, Row E, Grave 14
Husband of Lilian Robinson

Salisbury, Gunner Arthur 782157
Died: 25 March 1941 aged 29 Ismailia War Memorial Cemetery, Egypt, Plot 4 Row D Grave 1
Husband of Dorothy Salisbury of Aspley, Notts.

Seely, Lieutenant Colonel William Evelyn 7281
Died: 6 June 1942 Alamein Memorial, Egypt, Column 10
Husband of Lady Seely

Shepherd, Lance Sergeant Sydney 789294
Died: 27 May 1942 aged 32 Knightsbridge War Cemetery, Acroma, Libya, Plot 4, Row A, Grave 15
Husband of Doris Shepherd of Bulwell, Notts.

Slinn, Captain Graham James Stephen 113163
Died: 6 June 1942 aged 25 Knightsbridge War Cemetery, Acroma, Libya, Plot 12, Row D, Grave 7
Son of Reginald and Eliza Slinn of Thorpeness, Suffolk.

Smedley, Battery Sergeant Major Albert Clifford 888713
Died: 1 May 1941 aged 21 Tobruk War Cemetery, Libya, Plot 3, Row P, Grave 12
Son of Thomas and Florence Smedley of Nottingham.

Barkeley-Smith, Second Lieutenant Brian 179941
Died: 6 June 1942 aged 21 Knightsbridge War Cemetery, Acroma, Libya, Plot 12, Row A, Grave 21
Son of Rupert & Honor Barkley-Smith of Mettingham, Suffolk.

Smith, Lance Bombardier George William 887976
Died: 6 June 1942 aged 29 Alamein Memorial, Egypt, Col.12
Son of George and Esther Smith of Laindon, Essex.

Stanfield, Gunner William 880709
Died: 27 May 1942 aged 22 Alamein Memorial, Egypt, Col.14
Son of Thomas and Mary Stanfield of Cty Armagh, Nrthn Ire.

Steele, Gunner James Eric 1123227
Died: 6 June 1942 Knightsbridge War Cemetery, Acroma, Libya, Plot 12, Row A, Grave 14
Son of George and Caroline Steele of Hull, Yorkshire.

Stevenson, Gunner George 892619
Died: 6 June 1942 aged 21 Knightsbridge War Cemetery, Acroma, Plot 2, Row K, Grave 23-24
Son of Harry and Emma Stevenson of Arnold, Notts.

Tattersall, Gunner Edward 950806
Died: 6 June 1942 aged 22 Alamein Memorial, Egypt, Col.14
Husband of Mrs J O M Tattershall of Chard, Somerset.

Theaker, Lance Bombardier George William 938278
Died: 6 June 1942 aged 23 Alamein Memorial, Egypt, Col.12
Son of Mr and Mrs G Theaker of Staveley, Derbyshire.

Timms, Lieutenant Jeffrey Oliphant 151495
Died: 11 June 1942 aged 29 Benghazi War Cemetery, Libya, Plot 7, Row B, Grave 14
Son of Alec and Margaret Timms of Redhill, Surrey.

Tomlinson, Lance Bombardier Jack Wilfred 894799
Died: 27 May 1942 aged 22 Alamein Memorial, Egypt, Col.12
Son of Wilfred and Elizabeth Tomlinson of Old Basford, Notts.

Tyson, Gunner Robert 934540
Died: 31 May 1942 aged 24 Knightsbridge War Cemetery, Acroma, Libya, Plot 1, Row C, Grave 13
Son of Timothy and Sarah Tyson of Beckermet, Cumberland.

Watson, Gunner Henry Herbert 935653
Died: 6 June 1942 aged 23 Knightsbridge War Cemetery, Acroma, Libya, Plot 12, Row D, Grave 5
Son of Walter and Ada Watson of Ilford, Essex.

York, Gunner Geoffrey Kenneth 883479
Died: 30th November 1941 Knightsbridge War Cemetery, Acroma, Libya, Plot 10, Row G, Grave 11
No known next of kin details

Notes and References

1. Benson Freeman & George Fellows, *Historical Records of the South Nottinghamshire Hussars Yeomanry, 1794-1924*, Gale & Polden, Aldershot, 1928, p 2
2. Freeman & Fellows, *Historical Records of the South Nottinghamshire Hussars Yeomanry, 1794-1924*, p xv
3. Sir Lancelot Rolleston quoted in Freeman & Fellows, *Historical Records of the South Nottinghamshire Hussars Yeomanry, 1794-1924*, p 295
4. Sir Lancelot Rolleston quoted in Freeman & Fellows, *Historical Records of the South Nottinghamshire Hussars Yeomanry, 1794-1924*, (Foreword)
5. Known as 107 (South Notts Hussars) Regiment, Royal Horse Artillery
6. George Pearson, SR 10912, Reel 2
7. John Whitehorn, SR 11466, Reel 1
8. Ray Ellis, SR 12660, Reel 1
9. Frank Knowles, SR 11465, Reel 1
10. Charles Ward, SR 14728, Reel 2
11. As Major Gibson he was second in command of the regiment in 1944-1945

12. George Pearson, SR 10912, Reel 3
13. John Whitehorn, SR 11466, Reel 2
14. Fred Langford, SR 12240, Reel 2
15. Harry Day, SR 12412, Reel 1
16. Ted Holmes, SR 12409, Reel 1
17. Charles Laborde, SR 15103, Reel 3
18. Ray Ellis, SR 12660, Reel 2
19. Harry Day, SR 12412, Reel 1
20. Ray Ellis, SR 12660, Reel 3
21. Charles Laborde, SR 15103, Reel 3
22. Bob Hingston, SR 14789, Reel 5
23. Reg McNish, SR 12435, Reel 2
24. John Walker, SR 11464, Reel 4
25. Bill Hutton, SR 11957, Reel 2
26. George Pearson, SR 10912, Reel 3
27. Bill Hutton, SR 11957, Reel 2
28. Ted Whittaker, SR 12409, Reel 4
29. Albert Swinton, SR 14104, Reel 2
30. Ray Ellis, SR 12660, Reel 4
31. Norman Tebbett, SR 12410, Reel 4
32. Ted Whittaker, SR 12409, Reel 5
33. John Walker, SR 11464, Reel 4
34. Victor Harrold, SR 12682, Reel 1
35. Ray Ellis, SR 12660, Reel 5

36. ANONYMOUS
37. ANONYMOUS
38. Harold Thompson, SR 12242, Reel 5
39. Ray Ellis, SR 12660, Reel 6
40. Ted Holmes, SR 12409, Reel 3
41. Bill Adams, SR 14791, Reel 3
42. George Pearson, SR 10912, Reel 3
43. Charles Ward is now more usually known as 'Jim' Ward
44. Frank Knowles, SR 11465, Reel 2
45. Charles Laborde, SR 15103, Reel 4
46. Charles Laborde, SR 15103, Reel 4
47. Ted Whittaker, SR 12409, Reel 6
48. Charles Ward, SR 14728, Reel 4
49. Eric Dobson, *History of the South Notts Hussars, 1924-1948*, Heral Printing Works: York and London, 1948, p29
50. Ted Whittaker, SR 12409, Reel 6
51. Herbert Bonnello, SR 11959, Reel 4
52. Frank Knowles, SR 11465, Reel 3
53. Charles Laborde, SR 15103, Reel 5
54. Bill Hutton, SR 11957, Reel 3
55. Ray Ellis, SR 12660, Reel 7
56. Ian Sinclair, SR 11468, Reel 5

57. Ray Ellis, SR 12660, Reel 7
58. George Pearson, SR 10912, Reel 5
59. Victor Harrold, SR 12682, Reel 1
60. Ray Ellis, SR 12660, Reel 19
61. Herbert Bonnello, SR 11959, Reel 6
62. Ray Ellis, SR 12660, Reel 6
63. George Pearson, SR 10912, Reel 5
64. John Whitehorn, SR 11466, Reel 6
65. Albert Swinton, SR 14104, Reel 4
66. Albert Swinton, SR 14104, Reel 4
67. Ray Ellis, SR 12660, Reel 8
68. Bill Hutton, SR 11957, Reel 4
69. Bob Hingston, SR 14789, Reel 10
70. Captain Peter Gervase Birkin was known as Gervase Birkin but most of the SNH called him Gerry with a hard 'G'
71. Ian Sinclair, SR 11468, Reel 6
72. John Whitehorn, SR 11466, Reel 6
73. Ted Holmes, SR 12409, Reel 4
74. Charles Laborde, SR 15103, Reel 8
75. Fred Brookes, SR 14730, Reel 5
76. Harold Harper, SR 10923, Reel 5
77. Reg McNish, SR 12435, Reel 6
78. Fred Brookes, SR 14730, Reel 5
79. War Diary , 107 RHA, Public Record Office, WO169/1435, 10/4/1941
80. Dobson, *History of the South Notts Hussars*, p 71
81. Ray Ellis, SR 12660, Reel 16
82. Bill Hutton, SR 11957, Reel 5
83. Ian Sinclair, SR 11468, Reel 8
84. Albert Parker, SR 14788, Reel 5
85. Bill Hutton, SR 11957, Reel 5
86. War Diary, 107 RHA, Public Record Office, WO169/1435, 1/5/1941
87. John Walker, SR 11464, Reel 10
88. Albert Swinton, SR 14104, Reel 5
89. Harold Harper, SR 10923, Reel 3
90. Ray Ellis, SR 12660, Reel 16
91. John Walker, SR 11464, Reel 8
92. Albert Swinton, SR 14104, Reel 7
93. Ted Holmes, SR 12409, Reel 6

94. Herbert Bonnello, SR 11959, Reel 7
95. John Walker, SR 11464, Reel 10
96. George Pearson, SR 10912, Reel 8
97. Charles Laborde, SR 15103, Reel 8
98. Ray Ellis, SR 12660, Reel 19
99. Albert Ward, SR 15321, Reel 4
100. Bill Hutton, SR 11957, Reel 6
101. Harold Harper, SR 10923, Reel 6
102. Ted Holmes, SR 12409, Reel 7
103. Bob Foulds, SR 12715, Reel 9
104. Ted Whittaker, SR 12409, Reel 6
105. Ted Holmes, SR 12409, Reel 6
106. Ted Whittaker, SR 12409, Reel 10
107. Bill Hutton, SR 11957, Reel 6
108. Ray Ellis, SR 12660, Reel 19
109. Harold Harper, SR 10923, Reel 6
110. Harold Harper, SR 10923, Reel 8
111. Frank Knowles, SR 11465, Reel 3
112. John Walker, SR 11464, Reel 9
113. Victor Harrold, SR 12682, Reel 2
114. Ian Sinclair, SR 11468, Reel 8
115. Bill Adams, SR 14791, Reel 7
116. Harold Harper, SR 10923, Reel 6
117. Major R B T Daniell, unpublished typescript memoir, p75, IWM Dept of Documents
118. John Walker, SR 11464, Reel 9
119. Harold Harper, SR 10923, Reel 7
120. Bob Hingston, SR 14789, Reel 15
121. Victor Harrold, SR 12682, Reel 2
122. Victor Harrold, SR 12682, Reel 2
123. Harold Harper, SR 10923, Reel 7
124. Victor Harrold, SR 12682, Reel 3
125. Herbert Bonnello, SR 11959, Reel 7
126. Ray Ellis, SR 12660, Reel 17
127. Fred Langford, SR 12240, Reel 4
128. Ted Whittaker, SR 12409, Reel 6
129. Bill Hutton, SR 11957, Reel 5
130. Ted Whittaker, SR 12409, Reel 13
131. Harold Thompson, SR 12242, Reel 6
132. Albert Swinton, SR 14104, Reel 6
133. Ray Ellis, SR 12660, Reel 5

134. Ted Whittaker, SR 12409, Reel 15
135. Ted Whittaker, SR 12409, Reel 15
136. George Pearson, SR 10912, Reel 8
137. Major Gen I S O Playfair, *History of the Second World War, United Kingdom Military Series, The Mediterranean and the Middle East, Volume III*, HMSO: London, 1960, p46
138. Albert Swinton, SR 14104, Reel 9
139. George Pearson, SR 10912, Reel 10
140. Bill Hutton, SR 11957, Reel 8
141. Bill Hutton, SR 11957, Reel 8
142. George Pearson, SR 10912, Reel 10
143. Ted Holmes, SR 12409, Reel 7
144. Ray Ellis, SR 12660, Reel 25
145. Herbert Bonnello, SR 11959, Reel 9
146. Harold Harper, SR 10923, Reel 10
147. Bill Hutton, SR 11957, Reel 9
148. Major R B T Daniell, unpublished typescript memoir, p78, IWM Dept of Documents
149. Harold Thompson, SR 12242, Reel 11
150. Dobson, *History of the South Notts Hussars*, p 124
151. Ted Whittaker, SR 12409, Reel 19
152. John Walker, SR 11464, Reel 12
153. War Diary, 107 RHA, Public Record Office, WO169/4563, 5-6/6/1942
154. Major R B T Daniell, Unpublished Typescript Memoir, The Battle of the Cauldron, p2, IWM Dept of Documents
155. Major R B T Daniell, Unpublished Typescript Memoir, Autobiography, p80, IWM Dept of Documents
156. Jack Sykes, SR 11960, Reel 6
157. Albert Parker, SR 14788, Reel 8
158. Harry Day, SR 12412, Reel 8
159. Harry Day, SR 12412, Reel 8
160. William Pringle, SR 14790, Reel 8 & 9
161. Harry Day, SR 12412, Reel 8
162. Major R B T Daniell, Unpublished Typescript Memoir, p80, IWM Docs

---

South Notts Hussars interviews held at the Sound Archive, IWM